ROYAL MARINE

ROYAL

THE AUTOBIOGRAPHY OF

Colonel Sam Bassett, C.B.E., R.M.

STEIN AND DAY / *Publishers* / New York

MARINE

WITH A FOREWORD BY HIS ROYAL HIGHNESS Prince Philip

AND AN INTRODUCTION BY General Lemuel C. Shepherd, JR., U.S.M.C. (Ret.)

First published in the United States of America by Stein and Day, 1965
Published in England by Peter Davies
Copyright © 1962 by Colonel Sam Bassett
Library of Congress Catalog Card No. 65-13604
Printed in the United States of America

Stein and Day / Publishers / 7 East 48 Street, New York, N.Y. 10017

INTRODUCTION
To the American Edition

Colonel SAM BASSETT's autobiography of fifty-four years service as a Royal Marine will have a definite appeal to every American who served in the Armed Forces, as well as being of interest to those who enjoy a stranger than fiction story. His rise from Private to Commissioned Rank, although unique in the Royal Marines, parallels the military career of many officers, who through leadership and natural ability, came up through the ranks and attained positions as Senior Commands in our own Army and Marine Corps.

Colonel Bassett's suspenseful story of how the organization he commanded helped make D-Day a successful operation will be of great interest not only to those who recently commemorated the twentieth anniversary of their landing on the shores of Normandy, but also all those who were captured by the drama of *The Longest Day*.

Colonel Bassett's participation in a number of raids along the European Coastline will also bring back memories of landings by Marine and Army troops on Japanese defended islands in the Pacific.

During Colonel Bassett's illustrious career he was frequently assigned to the Office of British Naval Intelligence where he worked closely with the Admiralty. By his resourcefulness he was able to ferret out many items of confidential information which contributed materially to the war effort. On several occasions Sam made his intelligence reports directly to the Prime Minister, General Eisenhower, and other senior commanders. These top secret interviews, which have been buried in the archives of the Admiralty, are made public in his book. Among the interesting information revealed is the secret behind the Dam Buster's success in the destruction of the Moehne-Elder Dams which knocked out vast areas of German industrial plants and his location of the Tirpitz in her snow-covered lair in a Norwegian fjord.

Colonel Bassett tells his tale in a humorous and most readable form, which I feel sure will prove entertaining to those who peruse this book.

LEMUEL C. SHEPHERD, JR.
General, USMC (Ret.)

FOREWORD BY H R H PRINCE PHILIP

BUCKINGHAM PALACE

Colonel Bassett's record of service in the Royal Marines is unique, it is very doubtful whether it could ever be equalled. His autobiography covers two world wars, and is packed with incidents, exciting, tragic and amusing, which have happened to him since he took The King's Shilling as long ago as 1907.

Colonel Bassett has seen most things that can come the way of a Royal Marine, and the Corps by nature of its role sees a very great deal of life in all parts of the world, in war and in peace, at sea and on land, and he has related them with zest and humour.

30th January, 1962.

CHAPTER 1

I SERVED for fifty years in the Royal Marines, but not until very nearly at the end of my time in uniform did I pause to consider whether there was anything very unusual in this. Then at a party given in London in honour of the U S Marine Corps, which was celebrating an anniversary, Earl Mountbatten came up to me and shook hands. "Sam," he asked, "do you know if your record has been equalled by the U S Marine Corps?"

"I don't really know, sir," I said, at a slight loss, for it had never struck me that this length of service would be unique.

"All right, then, we'll ask the General," said Earl Mountbatten. He led me across the room to where U S Marine General Pate was talking to some other officers. "General," said Mountbatten, introducing us, "Sam here has just completed fifty years man's time in the Royal Marines. Have you anything in the U S Marines to equal that?"

General Pate rubbed his chin thoughtfully for a moment. "No, sir," he admitted at last, "I'm quite sure we have not. Why, only a few months ago I had to present a sterling silver tea service to an enlisted man who had served forty-three years, and we thought that pretty good."

I turned to my Commandant-General. "Sir, did you hear that?" I asked him. "A solid silver tea service—for forty-three years?" But without a flicker of expression, he dismissed my hint. "I'm frightfully hard of hearing, Sam—I didn't hear a thing!" was all he said.

And that was really about all the recognition I received for a record which the Chief of Naval Information in his hand-out to the Press has since informed all and sundry was unique; nobody in the British services, at any rate, could equal it and certainly nobody in the U S Marines. I was, therefore, just a little unprepared for the letters which I received in my office at the Admiralty four years later, on the day when it was finally decided that I should retire. The first came from Buckingham Palace. The

7

language was simple and formal, but not, I thought, impersonal; it warmed my heart to read it.

"Dear Colonel Bassett," the letter began, "His Royal Highness the Duke of Edinburgh, Captain-General of the Royal Marines, desires me to tell you that he has read of your approaching retirement and of your long and most distinguished service.

"His Royal Highness asks me to send you his best wishes for a very long, happy and full life on leaving the Corps to which you have devoted so many years.

Yours sincerely,
CHRISTOPHER BONHAM CARTER."

The second letter gave me equal pleasure; it came from the Duke of Windsor.

A third came from the Director of Naval Intelligence in the U S Navy to wish me well; and there were others, many from people with whom I had served, or whose lives had touched mine at some point.

I felt overwhelmed at all this, so unexpected and so gratifying. As I sat, the letters still before me on the desk, I seemed to see again some of the incidents of my life, some of the people with whom I had worked. It was too much; I could bear this mist procession of the past no more. On the impulse, I rose and walked out of the Admiralty, with no real plan in mind, but simply to give me time to compose myself. Aimlessly, and rather lost, I found myself wandering down Whitehall, past the mounted guardsmen.

As I stood and stared at them, my mind went back fifty-four years and I was surprised to realise that my life had turned a complete circle; I was indeed back exactly where I had started. Emotionally, there seemed little difference between the lad I had been then and the man that I was now. I had felt scared then; and now I was leaving my active service life, I felt just as apprehensive.

In 1907 I had only recently left the shelter of an ecclesiastical college and did not know what was going to happen to me. Now, after having been fed, housed, clothed, and with my whole life arranged for me through more than half a hundred years, I was faced with the same problem. Yet what memories I carried of the years between! What an exciting and varied life I had been

8

fortunate enough to enjoy—a life which had not only given me extreme satisfaction and pleasure, but had enabled me to meet and mingle with many influential and celebrated people who otherwise would never have become my friends.

All this had been made possible by Winston Churchill, who had enabled me to become one of the first men in the Royal Marines to be commissioned from the lower deck. Now this sort of progression is customary and expected; then, it was unheard of.

Fifty-four years earlier I had been standing in the same place in Whitehall, hungry, cold and lonely, lost in admiration of the soldiers sitting like statues on their horses. Suddenly I had felt a tap on my shoulder and, looking round, saw a most magnificent sight—a big, broad-shouldered man dressed in a gold and scarlet uniform, his chest seemingly covered with ribbons and glittering decorations for valour and long service.

"Look nice, don't they, sonny?" he remarked, nodding towards the Life Guards.

"Yes, indeed they do!" I agreed.

"How'd you like to be one of them?" he asked, after a pause.

"I'd like it very much," I replied with some earnestness—I had no idea what else I could be, for I was trained for nothing and knew no one who could help me to find a job, or indeed, even my next meal.

"But you know, you couldn't be," went on the stranger—I thought almost gleefully. "You have to be six feet tall and well built. They wouldn't take a little shrimp like you. Why don't you join the Marines instead?"

"If I joined anything, I'd rather join something with horses," I said uncertainly.

"Tell me, sonny"—and there was pity in his voice—"where did you go to school?"

I told him.

"Well, didn't they teach you anything about the Horse Marines there?" he asked. "It's the Horse Marines *you* want to join! Good pay—and a chance to see the world!"

"See the world?" I repeated, not quite understanding what he meant.

"Yes, and see it in comfort. Come on, I'll tell you more about it." He spoke briskly and at the same time gave my elbow a

9

gentle nudge. "By the way," he added in a stage whisper, to my complete mystification, "you're seventeen, if anyone asks you. What's your name?"

"Samuel John Woodruff Bassett," I told him.

He grinned. "Well, is it now? We've no Woodruffs or Marmadukes in the Marine Corps, sonny. From now on you're just plain Sam Bassett, and that's that!" And, to be fair, that's how it's been ever since.

He led me to the Marine recruiting office just behind Whitehall—I still had no idea that he was a Recruiting Colour Sergeant—and brought me into a small anteroom to see a doctor. This gentleman asked me to open my shirt, took a quick look at my chest, and then pointed to a big box of multi-coloured skeins of wool. "Pick out a blue," he ordered; I did so. He gave a nod to the Recruiting Sergeant, who ushered me out of the room. That was my medical examination. I had no outward signs of tuberculosis, and my vision was sound.

A Sergeant began taking down my particulars. "Can you read and write?" he asked.

"Yes," I answered.

"Anything else?"

"I have French, German and Latin—and some Italian," I explained diffidently.

He looked up, no doubt thinking that I was making fun of him. "In that case, sonny, you'll be an officer in no time. Right, sign your name here."

I signed my name and the big Colour Sergeant called me over. "Follow me," he said briefly. I followed him. He led me round to a nearby public house, the Silver Cross, and took me up to the counter in the public bar. He called the barmaid over to us. "Listen, love," he told her, "you're a witness. This recruit's getting the King's shilling." And he solemnly handed me a coin.

"Now," he said briskly. "We've got to drink the health of His Majesty—you've accepted his shilling. What'll you have?"

"I'd like some lemonade," I said.

"*Lemonade?*" A look of horror froze his face. "Listen, sonny, this is the Marines—you're a Marine now, not a Marmaduke. You'll drink a pint of beer, same as I do. Two pints, miss."

I took a sip of the stuff, and hungry, wretched and until then teetotal, was nearly sick.

"Here, give *me* that, sonny!" said the Colour Sergeant anxiously. "No point wasting good beer!"

He reached across for my tankard. I waited while he drank it —not a very long wait.

That afternoon, with two other recruits, I was put on the train for Deal where, it was explained, there was a Royal Marines depot. We didn't know each other and we didn't talk much on the journey, but just sat there on the hard third-class seat in silence munching the thick, dry sandwiches that we had been given as "rations".

All three of us were pretty frightened, although I gathered that the other two thought anything was preferable to living at home. One of them had had to sleep three in a bed with his brothers; such were the social conditions of the time.

At Deal we were met by a Corporal. He didn't seem a bad chap. "Look," he explained as we stood rather forlornly on the platform. "I'm going to take you to the barracks, to a place they call the Reception Room where you'll be kept until you pass a doctor and get fitted out with a uniform. Then you'll go before the Commandant to be attested and, once you're attested, then you're in for twelve years, unless you decide to buy yourself out—and that's bloody expensive. It's a hard life, but it'll make men of you. Later, I'll hand you over to a Colour Sergeant who's in charge of the Reception Room. Watch out for him; he's a Bible-thumper and he'll ram religion down your throat. But he's the biggest bloody hypocrite we've got."

We looked so blankly at him that he decided to give us an instance of this hypocrisy.

"When you're being measured for your uniforms, for example, he'll tell you he'll pack your plain clothes and send 'em home for you. Ignore this. All he does is to take 'em out and flog 'em! Tell him you'll send 'em yourself. Then he'll ask if you've any cigarette cases or watches and tell you you'd better hand 'em over to him for safe keeping as they're not allowed in the Corps. Well, if you do that, you'll never see them again. So don't say I didn't warn you."

None of us possessed such luxuries as watches or cigarette cases, but the moral was not lost. And with this warning the Corporal led us into Deal. It was six o'clock in the evening before we reached the barracks, where we met the religiously minded

Colour Sergeant who seemed, at the outset anyway, to be quite a pleasant fellow.

We were given a hot meal and an opportunity to wash. Then we were told to get to bed in the barrack room. Just before we jumped in, wearing our underwear—for none of us had any pyjamas—the Colour Sergeant reappeared and in a sanctimonious manner announced: "Now, I always make my boys kneel down by the bedside and say their prayers before going to sleep. It's a habit I try to get them to keep. Recruit Bassett, down on your knees and start praying!"

Dutifully I did as I was told. Only, unlike the others, I began to pray in Latin, as I had been doing for years; I don't think I could remember any prayers in English, anyhow. I didn't think there was anything unusual in my behaviour, but it was duly noted.

On the following day we were measured for our uniforms and, indeed, just as we'd been warned, the Colour Sergeant offered to send our plain clothes home and also asked us if we had any watches or jewellery which he could take care of for us. I didn't want my family to know what I'd done—and anyway the clothes weren't worth much—so I handed mine over. A pleasurable look crossed the Colour Sergeant's face as I handed him my bundle, but the other recruits stared at me as though I'd suddenly gone off my head.

Kitted out now in the smart Marine uniform, the three of us were led one by one before the Colonel-Commandant, whom I found smoking a big cigar at his desk. The Colour Sergeant who accompanied us introduced me. "This is Recruit Bassett, sir," he said. "The boy I was telling you about, sir. He says his prayers in Latin."

"Good for him!" said the Brigadier, puffing out a cloud of smoke. "Let him. I warrant he didn't learn that in the Salvation Army."

"No sir, he was in a religious school, training to be an Anglican priest."

"Well, Bassett," said the Brigadier, "you won't want Latin in this Corps, except for our motto: *Per mare, per terram*. I'm damned if I know whether that's Latin or not!"

"Yes sir, it is. *Per* means by, *mare* is sea, and *terram* land——"

"Good God!" shouted the Brigadier, dropping some ash on his

desk, "you're trying to instruct your Commanding Officer before you've even joined the Corps! Here, kiss the Bible and get out!"

I kissed the Bible as ordered and then repeated the Oath of Allegiance. And that was that. I was now a Royal Marine—and I'd be a Royal Marine for the next twelve years whether I liked it or whether I didn't. Indeed, as I marched out of the Commandant's office, my morale, for once, was scarcely buoyant. 'What', I thought to myself, 'have I let myself in for? How did I ever get involved in this? And what would my family think?'

My first vague connection with any of the services had been when Anne, our maid, had started to walk out with a soldier. My mother didn't like it; I remember she considered this sort of behaviour rather low and unbecoming. She said that Father's habit of backing bills had brought us all fairly low, but never as low as Anne walking out with a soldier. Father, I should explain, was a big-hearted man who had always found it difficult to resist a hard-luck story; which had led him to accept too many cheques which later bounced.

He was a journalist and had travelled over a great deal of the world. He had once been wrecked off the Coral Reef in New Zealand—I believe a part of it was later named after him—and he'd taken part in the Klondike gold rush. He was an amazing man and he lived to be eighty-six.

We were in Exeter at the time of Anne's infatuation with her soldier. Sometimes we seemed to have plenty of money; at other times it became extraordinarily scarce: I never remember a time when we seemed to have just enough. At one time we'd have a carriage and pair, then a very fine perambulator and nanny; next week we'd be reduced to absolute poverty with barely enough money to pay the baker and the milkman. We seemed to live on an inexplicable financial see-saw. Both my brother and I thought all this very exciting and it didn't worry us a bit. To us, our father remained a wonderful man with a fund of the most incredible stories.

He owned a big Family Bible which was the only thing he had saved from the wreck when he'd been almost drowned off the Coral Reef. He also had a box of exquisite New Zealand shells, and he'd named my sister Pepita after a Maori girl, who, so he said jokingly, had been an old flame.

13

Things came to a head one day, however, when we returned home to find two strange men wearing black suits and black bowlers in possession of the house; my mother explained that they were bailiffs. Once again my father had backed someone's worthless bill, and this time the bailiffs were going to take away our goods and chattels. They even tried to take my father's harmonium.

"You can't take that—you can't take the tools of my trade!" he appealed to them.

"These aren't the tools of your trade," one of the men pointed out. "You write with a pen and pencil. You can keep those!"

"Listen, I'm the local musical instructor to the Salvation Army, and that's a source of income," insisted my father. And, in the end, they actually let him keep it.

Afterwards my mother was very upset when she recalled this incident, for my father had been a practising Buddhist at the time. Earlier, he had been a follower of Confucius; once he had even tried to become a Roman Catholic. He changed his religion as he changed his style of living—as other men change their suits, and with as little concern.

In the end, we transferred to Portsmouth where we took refuge in the house of Aunt Emily, my mother's sister. She lived in Lombard Street, in the old part of Portsmouth, a place of wharfs and onion boats. Her husband Alfred was supposed to be a sailor—certainly he wore a beard and sported a sailor's jersey —but I think his connection with the sea began and ended when he was invited to pose in a sou'wester for the original painting which has since become the famous trade-mark of a brand of sardines. When we first went to Portsmouth, Uncle Alfred spent most of his time lolling about the house and smoking and drinking. Aunt Emily insisted that he'd have to earn some money, so out of her own resources she bought him a little boat, which was kept at a nearby wharf.

Purchase of this boat proved an absolute godsend to my brother and me. Uncle Alfred wasn't really fond of work of any kind, and we used to clean the boat for him and generally kept it in trim and seaworthy.

The only trade he could secure from the vessel was to take people over to the *Victory* in the daytime and, after the Gosport ferry had stopped, to ferry Marines to Gosport. Uncle Alfred was frequently reluctant to expend even this much effort. When someone approached and asked to be taken across, he would take the pipe out of his mouth just long enough to say: "Can't take you now. Getting my boat cleaned up. She leaks."

Often he'd refuse even to stir out of the house in the evening. My poor aunt would say: "Now, Alfred, go down to your boat."

Uncle Alfred would give a great puff from his pipe and answer: "I've just been outside, and it's enough to blow your entrails out!" Then he'd sit back and suck his pipe again, and that was that. Of course he was a wretched influence on my brother and me. Eventually, my aunt set my father up in a small business and we moved to Grigg Street—a rather tough quarter, which had earned itself a bad reputation.

Entertainment was naturally a great deal less varied in those days than now, and pubs and music-halls were about the only places where most people could find escape from the dreary rut of reality. Thus it was perhaps inevitable that in the crowded bars people who were forced to live drab and colourless lives should seek the spurious and passing excitement of an argument or a fight. There were certainly plenty of fights in Grigg Street.

Father prospered in his new business and even found time to take a mild interest in the education of my brother and myself. His ideas of education were strange and unorthodox. He used to read to us from Tolstoy's *War and Peace*, but insisted that it had lost a great deal in the translation, and so decided that one of us should learn Russian. I was chosen to study this language, while my brother was given the opportunity of learning the piano. This was a very disappointing decision so far as I was concerned, because I loved the piano; but this was the way my father had decided things and I had no choice but to make the best of it.

By now my brother and I were attending a Church School and also learning French. Eventually I became a server at the local church, which was extremely high—so high indeed, that the services were conducted entirely in Latin. The priest offered to teach me Latin, and so I found myself trying to master three new languages at the same time.

A dear and somewhat highbrow cousin sent me George Borrow's *With the Bible in Spain*, and followed this up with *The Bible in Wales*. I became so fascinated with this second book that

I determined to learn Welsh, because Borrow insisted that it was impossible to understand the beauty of Wales and its poetry unless you understood the language. So I added Welsh to my studies.

My brother, meanwhile, was trying to master both the piano and the organ. I had to blow the organ for him while he practised, but I finally rebelled at this and told him I would refuse to help unless he taught me the piano as well, and he agreed. I was twelve years old and, at that age, all things are possible.

One day I was wandering along Grigg Street when a very attractive girl appeared at the upper window of a house opposite and called out to me: "Would you like to earn some money? Perhaps you could run an errand for me?"

"I'll have to ask my mother," I shouted back.

"There's no time for that," she replied. "I've got a ruddy Bible-thumper coming to see me in a moment. He takes his pleasure and pays his money and then preaches me a sermon. He gives me the ruddy creeps! I can't stand it, I tell you, unless I have a drop of gin. Look, sonny, run around to the Clarendon and get me a quartern.[1] You can keep the change."

This was the first time I'd ever been inside a pub. With a half-penny of the three pennies change I bought some broken biscuits. When my mother caught me eating them she demanded to know where I'd got the money.

"That nice girl opposite asked me to run an errand," I said.

"That *nice* girl . . . ?" My mother became speechless. When she'd recovered her tongue, she raged at me. "Go straight up-stairs and take off your clothes and I'll scrub you! I might be able to get some of the dirt off your body even if I can't get it out of your mind!" She seized the rest of the change and threw it on the fire. "Wait until your father hears about this," she said grimly.

The upshot of this strange and really harmless encounter was that my parents took me to see a local priest, Father Mundy, with the idea that I should be sent away to an ecclesiastical college which trained young men for the Anglican priesthood.

My mother was determined that I should be removed as soon as possible from the pernicious influences of Grigg Street. After a talk with Father Mundy this was arranged, and I set out, forti-

[1]The fourth part of a pint, a measure in use in those days.

16

fied by five golden sovereigns given to me by Aunt Emily with the warning: "Don't tell your father I've given you this money —otherwise he'll try and borrow it and you'll never see it again."

The college was at Wimbledon; about twenty other young men were my companions as students. We worked at Latin and French, but the rest of the instruction was on religious subjects. We were not encouraged to leave the school and during the three years I spent there I did not go home once. We attended Mass every morning, helping as servers and sometimes acting as priests, without, of course, the power to administer the Sacrament.

I was just sixteen and looking forward to my final examinations when I suddenly decided that I could stand this life no longer and that the sort of closed-in existence I had been leading for three years or more would not suit me as a lifetime vocation. There and then I made up my mind to run away.

One morning, just after early Mass, with the balance of the money my aunt had given me in my pocket, I just walked out of the school, crossed Wimbledon Common and made for London. Where was I going? What was I going to do? I'd no idea, beyond a vague notion that I might be able to make my way to the docks and somehow go aboard a ship going . . . where? I didn't know and I didn't care.

I walked all the way to Trafalgar Square and then the sight of a crowd in Whitehall drew my attention. I walked towards them. They were watching the Life Guards at the entrance of Horse Guards Parade. I stopped and looked at them admiringly; watching the riders on the common from the college window had given me a great urge to ride a horse. So my interest in horses led a crafty recruiting sergeant to tell me the old, old story of the Horse Marines, and I arrived at Deal facing a minimum of twelve years' service.

I was put in a barrack room with about thirty boys like myself; I was the youngest by a year. Two old soldiers were around the place to see that everything was kept tidy and to prepare the food, and a Corporal was in charge.

I found myself a kind of odd-man-out in that barrack room. My physique was poor and I'd never learned to use my fists. I didn't, as they say, "speak the same language" as these chaps: most of them were almost illiterate; many were completely unable to write even their names or to read anything more than the shortest words in a poster. A great number of them had only joined the Marines in order to escape from trouble—usually the familiar experience of having put a girl "in the family way", as they said. Their conversation was dominated by three words— one I'd never heard of; the second "bull" and the third "bastard". They appeared to use these words because they lacked the education or the wish to use anything better.

The word "bastard" particularly coloured their language. The Adjutant was never referred to simply as the Adjutant; he was always "Bastard Adjutant". The Sergeant-Major was always "Bastard Sergeant-Major". Even I was referred to as "that Gentleman bastard Jack, the bastard"; I had become known as "Gentleman Jack" because my glossary was not sprinkled with crudities. This was a perturbing and difficult time for me, not made any easier by my inner feelings of guilt at having run away from the college in Wimbledon or by the realisation that through my own idiocy I faced twelve more years of this life.

I was alone and lonely, the crowd was no company, and I could find nobody with whom I could hold a conversation; they appeared to have no conversation, in fact. They never bothered to read anything—most of them couldn't, anyway—and were only concerned with the food, which was abominable, or the behaviour of the Drill Sergeant. This made a terrible limited world and one in which I had no desire to spend my days.

I also disliked the brutality that seemed an inherent quality of it. If something went wrong and I became involved in an argument with one of the other recruits, our discussion would inevitably be broken up by the Corporal sticking his head around the door and shouting: "All right, you two, behind the canteen!" We would find ourselves hustled behind the canteen—all the barrack room following, of course—and there I'd be forced to fight it out. Inevitably I came off second best, in every sense of the word.

I began to take extra gymnastic tuition to try and alter this state of affairs. An hour's P T was compulsory every morning, but one could also attend an extra class voluntarily in the evening. This helped to relieve the utter boredom—and my goodness, it *was* boredom!

One day, however, while on cleaning fatigue in the recreation room I saw a Corporal actually reading a book. Delighted to meet someone who appeared to be at least literate, I approached him. "Can you borrow books?" I asked him.

"Yes," he said. "There's a small library here, and they haven't such a bad selection. I'm reading Dickens."

"I've read most of Dickens," I said. "I think I must know many of his books by heart."

He smiled. "Oh, there are some other books," he said. "Tell me," he went on, "how on earth did you come to join this mob?"

I told him that I had a great urge to ride a horse and the Recruiting Sergeant had assured me that by joining the Horse Marines I would have the chance of riding.

"That's nonsense, you know," he said, not unkindly. "There aren't any horses in the Marines—it's just a silly phrase, the Horse Marines. Certainly some of the officers ride horses, but there's no such thing as promotion to an officer from the lower ranks. The highest rank you can ever hope to reach would be Quartermaster—and you'll be an old man before you work your way up to that. Even then, Quartermasters don't ride horses."

This was a bitter blow for me. It seemed to make my career worthless and without meaning. I'd been swindled and for the next twelve years I'd be little better than a prisoner, without friends and with no hope of regaining my freedom. My morale, battered as it already was by the stern, alien life of the barrack room, now sank to its nadir. If I couldn't ride a horse, what, in fact, was I doing here at all?

Schooling was, of course, compulsory. This was understandable, for the majority of the intake into the Marines in those days could neither read nor write, as I had already discovered.

It was the ambition of the Warrant-Officer Instructor to persuade or bully at least some of the men in his class to pass the Third-Class Certificate. This meant, in effect, that they had to become proficient enough to add two and two together and to read simple words; but with the calibre and quality of the men under their charge this was by no means easy.

After I had been a fortnight at the school, the Warrant-Officer Tutor came and looked at my work. "Here, where were you educated?" he asked me. I told him and then he said: "I want to make a prize thing out of you. I'm going to get you to pass both your Third and your Second-Class Certificates at one go. In fact, we might try for the first part of the First-Class."

I looked up, delighted; this was the best news I'd heard since my enlistment. The First-Class Certificate was extremely stiff; if I'd been in the Army and not in the Marines, a pass would have entitled me to be considered for a commission.

The tutor was as good as his word. He coached me assiduously and eventually I sat the examination. I passed all three Certificates at the first attempt. Nobody had ever done it before, and this moved the Commandant to record it in Daily Orders. That cost me a hiding from my comrades in the barrack room: I was immediately taken behind the canteen and made to suffer for my presumption.

I'd written to my mother, telling her that I was quite happy in my new life, and, rough as it might be, I still felt more fitted to it than to the priesthood; but I had mentioned the almost uneatable food. She replied saying that my father would have nothing more to do with me, but she enclosed a ten shilling note. Each month she sent me ten shillings, and with this I was able to buy my food outside.

There was a little shop at the barracks gate called The Burgoo Shop—here one could buy a plate of burgoo (porridge) for a penny. Every Tuesday they had fish and chips which cost three-halfpence, and on Wednesday they provided faggots at two-pence. I practically lived in The Burgoo Shop, rarely eating the barrack food at all. The two old soldiers who prepared the food for the barrack room continued to supply their burnt offerings—with no complaints from any of the other recruits who no doubt found it far superior to anything they had been used to at home; at least there was plenty of it. None, of course, could understand my attitude: this was simply another instance of my strange and unreasonable conduct, and they took it out of me accordingly.

Eight months after joining the Royal Marines, I'd progressed as far as section leader of my drill squad, which further inflamed the feelings of jealousy around me. But this was fortunate, for it led to an incident which at long last raised me in the estimation of my fellows, and rid me of some of the less tolerable aspects of life in the barrack room.

One Friday evening, while preparing for a ceremonial parade

the next day, I was sitting on the edge of my bed burnishing my bayonet. Behind me on the bed lay my white equipment which I had just blancoed, a chore that had taken me more than an hour. Into the room marched a huge, hulking brute of a man, a sadistic bully who had been trying since our first meeting to make my life unbearable. He had just come from the canteen where he had obviously been drinking quite heavily. Without a word he walked across to a table in the centre of the room, took a basinful of water from it and, with a dirty leer on his heavy face, he stalked towards me. Suddenly he threw the entire contents of the basin all over my newly blancoed equipment. Then he threw back his head and burst into a roar of laughter at my astonishment and anguish.

Maddened at the futility of this, and without really knowing what I was doing, I sprang up from the bed and ran straight at him. I still had the bayonet in my hand, and without a second's hesitation I plunged it deep into the fleshy part of his thigh. Immediately he fell to the ground, screaming in agony. I bent down and withdrew the bayonet, and then quietly went back and sat down on my bunk.

His screams brought the Corporal rushing from the cubicle he occupied at the end of the room. "What the ruddy hell's going on here?" he roared.

There was no lack of people willing to explain.

"Gentleman Jack's run him through with a bayonet," said the recruits.

"Send for the Sergeant-Major!" bawled the Corporal.

A moment or two later the Sergeant-Major appeared. "What goes on here?" he demanded.

"Gentleman Jack has killed a recruit," said the Corporal, not without some awe in his voice.

The Sergeant-Major walked over to my late antagonist and looked down at him as he lay curled up on the floor, his eyes closed. He gave him a hearty kick in the groin; the man moaned faintly. The Sergeant-Major turned to the Corporal. "He's not dead," he announced contemptuously. "What's wrong with him?"

"He's been stabbed," said the Corporal.

"Take off his trousers. Let's see."

They stripped off his trousers and had a look. The blood was

21

gushing from his thigh and seeping into the rough floor boards; and it certainly seemed quite a deep wound.

"Get the doctor," ordered the Sergeant-Major. "And keep your bloody mouth shut!"

In a little while the Corporal returned with one of the Sick Bay Attendants.

"Come and have a look at this chap," invited the Sergeant-Major. The Sick Bay attendant bent down and examined the leg.

"Blimey," he said in amazement, "he'll have to be sewn up!"

"Well, bloody well *sew* him up!" shouted the Sergeant-Major. "Why'd you think I sent for you?"

Still screaming, my old enemy was then subjected to the roughest piece of surgery imaginable. With no benefit of anæsthetic or even skilled surgical knowledge, he was held down on the floor while the orderly gingerly sewed the edges of the gash together. When this operation was over, the Sergeant-Major asked: "Will he live?"

"He'll be all right," replied the Sick Bay Attendant, rather surprised at his own competence. "But he'll have to miss parade for a day or two."

"All right, Corporal," said the Sergeant-Major, turning to him. "You don't appear able to look after a barrack room. Clear out of your cubicle and put this bastard in there instead."

When the wounded warrior had been carried off, the Sergeant-Major motioned all the recruits to gather around. Then he addressed them: "If any one of you blankety so-and-so's as much as breathes a word about this, you'll be put on fatigues for the rest of your time. Is that clear?"

Then he turned to me and I expected to have the handcuffs slapped on my wrists immediately.

"As for you," he said savagely, "one word of this from you and your life'll be made hell!"

And that was that.

There were two sequels to this incident. I'll give the last one first. Years later, my victim made legal history in a strange and infamous way. Having served out his twelve years in the Marines, he took a job as a night watchman. One night he raped and killed a girl. At his trial he put forward the defence that he was so drunk that he didn't know what he was doing. The case eventually went to the House of Lords where their lordships confirmed the judge's finding that drunkenness was no excuse. My old antagonist was hanged.

The other sequel was of far greater interest and importance to me personally; the incident of the bayoneting meant that my comrades in the barrack room suddenly began to treat me with a healthy respect. I was also by now learning how to take care of myself in other ways; to see the advantages in any situation, and to make full use of them. Until then, partly because I'd never complained before, and partly because I was small, I'd been given the worst fatigues possible; not one a week, as they should have been allotted, but every day. One was to clean the urine buckets which were placed outside the barrack rooms at night. The other was to swab out the wet canteen—where beer was served—every day. This was a filthy job, for drunkenness was common, and every day I had to clean up pools of sour vomit and worse, and scrub the stinking floors until it was all I could do to stop my own stomach from heaving.

Now I decided that I'd had enough. On the morning when the new fatigue lists were posted, I approached the Corporal when he'd finished pinning them up. Carefully I carried my burnished bayonet in my hand.

"Corporal," I said slowly, looking him in the eyes, "I'm not going to do that."

"*What* did you say, Gentleman Jack?" he asked, astonished.

"I want a change," I said quietly. "I'm not cleaning out the night-soil buckets or the wet canteen again ever."

As I spoke, I fingered the blade of the bayonet; it was as sharp as any razor. He looked at me in amazement and anger; and then he looked at the blade. I moved it ever so slightly. He took half a pace backwards, his eyes still on it. "Well, what d'you want?" he asked uneasily.

"Officers' Mess," I said at once. He hesitated briefly, and glanced again at the bayonet.

"Right, then, Officers' Mess it is!" he announced, with a heavy attempt at bravado. And for the remainder of my time at Deal, I did no fatigues but those in the Officers' Mess. I had begun to find my feet at last, in the Royal Marines.

I have made a lot of the awful life, but to be fair I must admit that this was partly my own fault. My family life had been

23

peculiar to say the least, but it was protected. I was never allowed to play with the 'rough' boys, as my very religious mother used to call them. The religious school was even more protected, and I was—to use a modern term—a bit of a cissy.

The PT Instructor at Deal summed me up: "Knock-kneed, pigeon-chested, flat-footed bloody waste of uniform!" However, when I went voluntarily to every gym, he took a personal interest in me and eventually became very proud of his efforts. I could box, bayonet-fight, and give displays on the horizontal bars and the horses. I became an expert swimmer and, although my languages suffered, I learnt more general knowledge than I had done in my previous schooling. I'm profoundly grateful to the Royal Marines for having made a man of me.

CHAPTER II

AFTER serving for twelve months at Deal, I was transferred to Portsmouth Barracks and appointed to "G" Company. I was no longer a recruit but a full Private and addressed as such (rankers were not called Marines in the Corps, until several years later).

Life became surprisingly different. First of all we were no longer recruits; we felt that we had left school and we were going to find out what a Royal Marine really did. Instead of being confined to a small town we were in a large naval port. It was the place we had given in our enlistment papers as our home, and we had relatives and friends there. We began to be proud of being Royal Marines and began to look forward to our training courses so that we could start our fuller life of going to sea and seeing the world.

Although conditions in our sphere of life in the service and outside were hard, we began to feel that we were privileged persons. I remember an old soldier arguing about church parade: he said, "When I joined I was asked what my religion was, and I said, 'Put me down to follow the band!' But now I've got a proper religion." Someone asked him, "What's that, mate, the Plymouth Brethren?" "No," he said. "The Royals. That's good enough for me!"

It intrigues me to look back on those years and reflect on changes in conditions then and now. I do not remember officers speaking to the men except on duty—but that wasn't because the officers didn't want to. It was just 'not done', and in any case the men would have been completely tongue-tied and embarrassed if they had done so, and any man so treated would have been regarded by his mates as a sucker-up type. Anyway, I suppose we had then advanced a little from the time when the officers kept a different step from the men so that it could not be thought that there was any connection between them! And on board a ship, where the Royal Marine officer had personal command of a relatively small number of men, this broke down class distinction more quickly than could happen in other services.

Now, of course, improvements in social conditions and in education have completely altered the picture. The first war with its close comradeship in the trenches and shared danger broke down a lot more of the rigid conventions, and with the advance of war techniques and the proved importance of initiative on the part of officers, N.C.O.s and men, after the war soldiering took on a new aspect. Gone for good were the days spent in pointless gravel punching on the parade ground.

When I did become an officer it was part of our training to talk to the men and encourage them to talk to us. In 'stand-easies' we would give them talks on anything that occurred to us—sometimes with mixed results. I remember talking about *esprit de corps*; the men were sitting around, and I noticed one old soldier looking as if he wasn't with me. So I called him out, and asked him, "Now, Jones, why is it that a Royal Marine should be prepared to fight and die for his King and Country?" He gave this serious consideration, and then answered, "You're quite right, sir. Why the hell *should* he?"

Every Friday night the officers, who lived in a completely different—and to me enchanted—world, held an official guest night. These were glittering occasions when red mess tunics and full decorations were worn, when the Royal Marines Band played and dinner consisted of at least half a dozen courses.

One night I was detailed to do washing-up fatigue. On the way back to the barrack room at the end of the evening, I said to the Mess Corporal: "That was the best night I've had since I joined

25

the Marines. It was wonderful to see that table, and to listen to the band."

"Would you like to do it again?" he asked.

"As often as you like," I told him.

"We can't pay you," he said, "but if you're prepared to come as an extra unpaid fatigue man, we'll make it a standing thing."

"I'd like that very much indeed," I said.

Eventually, I became an unofficial member of the permanent staff. I'd sit in the pantry, helping the Mess Butler, the Mess Sergeant, the Mess Corporal and the other servants and listening to the conversation of the officers. This I found fascinating because I had now begun to dream that some day, somehow, I would get a commission myself—although, I knew, of course, that this was impossible. Yet I felt, in my inexperience, that it might help in some way if I at least knew how officers behaved and thought.

One thing that immediately impressed me was that I rarely heard one of them talking about their work. The conversation ranged over hunting, grouse shooting, winter sports, cricket— matters of which I knew nothing. I even began to despair; clearly I was not of the material from which officers are made.

But my confidence was restored when I began to realise how much importance was attached to the ability to speak any foreign language or to play the piano. "Hear about old so-and-so?" somebody would say. "Gone to the Med. in the flagship."

"Lucky blighter!" would come the reply. "But then he speaks French, of course."

It seemed to me, from my lowly observation post, that the two—and only—keys I held to this world of privilege and grace lay in my ability to speak French and to play the piano. I determined to make the most of them should the occasion arise. More, I decided to specialise in languages and the piano and in that way fit myself for the rank which would some day be mine.

Working in the pantry also taught me something else of value: a knowledge of wines. Many of the young officers didn't drink much, and after the King's health had been drunk, glasses of port would be returned to the pantry, still half full.

I'd take a sip, and gradually I came to be something of an expert, extending my range of knowledge into all the wines

26

available. It was customary, of course, after the officers had left the Mess and gone off to play billiards or snooker or cards, for the Mess staff to sit down at table and lap up whatever food and wine had been left over.

One evening, after sipping a certain wine, I announced: "This isn't the wine we served at dinner!"

"Good God!" said the Mess Butler. "Of *course* it isn't! You don't think we'd give *this* to the officers? This is vintage Cockburn 1866, and there are only fifteen bottles left. It's far too good for *them*!"

I was delighted to realise that my knowledge of vintages had become such that I could not be easily fooled. This was an accomplishment that was to have a considerable bearing on my eventual promotion.

One day I was sent for by a certain Major French. When I reported, he looked up and said: "Bassett, I've been looking through your records and I find you're the only person with a First-Class Certificate." (By now I had passed the second part of this examination, a feat of considerable rarity.)

The Major went on: "I've been ordered to start a Signal Department. There are five other chaps with Second-Class Certificates, and they'll work with you. The Commandant has given me a room that'll hold only fifteen men. I'm having curtains put up there—at my own expense, I might add—and I have the Commandant's permission to draw these curtains and keep lights going until half-past ten every evening, so that you can study."

This was the start of a new and exciting phase in my life. To begin with, I was clear for a while of that big barrack room with its crowd of sex-starved men, and the horrors of those Friday nights when the drunks would come stumbling in blind with beer and lust, tripping over the beds cursing aloud in drunken blasphemy, and finally trying to wheedle their foul-breathed way into any bed. More important, this opened the way to a new and interesting study. I found Morse easy to learn and, after passing an examination, became an instructor myself. When the Royal Navy opened a new section called "Naval Examination Service"—which was to teach a specialised knowledge of naval signals as well—we were selected to take this course, and so I became proficient in all branches of signalling.

27

By now I had collected a good array of badges—crossed rifles for a marksman, star for judging distance and now crossed flags for a signaller. In my going-out tunic these were in gold and I thought it was a good opportunity to show myself at home. Carefully going to the lavatory and padding my chest with some newspapers, I proceeded to Portsmouth and was received with tears of joy by my father and mother.

One night, just before lights out, one of our sergeants burst open the barrack room door shouting: "Everyone out! The Black Watch've got some of our chaps in their guard room!"

Those already in bed jumped up and dressed. An old soldier asked me angrily: "Where's your belt, you bloody fool?"

"What do I want a belt for?" I asked in bewilderment.

"To hit the bastards with!" he roared, swinging his belt to show how to hit with the heavy brass buckle, a weapon that can easily rip a man's face like a razor, or strike out an eye.

We poured out of the barracks and down the road in an unruly mob. The gates of the Black Watch barracks were shut but we swarmed over the railings. We overwhelmed the guard room and I heard someone shout: "We've got 'em—back to the barracks!" And we led our men back in triumph, singing and shouting. Lights were on all over the Marine Barracks, and our officers were at their windows to cheer and wave to us.

I learned that there was a long-standing feud with the Black Watch, and feelings ran so high that the regiments had to be kept out of each other's pubs. Two Marines had apparently strayed into a Black Watch pub, and had been arrested—possibly for their own safety.

No one knew, of course, why there was a feud; its origins, like the beginnings of so many cases of bad blood, were lost long ago in the unremembered past. Our commanding officer eventually arranged a football match with the Black Watch, and then we became the best of friends.

Of "bull", of course, in those days there was plenty. Most of it was caused by the men themselves. For instance, there was keen competition to have the cleanest barrack room. With this laudable aim, floors would be scrubbed at six o'clock in the morning, and then spread with blankets to keep them clean and clear of footmarks. These blankets were then put back on the beds—with the result that men caught colds. This practice was absolutely forbidden by the officers. But the men insisted on doing it.

It was the same with our eating utensils. One set were kept highly polished and brought out for all parades, but the knives and forks and mugs in everyday use were filthy.

Again, great care was taken to go on guard duty scrupulously clean; some chaps even cleaned behind their buttons, and polished the brass oil-bottle inside the butt of the rifle. All this was done with the object of being hailed as the cleanest man on guard parade and thus becominging stick-orderly. To become stick-orderly meant that one did no night watch and carried a stick instead of a rifle.

I was selected once because I managed to give my trousers a razor-edge crease. The trick was to mix a little gum arabic with hot water and dab it inside the trousers, and then press them. This was frowned on, as it rotted the trousers. When the Adjutant questioned me about my creases, I said I had done it with a bottle filled with hot water.

The most boring job of all was this guard duty, especially night guard duty. I doubt if any sentry or N C O of the guard ever had the slightest idea of what to do in an emergency; or what or who he was guarding; the whole thing was purely ceremonial. I used to pass the time by practising my Morse with the trigger of my rifle and whistling.

One night I forgot I was on the Officers' Mess post, on the midnight to two o'clock watch. As I whistled, there was a shout from one of the windows and an officer said out of the darkness: "If you *must* whistle, do it quietly! And for heaven's sake keep to the same opera. What was that thing you were whistling?"

"Grieg's 'Schmetterling', sir," I told him.

"I learned that as a boy," said the unknown, unseen officer, "but I thought it was called 'Butterflies'."

"Grieg was a Norwegian and gave his compositions a German or French title, sir," I explained. "It means 'butterflies'."

"Thank you very much," said the officer caustically. "I'll have my next lesson when you do your next guard duty. In the meantime—will you bloody well shut up and let me go to sleep?"

After completing the various training courses such as musketry, field training and in my case signalling, we all became trained men and received another twopence a day in our pay. It was then time to go to a ship, and I was sent to HMS *Euryalus*.

I hadn't much enjoyed barrack-room life, but in this cruiser I soon found myself looking back nostalgically on the comparative comfort I had left! The ship was overcrowded—there wasn't even room to sling a hammock. The food was poor, and the officers had a mania for cleaning; shipboard life seemed to be an endless polishing of brass, and at this stage it seemed to me that there was simply no future for me in such an existence.

I was fortunate enough to meet one of the chaps who'd joined up with me and with whom I'd travelled down to Deal—a man of my own age named Homer. I discovered he hated *Euryalus* as much as I did. Talking it over together, we suddenly decided to desert.

When *Euryalus* returned to Portsmouth and we were given a week's leave, we planned to change into civilian clothes and make for the Continent. What we were going to do when we got there, neither of us had the slightest idea; but anything would be better than this fearful life.

We left our uniforms at the Naval Rest Centre in Portsmouth and caught a train to London where we made our way to the docks. We found a ship going to the Hook of Holland and signed aboard as seamen. The Master of the ship didn't ask for any papers, and we congratulated ourselves on the ease of the operation. Our plan was to duck the ship once it reached the Hook and then to cross over into France. After that—well, we didn't think any further. One step at a time seemed to be sufficient.

But when we reached the Hook we found that the Master was a far shrewder old bird than we had imagined; he had guessed all along that we must be deserters and he rapidly made it clear why he'd accepted us without any papers.

When we asked permission to go ashore, he said: "Certainly not. You'll return in this ship to London." And so back we went to London, having achieved precisely nothing. Worse, we were now three days over our leave and thus legally deserters. Yet we had no alternative but to return to Portsmouth and face whatever punishment awaited us; we'd run out of money, and had nowhere else to go.

I decided to leave the talking to Homer, who seemed to be more plausible than I was, but as we went up the gangway of our ship we were stopped by the Corporal of the Watch. "Where are you two going?" he asked belligerently. "Don't you know there's no lower-deck leave?"

We stopped and stared at him. I had no idea what he was talking about, but the tone of his voice and his general attitude were so fierce that I fully expected him to order up an escort to take us to the cells.

Homer was far more subtle and clever. "We only came aboard to get some clean washing from our kitbags, Corporal," he pointed out.

"All right," said the Corporal grudgingly, "but don't let the Sergeant-Major see you."

Lower-deck leave, I should explain, meant that in ports where accommodation was difficult one could officially go on leave during the day, but could return each night to sleep on board. The Corporal clearly thought that this was what we were trying to do. We soon discovered the reason. *Euryalus* was in such bad condition that further work on her was necessary before she could go to sea, and so an extra week's leave had been granted. We were, in fact, still officially on leave and not deserters at all!

This was a stroke of luck which I didn't deserve and which had an important bearing on my future career. My foolish act could so easily have blighted my future, for it would have meant that I could never be promoted.

Meanwhile, my signalling proficiency took me to Malta, where I found myself serving in a big signal station, the Auberge de Castille. This signal station was situated on the roof of the original building, erected by the Knights of St John, and it commanded the highest peak in the island. From this vantage point one had a view not only of the Grand Harbour itself, but of all the other inlets where destroyers were anchored. Signals in those days, of course, were entirely visual; we used semaphore and flags by day, and lamps by night.

Britain maintained an enormous Mediterranean fleet in those years before the First World War, and this spread itself over

31

several anchorages, each of them out of sight of the other but all within view of the Auberge de Castille.

When the flagship wanted to make a signal to the rest of the fleet, a flag was raised; this announced the intention to make a signal, which we were expected to spot immediately. We actually had a man whose eye was constantly trained by telescope on the flagship. The moment he saw someone going to the signal locker to hoist a flag, he'd shout: "Stand by for signal hoist!" We took pride in having our signal hoisted simultaneously with the one being raised aboard the flagship.

How crude and simple it all seems now, looking back! But then this was the most efficient way there was; and even when wireless came into use it was a long time before it was trusted as the flags were trusted. But Malta meant more to me than signals, much as I enjoyed that work. I'd looked forward to service there because I thought it would give me an opportunity to master the piano and perfect my Italian.

The first thing I did on arriving at the island, indeed, was to inquire about piano lessons. I discovered that one of the finest Italian masters lived in Malta, Chevalier Lancelotti. I sought out his address, and one free afternoon I went up to his house, wearing my best white uniform and sun-helmet. His secretary tried to find out what I wanted, but I refused to explain to her the object of my visit. I insisted on seeing the maestro himself. Eventually, I was admitted to his private room.

"You are a very persistent young man," he said, rather puzzled at my doggedness. "What is it you want?"

"I want to be taught the piano," I explained simply.

He spread out his hands. "Excellent. But why come to me?"

"Because I understand that you are the finest teacher in all Malta, possibly in Europe."

"That is so, of course," he agreed. "But I don't take pupils just like that. I've got a waiting list of hundreds of people who want to study with me. Isn't there someone else in Malta who would do?"

"Sir," I said simply, "I want the best; you are the best."

"I see." He hesitated. "You are, of course, prepared to pay?"

"Of course. I could pay you one-and-six a lesson."

He looked a little surprised. "One-and-six?" he repeated. "How much do you earn?"

32

"Four shillings a day, sir."

"H'm," he said. "Well, I suppose it's a fair proportion. You know, possibly, that I normally charge fifteen guineas a lesson. By the way, have you a piano?"

"No, but I could get one."

"You do play?"

"A little, sir. I have the rudiments of music."

"Well, play."

I sat down and played Faust's ballet music.

"You have the long fingers and you have the touch," said the maestro. "But you must have a piano. It is no good wasting my time if you haven't a piano to practise on."

I left him and went straight to the Y M C A where I knew there was a piano; but they refused me permission to practise on it. I searched Valetta, looking in second-hand shops and mission halls, but in the end I had to admit defeat. There seemed no place where I could borrow or rent a piano. I went back to the Chevalier to explain that I had failed in my search.

"What religion are you?" he asked. I told him, Church of England.

"Well, I know a Catholic priest who runs a club for boys. He has a piano. But I think in return for allowing you to practise upon it, he would insist upon giving you instruction in the one true faith."

"I don't mind that," I said. "I've always been interested."

He gave me a note to the priest, and in return for allowing him to give me a quarter of an hour's instruction every time I went to the club, I was allowed to practise as much as I liked. For the two years I stayed in Malta I was taught by Maestro Lancelotti, and at the end I played extremely well.

But the Chevalier's kindness did not end here. He arranged with the Director of the Malta Opera House for me to work as a stage hand when my duties as a signaller allowed. Some of the best Italian companies visited the island and I heard them all. Every night I lived in a different and wonderful world. And on top of this, I was able to earn an extra five shillings a week.

I was not promoted to Corporal until I returned to Portsmouth from service in Malta. I found myself back in my old barrack room, but this time as Corporal-in-charge. To begin with, my

33

former room mates played me up a bit, but they didn't really resent my promotion, and usually behaved fairly well, although they made it clear that they were not going to have me ticking them off.

One night, however, things came to a head. The men were particularly rowdy, so I left my cubicle and shouted: "Lights out, pipe down!" and then went back to bed. Everything was quiet. A big fire was burning in the grate. Very soon the skylarking started again. I went to the door and called for quiet.

"Oh, go back to bed, Corp!"

They produced a football from somewhere and began to kick it around the room. The door of my cubicle was selected as goal, and bong, bong, bong went the ball against it. I went out and said: "I thought I told you all to pipe down."

"Oh, go back to bed," said one chap, giving me a shove. I found myself being propelled backwards—he was a big fellow and kept goal for the barrack football team. I fell back on to my bunk, which collapsed; an iron leg had come off. I grabbed this leg and marched out again.

"Who pushed me?" I demanded fiercely.

"I did," said the goalkeeper. "Why, d'you want another?"

"No," I said, and hit him over the head with the bed leg. He went down as though pole-axed.

"Gor' blimey!" said someone. "You've laid him out!"

"Right," I said. "Does anybody else want some of the same treatment?"

"No, Corp," they muttered.

"All right then, back to bed now and pipe down. You,"—and I pointed to one man—"get the doctor."

The doctor came to have a look at the goalkeeper. "What's happened to him?" he asked.

"We were skylarking," said someone, "and he tripped and hit his head on the fender."

"Yes, that's it!" chorused the rest. "He bashed the fender."

"Well, he'll have to go to hospital," said the doctor. "Slight concussion. But he'll be all right." And with that he ordered the big fellow to be carried out on a stretcher.

Although it was a salutary enough lesson, I still had not finished with them. I had to consider that, although I'd dealt with the situation in the only way they could understand, I'd

34

succeeded only with their connivance, and I had to follow up my advantage and punish all of them.

"At half-past five you'll all get up and scrub the floor," I announced. Floors were only scrubbed once a week, and that was on Saturdays. Today was Wednesday. I don't think they believed me. But bright as a pin, I was up and at them at five-thirty as promised. I turned them all out and set them to it, and, by God, that floor had never been so well scrubbed!

Just before the Great War broke out in 1914 I was promoted to Lance-Sergeant and joined the Sergeants' Mess. By this time I had written to my mother telling her to stop sending me money; in Malta I'd even been able to send some back to her.

When war became imminent, a party of signallers was sent down to Portsmouth Harbour to join Commander the Hon. Cornwallis West, a retired naval officer who had been called up from the reserve and who was to run a Naval Examination Service boat. This was a section of the service concerned with stopping all shipping that came into ports in war-time, so that they could be examined before they were allowed to proceed to anchorages in defended harbours.

Our first assignment was to pick up a yacht at Southampton, which had been contracted for by the Admiralty for this work. We joined the ship four days before the war actually began, and were already anchored in the shadow of Culver Cliffs when hostilities opened. The yacht was beautifully appointed, with an elegant saloon where Commander West set up his quarters.

It soon became clear that our life aboard would be hectic; signals had to be hoisted every time a ship approached Southampton, and hundreds of vessels arrived there every day during the first days of the war. We were busy day and night, as destroyers or French torpedo boats brought ships in to us at our anchorage, under the guns of a battery on the Isle of Wight.

I had no idea, of course, that my life was approaching its turning point, and that the luckiest stroke of my career—apart from getting away with my 'desertion'—was to have been thrown into contact with Commander West.

One night we shared the middle watch. For once, there was no shipping seeking to gain entrance and, as is the way in the silent watches of the night, rank suddenly fell away and we found ourselves chatting quite normally and easily together.

"What do you miss most about this life?" the Commander asked me.

We weren't allowed to go ashore; and of course there was no question of leave. It was just hard work relieved by simple boredom.

"I suppose the one thing I miss most is not being able to play the piano," I replied.

"D'you play?" he asked sharply.

"Yes, but I can't keep up my practising."

"Well," he said, and his voice held a note of enthusiasm, "I like to sing. Look, the first time we go in to coal, we must find a piano, eh?"

He meant it. The moment we went into Southampton the two of us made straight for the shipping agent.

"Look," said the Commander. "D'you know where we could hire a piano?"

"Why?" asked the agent.

"To play, of course; what else do you think?"

"Why don't you use the one in the saloon, then?" suggested the agent with a smile, thinking, I suppose, that we were making fun of him.

"There isn't one," replied the Commander.

"There is! In fact," replied the agent with a bigger smile, "I'll come aboard and show you."

In the ship's saloon he crossed to the exquisite panelling along one wall and pulled at an embossed rose. Out of the wall appeared the keyboard of a most beautiful Steinway!

Following its discovery, I spent most evenings at this keyboard, accompanying the Commander who had an excellent voice. One evening, when I joined him after dinner, he said: "Good, Bassett; you're just in time to have a glass of port with me." He poured one for me, which I drank slowly. "Tell me," he asked, "does that taste like a vintage port to you?"

"No," I replied promptly, "it's good, but it's not a vintage port."

I told him the brand I thought it might be. He went into the pantry.

"My God, you're right, you know!" he called. "I'll have a word to say to the people who sent this to me as vintage!"

A few days later he came to me in great excitement, and told

36

me: "My cousin Millicent, Duchess of Westminster, is aboard this ship we're going to examine. She's going over to France to run a nursing outfit. If there's time, I should like to invite her to have dinner here with me."

I suggested that I should go ashore at Shanklin and buy some decent food and the appropriate wines. He greeted this idea with enthusiasm, and ordered a boat to take me ashore. "This evening you can wait at table, Bassett, and play the piano for us afterwards," he said.

I came back with lobster and some excellent white wine. I waited at table, and after dinner I played the piano for them. Both the Duchess and the Commander sang several songs and, as we were sharing a final whisky and soda before she left, the Duchess turned to Commander West. "I don't remember when I had such an enjoyable dinner," she said. "I didn't know you could do this sort of thing. The wine was excellent."

"You can thank my Sergeant," the Commander told her. "He arranged both the food and the wine."

"And he plays the piano so beautifully," the Duchess went on. "Why isn't he an officer?"

"Oh, there's no promotion from the lower deck in the Marines."

"What absolute nonsense!" cried the Duchess. "Most of my cousins are commissioned and, as you know, they're practically nitwits. Here you have excellent officer material like this and nothing's done about it! You must write to whoever it is at the Admiralty and *insist* that this Sergeant is commissioned."

And that was the last I was to see of her; a beautifully decorative woman who ran a team of nurses, all society women, like herself, among the blood and death and misery of Flanders.

Next day, Commander Cornwallis West sent for me. "I've written a letter to the First Sea Lord about you, as my cousin suggested," he told me. "Here's a copy for you to read."

I read the letter, and was astonished at the accomplishments he considered sufficient for my promotion. He emphasised my taste for wines and knowledge of various vintages, and pointed out that I played the piano, which, so far as I could see, was of no military advantage whatsoever. Still, there it was, the gesture was very kindly meant, and I was sincerely grateful; but I couldn't see that it would get me very far.

A week later all my dreams of advancement, and indeed of everything else, very nearly came to a sudden and terrifying end. At two o'clock one morning a French destroyer crashed into us in the dark and clove the beautiful yacht completely in two. We were tossed into the water, and only five of us were to survive. After what seemed hours in the sea, I was picked up by the destroyer. Commander West, who had again been sharing the middle watch with me, was among those saved.

The destroyer's captain, expressing his regret, explained that because the yacht was painted white and showed no lights, she had not been distinguishable against the white cliffs in the background.

I was given a week's 'survivor's leave'. But on the third day I received a telegram: "Return to barracks," I read. "Report to Orderly Room."

When I went back to barracks I learned that the Adjutant wanted to see me. I reported to him, and he said: "I'm taking you to see the Colonel-Commandant—you've been selected for a Corps Commission!"

I almost dropped at his feet. I felt lightheaded, dizzy; the impossible dream I'd nursed so long was about to come true!

"There's no such thing," I managed to say.

"There is now," replied the Adjutant. "The First Lord, Winston Churchill, has introduced a new system of promotion from the lower deck. It's called the 'Mate System'—any young man of twenty-five or less, who has a clean record sheet" (I remembered my attempt to desert!), "is unmarried, and has a First-Class Certificate of Education, can be considered for promotion to the quarter deck.

"Your case was the outcome of a letter which your commanding officer sent to the First Sea Lord, although I don't think that influenced the Commandant-General very much. You're the only person in the Portsmouth Division with a First-Class Certificate, so you're considered for a commission. Don't bother to kit yourself up again as a Sergeant. You can go on leave until we send you final instructions."

I listened to him in a daze. Would my wild flights of fancy, my dreams, come true? It seemed incredible.

Then I was called before the Commandant-General who, with some compassion, explained that unfortunately I had seen no

38

active service, which was necessary before I could be commissioned. Serving aboard the Naval Examination Service vessel apparently didn't count. Neither did being tossed into the sea and almost drowned when our ship was cut in two by the French destroyer. I was to go to France, to experience service with a battalion and be tried out under actual service conditions.

I was posted to a Marine Division fighting on the Western front. Whether the Commanding Officer had decided for himself that rankers were not wanted in the higher echelons of the Corps, or whether he had been given instructions really to put me to the test, I never knew; but I found myself being sent out on every raid, every dangerous mission, he could organise. Casualties were extremely high, and yet, by the grace of God, I came through without a scratch. I've tried to recall places and names, but I don't think I ever knew them. I went to some base and I imagine that the orders were that I should be temporarily attached to some unit in the firing line; but I don't believe that the N C O or men had the foggiest idea where they were or indeed what they were there *for*.

I vividly remember my first task on arrival with the battalion. I had a platoon and the Company Sergeant-Major said : "Come on, you, I want this 'ole filled in."

It was a tremendous hole which must have been caused by an outsize explosion, a mine or some very heavy shell. I asked : "Where do I get the material to fill it?" All he said was : "Use your loaf, Lance-Sergeant! There's a village 'ere and the 'uns 've knocked it down, so all you got to do is move it to this 'ere 'ole!"

I lost count of the numbers of houses we put into the hole, but we did eventually fill it.

When the war settled down to trench warfare we had trench parties. Officers and men came to France for a spell in the trenches. Life in a ship like the *Dreadnought* lying at anchor in Scapa Flow was as comfortable and indeed as luxurious as could be imagined. Comfortable cabins, hot baths, a servant, excellent meals with a full dinner at night, duty-free drinks and wines; and yet the officers seemed to be always anxious to get back to the trenches with all the danger and filth. Their explanation was that in the trenches there was always a chance, but if the ship went into action and was sunk everybody would be lost without even seeing the enemy.

I found out that this was indeed true. Whatever the task I was given, repairing the barbed wire, raids on the German lines to bring back prisoners, etc., one was always convinced that no matter who was killed or wounded it wouldn't be you.

After a few weeks of this the C O called me before him and told me that I was being sent back to base. "You've carried out your duties extremely well, taking into consideration that you had no actual service experience before you came out here. I shall be putting that in my report."

And so I finished my first taste of active service. Shortly afterwards, I found myself commissioned a probationary Second Lieutenant in His Majesty's Corps of Royal Marines.

Just before that happened officially, I was sent for by the Adjutant-General. "You're going to be commissioned as a probationary Second Lieutenant," he told me. "It will be slightly different to those colleagues from the lower deck who're being commissioned by the Navy. We're doing this deliberately. The Navy intends to promote its men as Mates, and that title, we think, will remain with them for the rest of their careers, and possibly handicap them.

"We don't want this to happen in the Marines. You'll be commissioned exactly as all other Second Lieutenants are. You'll join a different division where no one knows you, and you'll join on the same day as probationary officers coming in from the public schools. No one, in fact, need ever know that you came from the ranks."

I thought at the time, and I still do, that this was the best attitude. The stigma of Mate—and it *was* a stigma—even when a man had risen to the rank of Captain, there were people who'd remember that he'd once been a ranker—was never mine; and I'm not ashamed to say that I was glad of it.

The Adjutant-General gave me a bit of advice which I was very glad to take. "Buy your uniforms at the tailors who specialise in R M officers' dress," he said. "They may be a bit more expensive, but you don't have to pay for them until you become a Major, by which time you'll be able to afford the difference. The important thing is that you don't look different from the other officers. Buy your sword at Wilkinson's, and have your boots hand-made."

I arrived at Plymouth by the same train as the other probationary Second Lieutenants. We were greeted by the Adjutant, allocated individual batmen, and given quarters.

I passed all the statutory courses quickly, and joined up with the more senior group of officers, one of whom was "Jo" Hollis (afterwards Secretary to the War Cabinet, later Commandant-General, Royal Marines, and now General Sir Leslie Hollis). We became firm friends, and have remained so right up to the present day.

The fact that I knew all the drill and was a good rifle shot was not too obvious, as a large number of the new temporary commissioned officers had done cadet training. But I was a little hurt at being bowled out twice by senior officers.

Coming in for a ten-minute break we were allowed to keep our swords on and go to the anteroom for coffee. A Lieutenant-Colonel came up to me and demanded, "Is your sword a Wilkinson's?"

I said, "Yes, sir."

He asked: "Has it the proved steel mark?"

I hadn't the slightest idea, and he said: "Oh, give it to me" and I drew my sword from its scabbard. He went straight to the bell and, when the Mess Corporal came in, he said: "Take this young gentleman's name. He will stand a round of port tonight for drawing his sword in the Mess!"

At dinner one night I was sitting next to another Lieutenant-Colonel; he asked my name and then asked me, "What do you do with yourself in the evening?"

I replied that last week I had been to the local music-hall and listened to a famous singer.

"Oh, yes? Now what was her name?"

I told him. He tapped the table and ordered the Mess Butler to charge a round of port to me for mentioning a lady's name in the Mess.

I realised that had either of these senior officers known I was promoted from the ranks they would never have dreamt of putting me to this extra expense, so I was greatly comforted.

Both Jo and I found parade work dull and unnecessary, so one day we approached the Chief Instructor, a Lieutenant-Colonel, and asked whether we could be excused so that we could study for the Staff Course examination. This was agreed to, although the Instructor pointed out that he was too busy to give us special instruction. We hadn't expected any extra instruction; we were content that we could study in our quarters.

The next morning we went to the Mess library, but the only books we could find there were a wonderful unexpurgated set of the Arabian Nights. We took a volume each to our quarters, and spent the time playing cards and betting who could find the best story in the Arabian Nights. After some days of this we grew bored and decided to ask the Chief Instructor for some tuition. With some difficulty we tied him down to a time when we could meet in the library. We'd managed to obtain some Staff College examination papers, and we asked him to help us with these.

The first question on the paper was on map reading, and called for definitions.

"You know all about this," said the Chief Instructor.

"Oh no, we don't!" we chorused, and we made him explain. The first question was: 'Define a hill'.

"Damn silly question!" commented the Instructor, and tried to pass on.

"But exactly what is it, sir?" I asked.

He made a motion with his hands. "Even a child knows that it comes up from the ground like this."

"Oh yes," I said. "But so does a hillock, a knoll, a mountain, a spur and a cliff."

That fixed him; he dropped the paper and said that he had an urgent board of survey to attend to, and couldn't waste time on our instruction. So we never found out what a hill really was.

My first appointment as an officer was to H M S *Dreadnought*, then anchored at Scapa Flow. As an officer, I travelled to join the ship in a first-class compartment; my Marine servant travelled third.

As we stood on the jetty at Scapa waiting for a boat to take us out to the battleship, I asked him: "Have you worked as an officer's servant before?"

"Oh yes, sir," he replied.

"Then you know the routine. What do I do when I go on board?"

"Well, sir, go to your cabin, and I'll unpack your gear. After that, I'll find out what the routine is for you."

After I'd reported to the Officer of the Watch, I went down

to my cabin. My servant laid out my Mess kit and then went away to make inquiries. When he came back he reported that the Major of Marines—whose subaltern I was to be—always went into the wardroom at six o'clock for a glass of gin, and he suggested that I go there a quarter of an hour earlier and wait for him.

The wardroom was empty when I arrived there. I waited for a few minutes, and when no one came in, I sat down at the Bechstein grand in the corner. Because of my service in France, and the various courses in gunnery and instruction I'd been taking since being commissioned, I hadn't practised in a long time. I thought I'd see if my fingers were still flexible.

I was playing when the Major walked in; I stopped and rose to my feet. I'd met him when I was stationed at Plymouth as a ranker, and I felt sure he recognised me. But he said nothing. He rang the bell; I imagined that he wanted to order a drink. But when the Corporal of Servants came in, the Major demanded in a very loud voice: "Who is this bloody person playing the piano?"

"Your subaltern who's just joined, sir."

"Well, tell him to get out!" roared the Major.

The Corporal approached me and said very quietly and stiffly: "With the Major's compliments, sir, will you leave the wardroom?"

I returned to my cabin and found my servant polishing my buttons. I told him what had taken place in the wardroom. "Cor! I'd better go and see what happens now," he said, and disappeared.

The news he brought was not very comforting. "The Major's furious, sir; you'd better not go in to dinner. I'll bring you in a tray." And so, on my first night aboard, I sat alone in my cabin, eating from a tray.

Each morning, the whole ship's company attended divisions, assembled on the quarter deck. The Padre read the prayers, and the Major, of course, gave the Marines the order to disperse after the Padre had finished. On my first morning, after giving the order, the Major shouted: "Stand fast, Mr Bassett, stand fast!"

He came up to me. "Now, Mr Bassett," he began sternly, "let me make this quite clear. I got rid of my previous subaltern because he was no good. This time I asked the Marine Officer to

43

send me a soldier. And what do they send me? A bloody piano-player! I don't want you playing that piano just as long as I'm in this ship. D'you understand me?"

"Yes, sir," I replied, outwardly calm. But I was seething, for I knew this man had never heard a shot fired in anger in his life. My only course was to obey him. For a very long time I was unable to touch that beautiful piano, although I discovered a little one in the gunroom, where I practised.

Eventually, *Dreadnought* was made flagship, and we went down to Sheerness where an Admiral joined us. As was customary, he was invited to dine with the wardroom officers. The Commander, rather foolishly, had neglected to inquire what he liked to do after dinner and when the port was being passed around he said: "Sir, I've arranged a game of bridge for you."

"I don't play bridge," the Admiral replied sharply.

Disconcerted, the Commander tried to smooth things over. "Perhaps a game of poker for small stakes, sir?"

At this the Admiral gave the Commander a piece of his mind: "I sincerely hope there's no playing of cards or gambling in any ship under my command. I loathe and detest cards: I consider them the devil's playthings!"

Hurriedly, the Commander signalled up the port again. "How about a game of billiards then, sir? There's a nice table in the gunroom," he ventured.

"No, I couldn't do that," said the Admiral, his temper not improving. "I'm having dinner there next week, and I can't anticipate that. Besides, I like to be entertained *where I dine*."

The table was a very large one, with the Admiral and the Commander seated at the top, and us junior officers at the other end. We could hear this conversation very clearly, and were very close to laughter. Suddenly the Admiral relieved the situation. "That's a nice piano you have there. Does anybody play?"

After a swift glance around the table, a voice replied: "Yes, the young soldier plays."

The Commander, who had no idea whether I could play or not, broke in quickly: "Oh yes, the young soldier plays!"

"Come on then, let's hear you," called the Admiral to me. It was with pleasure that I sat down at the Bechstein and played a couple of pieces.

44

"You play very well; d'you read music?" the Admiral barked.

"Yes, I do, sir. These are just some pieces I've memorised."

"Flags!" bawled the Admiral to one of his officers, "Haven't I got some music in the cuddy?"

"Yessir!" said Flags, springing to attention.

The Admiral, in fact, considered himself a singer of distinction, so much so that he had some music that had been specially arranged for his singing.

Flags quickly produced several ballads, I played three or four, and when I came to the 'Indian Love Lyrics' I turned to the Admiral. "Sir, I can only play the accompaniment here; someone'll have to sing," I told him.

"Has anyone got a *voice?*" barked the Admiral in a tone that might have sent the entire German Navy running for cover. No one wanted to see the inside of the brig, so there were no volunteers.

"Well, *I* can sing that," he said smiling. He sang it, and many others, and in fact it was two o'clock in the morning when he stopped singing. He left saying that he'd never had such an enjoyable evening in his life.

When he'd gone, the Commander called for me. "Come here, you! We've been in this stinking hole for three weeks, with nothing to do in the evening, and you've been able to play the piano! Why didn't you?"

"Because of the Major's orders, sir."

"Major's orders, my foot! I'm the senior officer in this wardroom, and you'll play that piano every evening! Understand?"

I nodded. I was only too pleased to understand.

My experiences in the lower deck had given me a loathing of the word "bastard". As I marched beside a shore detachment one day, I became more and more irritated by the continual and meaningless use of this word in every context and situation; it was a noun, an adverb, and a verb. We were on a route march, and the men were marching at ease, and so were talking. During a break I called them around me, and explained that I was sick and tired of hearing nothing but this word "bastard". It was bastard boots, bastard collar, bastard pack, bastard everything. Did they know the meaning of the word?

"I don't, sir," said Private Smith.

"Well, you've been using it more than anyone else. Does *anyone* know?"

"It means being born the wrong side of the blanket," one of the men replied.

"Right!" I said. "Now I'll give you an example of the proper use of the word. A father on his death bed sent for his three sons and said to them: 'Boys, I've a confession to make to you. Your mother and I were never married.' And then he died. The eldest son turned to his brothers: 'Well, I don't know what *you* bastards are going to do,' he said, 'but *I'm* going to the pictures.'"

In the wardroom I had to be careful of my own speech. One can't spend eight years in the lower deck and remain entirely unaffected. I realised that my speech left much to be desired, and I decided the easiest way to handle the difficulty was to invent a way of speaking of my own. I therefore began to deliberately mispronounce words—Daffodil; Tra...falgar; Ad...mirality—in this way many of my genuine mistakes passed unnoticed.

My knowledge of French, of course, proved to be of great advantage. I translated *La Vie Parisienne* for other officers; it seemed to be the only French reading in which they were interested. I found this book difficult, for I'd learned my French at that religious school, and much of *La Vie Parisienne* contained words and sentences which had never entered my vocabulary at school. However, no one raised any objections to my translations.

The Major who'd forbidden me to play the piano was transferred shortly after this. I heard nothing further of him until just after the war, when he commanded a Marine Battalion which was sent to occupy Murmansk and fight the Bolsheviks. This battalion was in fact tricked into going out there—only volunteers were supposed to be accepted for service in Russia—and these men were told they were going to Schleswig-Holstein.

Everything seemed to go wrong from the moment they arrived in Russia. They were surprised by the Bolsheviks and suffered great losses. Later some of them retreated without orders, or because of conflicting orders, and there were many courts-martial.

My Major, who had apparently shown extraordinary incompetence, was hurriedly retired. I'm not sorry to say I didn't meet him again. His confidential report on me read as follows: "This

46

officer has served under my command for six months. He plays the piano."

He was replaced aboard *Dreadnought* by an incredible character known as Major What, a nickname we gave him because he used this word about three times in every sentence. He fancied himself as an artist and spent most of his time in his cabin, painting. Every morning I had to inform him of defaulters. The accused would be kept outside while the Major, still in his bed, listened to me, or pretended to listen to me. I would explain the crime and suggest an appropriate punishment. Without hearing one word, he'd repeat the punishment, parrot-like.

On one occasion I had a really serious case to report to him. A Marine had gone ashore with a party of sailors and wrecked a pub. When a patrol tried to arrest them, they'd fought the patrol. This was a serious offence, for Petty Officers had been struck, and the affair would have to be reported to the Commander, who'd report it to the Captain.

As well as this man I had a second defaulter, a Marine who hadn't left his hammock promptly at reveille; a very minor offence indeed. I explained both cases carefully to the Major, and he rose from his bed and came outside. I read out the serious charge, and evidence was given by a Petty Officer, but I could see that the Major wasn't listening.

"That's all, sir," I said when the case had been presented.

The Major stared at the man who'd been involved in the patrol fight, and who was standing sullen and crest-fallen. "The trouble with you is that you're sleeping in a hammock under a police light, what," said the Major stupidly, repeating exactly what I'd told him about the second defaulter. "Move your hammock to another place and then you'll be able to get some rest. What, what! Dismiss!"

And he went back to his cabin and his bed. I followed him to explain his mistake.

"What can I do now?" The Major laughed as though it were a great joke. "I've dismissed him!"

Indeed, that might have been the end of it but for the fact that the other men in the affair were taken before the Captain, who gave them ninety days in cells. They complained bitterly that their ringleader had received no punishment whatever. The

47

Captain called for an investigation, and Major What was hastily returned to barracks.

We had another extraordinary character on board at this time, whose nickname was "Skintight", because although he drank a great deal he never became intoxicated.

Aboard ship, a Marine officer has practically nothing to do. He cannot even, in many cases, punish his own men; sometimes this is the prerogative of the Commander or the Captain. "Skintight" could find no way of passing the time and relieving the boredom other than by drinking. One day we were talking in the wardroom. He asked me where I'd been educated, and I explained that I'd been promoted from the ranks.

"Why on earth did you select the Marines?" he asked me in astonishment. "You know what they say of us. The two people aboard a ship who have absolutely nothing to do are the Padre and the Major of Marines. And the Major's in the worst state, because he has a subaltern to help him! Get out of it, laddie. Go anywhere. Join the Egyptian Army or something. Anything but stay in the Marines!"

"I don't think I'll leave, sir," I said. "I'm anxious to make a success in the Corps."

"Well, in that case the only advice I can give you is . . . never fornicate with suède shoes on; it makes the toes shiny."

Looking back, I remember those days as extremely happy ones. On one occasion, four of us pooled our resources and decided to have a night out in London. We agreed to go to the Savoy Hotel and see a show called *The Bing Boys On Broadway*, starring George Robey.

We'd heard there was a zoo scene during the show, when the audience pelted the players with stuffed animals. We decided we'd go one better, so we went to Harrod's zoological department with the intention of buying a lion cub, which we intended to present to Robey. No lion cubs were available, and finally, after declining various substitutes, we decided to settle for a snake. This was completely harmless, of course, but it's strange how some people react to any sort of reptile.

During the interval we went into the bar. We had the snake inside a chocolate box, perfectly safe. The barmaid saw the chocolate box and remarked what a nice box of chocolates we had. One of my friends asked: "Would you like one?"

48

She nodded, and leaned over as he lifted the lid. The snake reared its head, and the barmaid fell to the floor in a faint. Glasses smashed everywhere as other women saw the snake and rushed screaming from the bar.

We put the snake back in its box and considered whether we'd be wise to throw it on to the stage; it could so easily start a riot. We decided the best thing was to take it to George Robey in his dressing-room and present it to him in person after the show. And that was what we did. But when Robey heard we had a snake for him, he bawled: "Get it out of here at once! I'm absolutely terrified of snakes! If you'd thrown that thing on the stage, it would have been the end of the show!"

We were now stuck with the snake. One of the officers—the Padre's son—invited us to spend a few days of our leave with his people. We took the snake with us to their house in Plymouth, and he told his mother about it. "All right," she said anxiously, "but make certain it's locked up."

Two days later we went to look at the snake and see that he was all right. We opened the box; it was empty. The Padre's wife ran from the house, screaming that she wouldn't come back until 'George', as we called him, had been found. We never did find him, and to this day I don't know what happened to him. Nor do I know if our hostess ever returned.

Life at Scapa Flow could be very boring. Occasionally we'd receive an alarm about the German fleet, and steam out to challenge them. But we never found them. I suppose some scouting cruiser or destroyer had seen something, but so far as the great capital ships were concerned the German Grand Fleet remained for us the figment of somebody's imagination.

My life was made tolerable because I was serving under a most admirable Major of Marines, Eric Weston. He taught me to play golf, and many of our days were spent going around the nine-hole course the Navy had constructed at Scapa.

About this time, as subaltern, and in charge of sentries and guards, I was ordered to investigate the strange case of the drunken watchkeepers. A number of people were found to be drunk and incapable in the middle and morning watches, the hours between midnight and eight in the morning.[1] The Corporal

[1] Middle watch = 12–4 a.m., morning watch = 4–8 a.m.

of Marines, the signalmen, even the Quartermaster, would be found unconscious. It was very mystifying, because when we checked the supplies of spirits on board everything was found to be in order; nothing had been stolen from stores. There was no way in which spirits could be smuggled into the ship; every possible check had been made on all the traditional and modern methods. I was informed that my leave would be stopped until I solved the mystery.

I found this an impossible task for some days, and I couldn't go out for my golf with the Major, which made me more irritable about my job.

One day, when I was wishing I could have a game, my servant gave me the first clue to the mystery. "Are you playing golf this afternoon, sir?" he asked me.

"You know damn well my leave's been stopped," I shouted.

He grinned. "Yessir, I forgot." As he was going out of the door, he hesitated.

"Of course, water can always be put in a rum barrel, can't it?"

"Hey!" I called after him as he tried to duck away. "What did you say?"

"Nothing, sir, nothing at all," he muttered, his face a picture of innocence. I realised that he wouldn't tell me anything else, because he didn't wish to give his friends away openly; but what he'd said was enough to give me a hint. I called for the Corporal of the Guard.

"How are these chaps getting the rum?" I asked him.

"Dunno, sir. All the rum's been mustered and found correct," he said.

"All right, let's follow it through. What happens to the rum?"

"Well, sir, it comes up from the rum store, which is locked, and then put into the cask that has 'God Save the King' round it in brass letters. This cask stands in front of the Captain's cabin. The spirit inside's pure rum, but when a man gets a tot it has to be watered.

"What happens is that this ornamental sort of barrel's taken up on deck under guard, and the rum is poured into another barrel that already has water in it. Then it's returned to its stand. The men are served from the watered barrel, and the cask gets filled again every morning. It stands empty during the night."

"Could the men be putting water into this cask when it's

50

empty?" I asked "The wood must soak up a great deal of the neat rum, and if it were swilled out with hot water it might yield a potent drink. What d'you think?"

"It's possible, sir," agreed the Corporal.

I arranged for the Corporal to stay in a cabin overnight where he could spy on the barrel. The following morning he made his report to me. "You're right, sir," he told me. "The people on the first watch're allowed to go to the galley at eleven o'clock for cocoa. Instead, they come down with the water they've boiled and pour it into the cask. A second group—on the middle watch—go to the galley at three o'clock, also to get cocoa. But they never bother about the cocoa; they turn up the barrel and take out this rum swill."

So that was the answer—I'd solved the mystery, and I felt like Sherlock Holmes. If the men had been content to take only a small tot at a time they could have kept up this trick indefinitely, and nobody would have minded much. But as it was they'd left themselves open to the charge of stealing rum, and they were all sentenced to thirty days in the cells.

The important thing, however, so far as I was concerned, was that I could return to my golf; if you've ever been as bored as I was at Scapa, you'll know what that meant to me.

It is very sad to relate that when the great naval battle of Jutland was fought we were in dry dock at Invergordon and all we knew of the battle was the meagre and conflicting wireless reports. When the battle-scarred ships returned, the dockyard 'maties' had heard that we'd been defeated by the Germans, and they booed the ships as they came alongside.

My melancholy task was to go on board one of the ships with some of my Marines to get the drowned Marines out of the magazines—which had been flooded by Major Harvey, thus saving the whole ship from being blown up and winning him the V C.

In February 1918 I was appointed to H M S *Isis*, where I relieved Lieutenant Robert Sturges, now Sir Robert Sturges. *Isis* was an old cruiser employed in convoy work between Glasgow and Nova Scotia. The other end of the line was actually not Nova Scotia at all, but the United States, because convoys usually gathered in Chesapeake Bay, and *Isis* used to pick them up there and escort them to Nova Scotia before making the Atlantic

51

crossing. She was a slow cruiser, but so were the convoys, and crossings normally took twenty-eight days.

There was no bakery on board, and of course no refrigeration, so three or four days from port we were forced back on to hard tack. This was an abysmally dull sort of life, even worse than Scapa—where at least I had my golf!—and only on two occasions were we ever attacked by submarines. Once they downed a transport carrying army mules, and I had to order my Marine detachment to shoot the poor beasts as they struggled in the water. On another occasion *Isis* was rushed to Halifax on rescue work after the port had been almost destroyed when a T N T ship blew up.

When we arrived in *Isis* on her next trip we found desolation; reconstruction had been hampered by the hard winter. The crew of the *Mont Blanc* were still there attending courts of inquiry, and we put some of them up in our mess and heard their story. The *Mont Blanc* had had to call at a port for fuel on her way from New York to Halifax; the port agent had some cargo for France, but the ship's master declined to open his holds: his orders were secret, and he didn't disclose why. He was told "That's all right—it's all cased, so you can carry it on the upper deck."

All might still have been well if the ship, as it was about to enter Halifax harbour, hadn't unfortunately collided with another ship coming out. The petrol cases broke open, the liquid ran out along the decks and reached the galley, which had been transferred to the upper deck because of the dangerous cargo in the hold. Within seconds the ship was an inferno. Captain and crew, realising that she'd explode any minute, launched the lifeboats.

Before leaving the ship, the captain lashed the wheel so that the vessel would circle around inside the harbour, and not crash into the jetties where there were other ships anchored. Even so, when she eventually did explode, the damage was appalling. Thousands of people were standing at their windows, gazing down at this brilliant sight of a ship circling in flames. Most of them were blinded by glass splinters. The ship's gun was found three miles inland. Other ships were capsized, and dockers injured and killed.

When we went ashore we found rescue work most difficult.

52

It was the depth of the severe Canadian winter, and we were not prepared for the extreme cold. For instance, when any of our men tried to lift a girder, his fingers stuck to the freezing iron.

But service with the *Isis* had its compensations. On the 4th of July I found myself in Washington DC, taking part in a ceremonial parade before President Wilson. The President had conceived the idea of a great parade of Democracy to mark America's National Day. He overlooked the fact—until the last moment—that he'd neglected to invite a British detachment to take part.

HMS *Isis* was ordered to proceed to Chesapeake Bay at full speed, and I received orders to hurry with my men to the US capital to take my place with the other detachment as the British representatives. We arrived just in time, by travelling up the Potomac in a paddle steamer. It was incredibly hot weather in Washington then, and on 4th July—Independence Day—the Colonel at the US Marine headquarters asked me what sort of food my men liked. I told him they liked roast beef, Yorkshire pudding, and prunes and custard.

"Well, it's a bit unusual," said the Colonel. "My chaps can stand only cold meats, salads, iced coffee—that sort of thing—in this heat. I guess I'll have to ring up a hotel." This he did, and that night the Royal Marine detachment solemnly scoffed their roast beef and Yorkshire pudding with every sign of satisfaction during the very height of the Washington summer.

Before the big parade began, the Pageant Marshal approached me and asked if the Marines were well disciplined. I rather bristled at this until he explained the reason for this question "We have to be careful, you see. The last time you Marines were here in Washington, you burned the White House. The crowds might remember this and throw something at you; if they do, take your detachment off the line and we'll pick you up."

Fortunately, this didn't become necessary. The American crowd loved the smart display the detachment gave them, and we were greeted with roars of applause as we marched to the Capitol. The following day the British Ambassador, Lord Reading, asked to speak to us. He insisted that there must be no reporters present.

We fell in on the barrack square of the US Marine Corps. "First of all," began Lord Reading, "I'm going to tell you what

53

the President said. He said: 'Those troops from India were magnificent.' I had to tell him that there'd been no Indian troops.

" 'What about those chaps in white helmets and uniforms?' he demanded. 'They, sir,' I replied with some pride, 'are the Royal Marines!' "

CHAPTER III

AFTER the war I was sent to the island of Lemnos in the Aegean as Signals Officer. I went as relief to an officer who'd been in the service only for the duration of hostilities. A Royal Marine Battalion had been stationed in Lemnos with detachments in Imbros and Tenedos, because there were still large German forces in south Russia and it was not known whether these would attempt to fight their way out. Lemnos had been General Hamilton's old G H Q during the Gallipoli campaign. G H Q was a big bungalow situated on one of the highest points in the island, overlooking the harbour of Mudros. I was attached to the staff of the Military Governor, who was General J. B. Finlaison, Royal Marines.

It proved to be a pleasant life—certainly a great change from convoy work—and the war in Russia was far from our thoughts. There were good bathing and an excellent local drink called Mastic, which is made by the Greek monks. I even managed to find a piano, one that had been washed ashore from a wreck. The casing was being used as a sideboard in the Quartermaster's offices, and the works were lying rusting; but with a bit of ingenuity and some hard work I managed to bring both parts together and make an instrument that I could play.

Some weeks after my posting there, one of my signallers came to me to say that a destroyer was entering the harbour; this was a great occasion indeed, for shipping usually only came about once a month with mail and stores. I went down to the pier and saw several people on board wearing unfamiliar uniforms. They were a White Russian general and his staff, who'd come to make arrangements, in case it became necessary, to evacuate troops and families from south Russia.

54

"Should this occur, you are to expect some forty thousand men, women and children," the General advised me through the interpreter.

You may remember that my father had insisted upon my studying Russian. Some smattering of it still remained with me, and I was certain the General had said 14,000, not 40,000. Lemnos was barren, even the water had to be distilled; we could never have handled 40,000 people. I broke in and asked the General if he meant 40,000 or 14,000. "Fourteen thousand," he replied in Russian.

The interpreter, a young Grenadier Guards officer, turned to me, surprised. "D'you speak Russian?"

"Yes, but only a little."

"Well, for goodness' sake, you carry on!" he said. "I've been doing a Russian course at Constantinople, and suddenly I was called to do this job. But I really don't know enough Russian to handle it."

So I finished the conference in Russian. There was an astonishing sequel to this. Two months later when the mails arrived from England there was an official letter for me from the War Office. It informed me that I had been appointed Staff Captain to the Army of the Black Sea, and accordingly my pay had been transferred from the Royal Marines. There was an accompanying form on which I was to claim army allowances. These seemed extraordinarily generous compared with those we had in the Navy. This aspect was certainly satisfactory enough, but it all seemed the most utter nonsense. What did the Army want with me?

Two days later a telegram arrived from Constantinople, instructing me to report forthwith to Army H.Q in Constantinople. I went immediately. But first I tried Naval H Q to see if they could throw any light on this extraordinary appointment; they knew nothing. At Army H Q, however, they knew all about me.

"You've been appointed Staff Captain, old chap."

"But why?" I asked. "I can't understand it."

"Apparently you speak Russian."

It appeared that the Russian general at Lemnos had reported that I spoke excellent Russian, and it had therefore been decided to appoint me liaison officer.

"You'll be sent to Russia. We have an Army Mission there, and you'll be attached to them. In the meantime, you'd better start reading papers."

I was hustled off to study the latest reports on the war between the White and the Red armies. Among my reading matter was a most interesting pamphlet. It was signed by Winston Churchill, and gave advice to officers joining the Army of the Black Sea. Among other things, it explained that the Russians were very like us, possibly more so than any other nation; but they had one extraordinary custom to which we should pay particular attention. They loved shaking hands. They would shake hands with one before visiting the lavatory, and they would shake hands again when they came out, such was their enthusiasm.

I travelled by destroyer, and landed at Novorossisk, where a detachment of our Army Mission was working with the Russians. The first night there, with Churchill's advice in mind, I tried to shake hands with the Russian liaison officer; he'd been at Oxford and spoke excellent English.

At first I wasn't sure whether it was my imagination or not, but he seemed to withdraw his hand. After tea I made a second attempt, and this time there could be no mistake. He'd definitely withdrawn his hand.

"Look," I said, "I don't want to make any mistakes. We were warned that you Russians liked shaking hands and insisted on doing it at every opportunity."

He laughed. "Well," he replied, "we were warned that you British *never* shake hands unless you're going big-game hunting in Africa, or when you're on your deathbed."

From Novorossisk I went on to Rostov, where the main party of the British Military Mission was stationed. The English commanding officer there was a Colonel Cox, 15th Hussars; a Russian speaker, he'd been christened Coxinka by the Russians. He explained to me that the war was going very badly for the White Russians. They were being beaten for political reasons. The Bolsheviks were promising the peasants land, and as there were something like 140 million peasants, this was naturally attracting massive support to the Red Army.

The White Russian general was doing his best to counteract this by promising land reform and redistribution, but every time he made another promise he antagonised his own officers who owned the land he was giving away.

It was not a happy situation. Bribery and corruption existed on a large scale; when stores were landed at Novorossisk or Sebastopol, the people at the base picked over the best items and either stole them or sold·them. This meant that while the people at the base were well-clad and warm, the troops in the fighting line remained ill-equipped, and the biggest casualties were caused by frostbite. The fatal word was 'nichevo' which means: "it doesn't matter, everything'll be all right." But of course it didn't come all right.

Things were going extremely badly for the Whites. General Denikin's forces had advanced to Orel only some eighty miles from Moscow. There did not appear to be set battles and planned operations and the English officers were extremly worried at the lack of consolidation after each skirmish and the entire lack of concern at the ever-increasing lines of communication.

General Denikin's attitude was that they did not understand the Russian temperament, nothing he or anyone else said would stop the victorious march of his army and that was that. Moscow, of course, was never reached. A partisan force raised by someone who had enjoyed no previous military experience—a shoemaker, I was told—cut the communication lines between Orel and the south, and the White Army beat a hasty retreat only to find their way blocked and their supplies cut off. It was soon obvious that if anything was to be saved a general retreat to the Crimea would have to be made, and artillery units were sent to build up defences at the Perekop Isthmus. The Army Headquarters and thousands of civilian refugees moved to the port of Novorossisk.

Our orders emphasised that we were not to pick up any refugees on the way—there'd be many thousands of them, and we must make no distinctions; better to leave all than to help a few and so create ill-feeling. Thus we had to push our way through the ghastly hordes of refugees carrying pitiful possessions on their backs, many with small children toddling along beside them. It was a sight to stir even the most hardened heart.

At one halt I noticed three girls walking along painfully. The one in the centre—a lovely, fair-haired girl—had no shoes, and her feet were badly cut and bruised. The other two were trying

57

to help her. Although we weren't allowed to pick up any refugees, there was nothing in orders forbidding us to help them. I
undid my pack and took out a pair of canvas shoes and tossed
them down to the girl. And then we drove on.

We were held up by a White artillery brigade which had been
sent down ahead of the army to build up proper defences, but
hadn't done anything at all. The Red Army, meanwhile, was
almost on top of us, and there was nothing to stop them. The
British Mission, being only administrative, was not supposed to
engage in any fighting, but we had to; we knew what our fate
would be if we were captured. We were forced to leave two of
our officers behind after a skirmish, and we learned later that
both of them had been tortured and killed.

I didn't exactly cover myself with glory during our efforts to
escape. Our Russian driver told us that he thought he could get
us away by encircling the battlefield. We set off, driving through
masses of White Russian guns and transports, and after a nightmare journey, which was made bearable only because we
thought we were escaping, arrived back at precisely the spot
from which we'd started! This was entirely my fault. In my
panic, I'd neglected to undo the clip of the compass needle, and
so had given the driver the wrong directions. It's a story of which
I am, to this day, thoroughly ashamed.

We tried again, this time successfully, and arrived safely at
Novorossisk where we boarded a British destroyer. Hundreds of
ships of all nationalities were anchored in the harbour, waiting
to take refugees aboard. We stood off for some time to see if
we could help, and in fact took on many Russian officers.
Refugees were being embarked at a very fast rate but, no matter
how many thousands were loaded, still more thousands were
arriving at the small dockyard.

We were forced to leave the harbour when our reconnaissance
party on shore reported that the Red Army was approaching
at speed and bringing up artillery.

The C-in-C knew that the transports, most of which had
been built to carry only 3,000 people, were in many cases
crammed with more than 10,000. It would have been suicide
to remain in the harbour and risk having many of them
sunk by the Bolshevik artillery, in order to cram perhaps
another few hundred on board. We'd done the best we could,

and had no need to feel ashamed of the help we'd given.

The destroyer sailed for Lemnos, and I reported to General Finlaison, who welcomed me back and asked me to stay on the island to help to organise and run the refugee camp which we knew was going to be established there. The transports began to arrive a few days afterwards packed with the soldiers and the refugees.

Our main worry was medical. Many of the refugees were likely to be carriers of typhus, smallpox and other diseases prevalent in revolutionary Russia. Our Surgeon-Commander, who had only two doctors to help him and a very small hospital in which to work, was insistent that the most rigid precautions should be taken, for if an epidemic developed there were no resources in the island with which to tackle it. He therefore ordered that the refugees be segregated in their camps and forbidden to mingle with the islanders, so we threw barbed wire around the camp to make sure of this.

His main demand, however, was for a proper system of sanitation. This presented some difficulties, for it was impossible to dispose of the sewage in the non-tidal sea, and we had to dig pits on one of the sandy beaches some distance from the camp. Collecting the sewage was to pose an even more difficult problem. We detailed working parties of Russians to deal with this, only to find that they were all officers—many of them princes, barons or members of the Czar's bodyguard—and they absolutely refused to do it.

Could we not get the Greeks to do this work, they asked? Certainly, we said, if you pay them. But they had no money! Well, what about the Marines? I had to tell them the Marines were not on the island for that purpose.

The Russian women had formed themselves into Ladies' Committees, and one of the senior ladies in the camp came to me and told me that the women would do the job if the officers refused.

I told General Finlaison of this proposal, but he replied he'd order the men to do it. So at seven o'clock in the morning he paraded the Russian officers and addressed them from horseback. He explained that the first and most important need was sanitation and, if this were neglected, then their children would die. They *must* clear the lavatories.

59

Not a Russian moved.

"Well, I'll give the order a second time," said General Finlaison.

He gave it, but still the men stood there as stubborn as mules.

Then suddenly the women broke through their ranks. They went into the lavatories and began carrying out the buckets. The shame of watching their women do this proved too much for the gallant officers, and they gave in.

General Finlaison and I soon realised that the attitude among Russian officers was that a prince or a baron should not be asked to do a menial task. General Finlaison issued a firm order reminding them all that they were guests of H M Government, and that in future there were to be no ranks or titles among them; all were to be addressed simply as refugees. They drew the same rations as our Marines. Contrary to our belief that this might cause ill-feeling, most of the Russians welcomed it.

They quickly adapted themselves to life in tents, sometimes with as many as twelve in each; and in order to keep up their morale we encouraged them in the belief that they were there only temporarily. They remained very cheerful and we thought they were behaving extremely well, remembering that most of them had been brought up in great luxury.

Within a short time they'd requested a marquee for a church, another for a school, and one for a club where they could enjoy some kind of social life in the evenings. We sent for pianos, violins and other musical instruments, and as there were many talented musicians among them we had excellent concerts every night.

A number of these White Russian refugees owned villas in France, or elsewhere, and had money abroad, but no government would grant visas because of the fear of Communism. As an interpreter I was beginning to find the strain very wearying. Refugees from Riga spoke German, others spoke French. Sometimes I had to try to speak three languages at once. Finally, I could go on no longer, and so I went to General Finlaison to ask for help.

"I can't stand this," I told him. "I'm spending most of my time acting as a bad interpreter. Surely there's someone in the camps who can speak all these languages, someone we could appoint as official interpreter?"

"There's a girl in No. 3 Camp," said the General. "She has quite good English, German and French—even a little Serbian."

"Well, let's appoint her right away," I suggested. The General grinned and sent for the girl immediately.

The orderly ushered in the fair-haired girl to whom I'd thrown a pair of shoes during the retreat into the Crimea.

She proved absolutely superb in the job. Her duties normally threw her into some proximity with me and, when General Finlaison invited high-ranking Russians to dinner or to lunch, I sometimes invited her along as guest. In a very short time I realised I was in love with her and wanted to marry her.

We would have to be married on the island, otherwise she wouldn't be allowed to leave it. And while we remained on the island this meant difficulty over accommodation. I approached the General. I knew he was fond of the girl and I expected every assistance. "Sir," I said, "I intend to marry Zoya, and I want permission to live in one of the villages after the ceremony so that my fiancée can leave the camp."

I was astonished at the General's reaction. "Oh, no!" he replied sharply. "I couldn't give you permission to do that!"

"Well, sir," I asked, angry and surprised, "could I have permission to live in one of the spare tents?"

"No, no!" he said, "I couldn't consider that either!"

Such a reaction seemed inexplicable to me: we'd been the best of friends until now.

"In that case, sir," I said stiffly, "I must beg permission to return to England."

He looked up at me in surprise and a grin crossed his face. "Why the devil don't you come and live with me, Sam?" he suggested. "We can get another room built on to this bungalow."

I felt a bit foolish; he'd been joking with me.

People were kindness itself. When I told the Captain of HMS *Dublin* (a cruiser detailed to stay at Lemnos to act as wireless unit) of our plans—his Padre was to marry us—he said that as a wedding present he'd send a party ashore to paint and decorate our new room.

61

This led to the only sour note in the whole proceedings. For some reason a Marine Colonel down at the camp thought the extra room was being built for him. I did nothing to disillusion him, and one day he approached me in a fury. "There's a Navy party painting my room like a whore's boudoir!" he stormed. "I don't *want* those colours! Where's the General?"

The General, warned that he was coming, had jumped on his horse and ridden away. So I had to break the news to the infuriated Colonel that the room was for Zoya and me, and he didn't take it at all well.

My wedding was to prove quite an elaborate affair. There were to be no less than three ceremonies—one in Russian in the Greek Orthodox marquee, another on board H M S *Dublin*, and a third before the Civil Governor of Lemnos—with two receptions.

The Russian service was held in the marquee at ten o'clock in the morning, the Russian priest supplying us both with crowns made of flowers. I didn't understand a word of the service; the language wasn't Russian but Old Slav, the language only used in the church. At the communion service I made a bad mistake. When the cup was passed to me I drank too deeply. As everything's done in threes in the Russian church and I'd drunk all the consecrated wine, they had to go to the trouble of consecrating another lot.

As we left the marquee, I noticed that my wife was walking with a limp, and I thought I'd married a cripple; but she explained that she had a golden ten-rouble coin in her shoe, a Russian custom to ensure that she would always "walk on gold". This hasn't come true yet; but who knows?

Then we went on board *Dublin* where we were married again under the Foreign Marriage Act. The Captain and officers gave a reception for us, and at five o'clock we set off on so-called riding mules to be married by the Civil Governor at Kastro, whose permission was necessary if Zoya was to be allowed to leave.

We hadn't anticipated another reception, but when we saw the trouble that the Governor had taken we were pleased to join in. He'd arranged for a whole sheep to be cooked in our honour, and it was a custom that we had to eat everything—including the animal's eyes—using our fingers instead of knives and forks.

Outside, a boy was playing a flute; this was not as pleasant as it sounds, for in our honour he played the only British tune he knew—'Tipperary'—and we had to endure it continually for several hours.

The quite extraordinary sequel to this enchanting day was that all three 'marriages' proved to be illegal! The priest should not have attempted to perform a marriage in the marquee because the ground had not been blessed by an archbishop. The Captain of *Dublin* was wrong to marry us under the Foreign Marriage Act; he had to be outside the three-mile limit before he could perform a valid ceremony.

He had taken the precaution of hoisting the anchor and putting up the Union Jack and then lowering it again to show that officially we were at sea, but the Officer of the Watch, noticing that the ship was drifting towards the shore during the ceremony, shouted: "To hell with this, let go the anchor!" This meant that we were not at sea in *any* sense. Further, the banns should have been posted on the ship's notice board for three weeks in advance; and this hadn't been done.

Lastly, the Civil Governor had been no longer Civil Governor when he performed the ceremony! Two weeks earlier he'd been deposed by the new Greek Prime Minister.

In order to obtain my army marriage allowance I had to produce certificates of these marriages, and then the trouble started. Somerset House managed to sort out the confusion. They said the religious marriage didn't matter; the only one that counted was the shipboard marriage, and the essential thing about a marriage ceremony under British law was evidence of intent. If anyone had shown intent, I certainly had—and so they provided me with my marriage certificate!

All this time British and French stores had been pouring into the Crimea. General Wrangel had taken over command of the White Army, which had been reorganised, and a signal was sent to all refugee camps ordering all fit men to report to him there. I was dispatched to Constantinople to continue my job as liaison officer to the Army of the Black Sea in the Crimea. I left my wife in Constantinople and went on to Sebastopol and eventually joined General Wrangel's staff. There were no major operations, and Wrangel's main task was to get food for his army; this involved sorties into the rich grain lands outside the Crimea. Large numbers of White Russians continued to make their way to the Crimea but no one knows how many were caught and disposed of.

I had a chance to talk to a captured Russian Commissar who spoke excellent English. When I mentioned that the Bolsheviks were wrecking everything, he answered that it was necessary to pull down before you could build up again. He made much of White Russian atrocities and of the plight of the Russian peasants before the Revolution.

"Will you be any happier when the country is run by the State?" I asked.

"Yes, I think so, although it'll take some time," he replied. "But with Russians it's all a question of relativity. Russia had endured 400 years under the Tartars, and 200 years under the Czars and then the German war.

"I'll tell you a story. Once a Russian peasant had two sons. The boys married, and brought their wives to live in the house. Then they began to have families, and the house became so crowded that the peasant went to the village priest and asked permission to commit suicide with the church's blessing.

"The priest said: 'I want you to obey me in several things, and if at the end you are not satisfied, I'll give you the church's blessing. Now go home and take your two cows and three calves into your house right away.' (They did this in the winter anyway.)

"The peasant did so, and returned in two days' time, to say that the house was even more unbearable.

" 'Now,' said the priest, 'go home and take your chickens and turkeys into the house, and then come back to me in two days.'

"The peasant did so. When he returned again the priest said to him: 'You've still got three goats which are not in your house; take them inside too, and come back again in two days.'

"When the peasant returned again he said: 'Father, this is the end, I cannot even get over the threshold.'

" 'Right, my son,' replied the priest, 'now go home and kick all these animals out.' The peasant returned home and did so, and then came back to the priest.

64

" 'Father, I've done as you said, and it's wonderful!' "

I liked this man. The following morning I asked permission to see him again.

"Certainly," replied the White Russian officer, in whose charge he had been left. "But he won't be saying much. He's hanging from that tree. . . ."

General Wrangel, who'd returned from a visit to the front line, held a ceremonial parade at which he invested me with the Order of St Stanilas—a very high decoration indeed. The honour led to an invitation a few weeks later to be the guest of the Don Cossacks.

To my surprise, I found myself the only guest. Toasts were on all the evening and, just as I was about to slip under the table, there was a rush from the marquee and I was seized and tossed in a blanket. The Cossacks cheered and sang, and kept tossing me. Finally they let me go and I went behind a tree and was sicker than I'd ever been in all my life.

Then I was being lifted on to the table, in the centre of the marquee, where there was a chair. I was placed on the chair and solemnly invested with the uniform of the Don Cossacks—cloak with decorated cartridges and beautiful silver filigree work; jewelled dagger and a big fur hat. Then more toasts were drunk.

In the end I managed to escape from the table, and I asked a Russian Colonel who spoke some English why I was being so honoured.

"You have been promoted a Major in the Don Cossacks," he explained.

"What on earth for?" I demanded.

"Well, General Wrangel invested you with the Order of St Stanilas. But you weren't really entitled to it. Only a field officer can rightly receive that decoration, and you were only a Captain. So someone decided that the only thing to do was to promote you Major."

I was, indeed, very pleased about this honour. Normally, British officers are not allowed to accept foreign decorations without permission, and I was not hopeful of being allowed to retain this one. However, when I returned to England more than a year later, His Majesty gave me special permission to wear it.

It's a unique decoration—the last Czarist one given to a foreigner on Russian soil.

But to return to that night in the Cossack tent—I asked the Russian Colonel why I'd been tossed in the blanket.

"To be a good Cossack officer," he explained, "you have to be able to take your drink. This was a test. If you'd been sick while being tossed, you wouldn't have been promoted."

Luckily, no one had seen me behind the tree.

By now it was realised by both England and France that it was hopeless to continue military aid to the White Army. The Bolsheviks were firmly in power and growing stronger every day. What arguments were used to convince General Wrangel that his cause was hopeless I do not know but eventually came the decision to evacuate the Crimea and the second great refugee exodus took place. This time the soldiers and refugees were more numerous and large camps were set up on the Dardanelles, Greek Islands, Cyprus and one of some forty thousands at Touzla, opposite the Island of Prinkipo. It was to this camp that I was sent. The huts were in reasonable condition, rations were supplied by the French and large numbers of the Russian men, Generals down to privates, got jobs in Constantinople.

Previously Touzla had been a Turkish P O W camp for British prisoners captured at Kut in the Mesopotamian campaign.

Nights here were hideous with noise. We were kept awake for hours by thousands of pariah dogs which came to drink the water we'd laid on.

Owing to the stony ground, burials in this part of the world were in shallow graves, and the dogs used to dig up human remains which they'd bring up to the camp before making a meal. When they'd finished eating they'd slake their thirst from a small pool outside the hut, which the Turkish officers washed their feet in before entering their hut.

While here I became friendly with an old Turk called Race Bey, captain of a Turkish cruiser called *Yagouse*, meaning 'The Magnificent'. (This was the German battleship *Goeben*, which had escaped from the British fleet and been handed over to the Turks.) He was a charming old chap, part of his charm being his fluency in Cockney. His favourite expression was "Gor' blimey! Pass the cow's grease, mum!" (for butter).

On one occasion he rang me up to ask whether I'd send some Russian troops down to Touzla village, as he'd heard that the Armenians there were planning a massacre of the Turkish population. I replied that I was sorry, but I couldn't do anything like that without permission from British H Q in Constantinople—and I personally had no British troops I could send. However, I'd see what I could do.

In fact, I ordered one of my signallers to jump on a horse and ride down to the village to find out what was happening. He was to take a field telephone with him and report back if he saw any trouble. I would then contact Constantinople. However, I heard nothing further from him until he returned several hours later.

"What happened?" I asked.

"Oh, I quelled the disturbance, sir."

"What the hell d'you mean, you quelled the disturbance?"

"Well, sir, when I got to the hill outside the village I could see lots of people in the street, but they didn't seem to be doing much harm, and I thought I'd better go and have a look.

"I went down and there they were, all jabbering away and flashing knives. I rode straight up to them and shouted 'You shove off!' And they shoved off, sir."

One day our transport section reported that the rations for women and children in the camp had failed to arrive. I telephoned to my superior in Constantinople about this.

"Sorry, old chap, there's been no mistake," I was told. "The French Government's simply stopped all aid. General Wrangel's apparently broken the terms of his agreement with them by going outside the Crimea.[1] Apparently he's gone into the rich cornlands to get grain, and this is just the excuse the Government've been waiting for. They know the White Russian adventure's useless now."

I immediately approached our Naval C-in-C, Admiral de Robeck, and explained that something would have to be done for these starving people. I suggested that if I could go around all the ships and collect the stuff which was normally sold to farmers for feeding their pigs, this might help. Bones, for instance, could be used by the Russians to make soup.

[1]Both the French and British Governments had promised to keep him supplied as long as he stayed in the Crimea.

The Admiral at once sent a signal to the Fleet asking that any stuff which could be used for making soup should be collected. The response by the Fleet was quite magnificent. Canteen Committees met immediately, and every sailor volunteered to surrender one day's rations each week to help the refugees. This was a wonderful effort, for it included milk, jam, tea, meat and potatoes; we continued to collect this magnificent aid from each ship until eventually the League of Nations took over responsibility from us.

When this happened I was ordered to Constantinople and informed that I was to be sent to Belgrade. Serbia, which had been badly overrun and devastated during the war, had agreed to take all refugees who wanted to go, especially as the British and French Governments were to contribute a subsidy for every man, woman and child admitted. I was to superintend the arrangements for transporting and finding accommodation for these thousands of refugees. As I'd be away indefinitely, I could take my wife with me as official interpreter.

In Belgrade I met Government officials and worked out a scheme under which educated refugees would be given accommodation and employment in the big cities, and the others would go to farms where there was a desperate shortage of manpower. After a few weeks in Serbia, my wife and I returned to Constantinople, and to Salonica where we watched the final disintegration and dispersal of the White Russian armies, those infinitely sad remnants of that great empire which had once been ruled by the Czar of all the Russias.

On my return to Constantinople I went to see the Naval C-in-C, and he said that he could give me a passage home in a cruiser. I explained I had my wife with me.

"In that case, your wife can travel with you," said the Admiral. "After all, she's been helping us with the White Army."

I believe I am right in saying that the Captain of *Centaur* received orders that Mrs Bassett was to be given an official passage, not as a refugee, and that this was unique. What's more, she was given the Captain's sea cabin and ate with the Captain whilst I fed in the wardroom.

So we returned to Plymouth, and here I ceased to hold the rank of Staff Captain and reverted to that of Marine Subaltern. I found lodgings, by regulation, "within a bugle call" of the

Marine Barracks. At first my wife had some difficulty with the shopping. I noticed that we seemed to be eating an incredible number of chickens. Then she explained: "Well when I go into a shop and ask for lamb, the butcher asks me do I want home or New Zealand? As I don't like displaying my ignorance, I always have to say, 'In that case I'll have chicken!' "

As I could not afford chicken every day on a subaltern's pay, I arranged with my Marine servant to help my wife with the shopping, and she began to pick up English fairly quickly.

We were so hard pressed for money in those days that when I was posted to Scrasedon on the other side of Plymouth I couldn't leave my lodgings near the barracks because I hadn't the money with which to pay the rent, and our landlady wouldn't release our baggage until I'd paid her in full. I was thus forced to sell for £80 a motor-cycle that was worth a great deal more. In addition, my mother-in-law had come to live with us by now, having managed to escape from Soviet Russia by contracting an arranged marriage with a Swiss baron.

One day the Adjutant-General sent for me and said he wanted me to take the Army signalling course. If I got high marks I'd be appointed Superintendent R M Signals, a Corps appointment.

First, of course, I'd have to pass a medical test before I was posted. The young doctor examining me, said: "I see on your paper you're taking an Army signalling course, and they make a particular specification for eyesight."

He explained that he'd have to give me an extra test. "How's your colour vision?" he asked me.

"Perfect," I replied. "I've been reading flags for a great number of years."

He put me through the test and the result was that he discovered I was colour-blind! Not only would I be unable to take the signalling course, but I might well be invalided out of the Corps altogether.

I went back to barracks and that evening, as usual, went in to the Mess. The Commandant usually came in about six o'clock; fortunately he did so on this occasion. "You're looking very miserable, Bassett," he said.

"I've just been bowled out for being colour-blind," I explained.

"Good gracious, that explains it!"

"Explains what, sir?" I asked.

"Why we've often had to wait for you when we've been playing golf together. Obviously, you couldn't find your tee—if it were red or brown it'd be lost in the grass for you."

"Well, that doesn't help me."

"Nonsense," he said. "This signals job is purely an administrative one. I'll write to my friend the Medical Director-General of the Navy and tell him that this colour-blindness of yours is of no importance." And so it was all solved: I was allowed to go ahead with the course.

But I knew that in order to compete with some forty military officers who were under no such handicap as colour-blindness I'd have to watch my step very carefully. I therefore decided to improve my speed of reading and sending of both Morse and semaphore, and asked the Wireless Signals officer at the Admiralty: "Have you got anyone who can send Morse very quickly?"

"I suppose we've got the fastest sender in the Navy," he replied, knowing why I wanted this information. "Spend an hour every evening with him and in a month you'll be able to blind these military wallahs."

I did, and eventually I was able to read at a speed almost up to that of the automatic. On joining, we had to pass an entrance examination, and I received 100 per cent in all the reading and all the sending. Afterwards, we were interviewed by the General commanding the Signal Corps. He remarked pleasantly that I'd passed 100 per cent in all the tests; so then I had to put my oar in. "Oh, but we read and send at *incredible* speeds in the Navy, sir!" I told him rather condescendingly.

He was a little nettled at this information and replied coldly: "We also have people who can read and send incredibly fast— Royal Corps of Signals instructors."

"Well, sir," suggested the Adjutant, who was in the room, "let's test him out after tea."

"Yes," agreed the General. "I think he'll find that some of the Royal Corps of Signals can send just as fast as the Navy—and some probably faster."

After tea I sought out the Adjutant.

"I spoke out of turn this morning," I told him, "although I do think I can send and read fast; but I'd like this test to be fair.

The man who writes down the message has got to be good too. If you're reading fast he has to be just as fast."

The Adjutant agreed.

"I'll write down," he promised. "I'll see that you get a fair deal, and I'll watch your sending."

Well, I absolutely astonished them. The General could hardly credit our speed. "We've never known any person to send and read as fast as you. How did you?"

"Well, sir, you know, in the Navy . . ." I said deprecatingly. I didn't bother to mention my two months' intensive practice!

I finished this course with a "Special", the highest qualification. But despite this, I didn't get the job for which I'd been tested. The officer holding the post decided to stay on for another year, and so I went off for a spell at sea. I was appointed to H M S *Ceres* in the Mediterranean.

Although my wife and our young daughter, who was born shortly after we arrived at Plymouth, and my mother-in-law, had to travel third-class to Malta, we found life there extremely congenial, and we were soon able to afford a champagne standard of living on a ginger-beer budget. Our maid, for example, cost us only ten shillings *a month*!

Ceres was a newly commissioned ship and she proved a pleasant appointment. I brought my dog Jack aboard and he rapidly became a favourite with the crew. Jack was a Welsh terrier and had come into my possession in a curious way.

He'd originally belonged to an R A S C Major who turned up on Lemnos one day, beautifully dressed. Apparently he'd been an extra military attaché to the court of the King of Greece, living in the utmost luxury. One day his dog Jack had a fight with the King's pet monkey; the King apparently tried to separate them and His Majesty subsequently died. His successor, pro-German and anti-British, immediately turned out the British Mission, including the Major. As he had no job, he was sent to Lemnos.

He'd brought no field equipment with him, so I fixed him up in a tent at the camp base. The next morning he reported to H Q, and his clothes, which had been among the most impeccable I've ever seen upon any officer, were in a sorry state. He was even wearing shoes.

"Where are your field boots?" I asked.

"I took them off last night and when I awoke this morning

71

there were only a few pieces of leather left. The rats ate them."

"Didn't your dog attack them?"

"No, he slept through the whole thing. Damn it, I'll have to get rid of him! First of all he lost me my job in Athens, and now he's allowed this to happen. D'you want him?"

Which was how I came to own Jack. The Quartermaster aboard *Ceres* fixed up a tree trunk on the quarterdeck for him. One day I found him in my cabin, crouched in the corner and looking ill.

"What's the matter with Jack?" I asked my servant.

"Oh, nothing, sir. We ran into a bit of a storm, and a wave washed over the poop. Jack arrived on deck just as this water was pouring off the poop and the Quartermaster pointed at it and said: 'Jack, you naughty boy!'"

He was certainly an intelligent and lovable dog. He'd line up with the ship's company when they were going in for a swim, and wait for the bugle call before diving in with the men. One night in the wardroom I noticed that after all the guests had taken their seats an extra place had been laid. The Commander turned to the Corporal of Servants and said: "Has our other guest dressed for dinner yet? If so, please tell him we're ready."

The Corporal went away and to my astonishment returned with Jack all dressed up with a collar and bow tie. He was placed on the extra chair and when the Padre began grace put his head between his paws. When dinner was over and the port passed round, the Commander said: "Gentlemen, the King." Immediately Jack sat bolt upright with his right paw to his head.

After the Royal toast had been drunk, the Commander solemnly turned to Jack. "Master Jack," he said, "you can now leave the table," and down Jack jumped and scurried away to my cabin, possibly the only dog in the Fleet ever to have been the guest of a wardroom. All this had been rehearsed by the Corporal of Servants and my servant without my having the slightest idea what was going on.

A summer cruise brought the *Ceres* to Palestine along with the rest of the Mediterranean Fleet. To mark the occasion the R A F at Sarafand arranged a gymkhana. The outstanding event, it was decided, was to be a team race, each ship contributing a team of three riders.

I had rather undeservedly earned myself a reputation as a jockey. Nothing, of course, could have been farther from reality, but it was common knowledge that I'd only enlisted with the Marines because I wanted to ride a horse. In addition I'd undertaken a full-scale riding course at the Royal Artillery Riding School, Woolwich, and my experiences among the Cossacks added to my reputation, which, though entirely undeserved, was considerable. But probably the real reason I was chosen can best be summed up in the Commander's own words: "We know you're a bit of a jockey, and anyway there are only two others of us who can ride, and we've got to make up a team somehow."

I think I must explain what kind of a team race it was. To start with, there was a field of twenty-eight horses. The winning horse was awarded twenty-eight points, the second twenty-seven, and so on. The team with the highest collected a cup.

I didn't even have a proper riding kit. This didn't worry me, however; I gathered that the whole thing was meant to be informal. I therefore togged myself out in a pair of khaki riding breeches and trench boots. I borrowed a Norfolk jacket from my servant, and his "gor-blimey" hat. To my horror, when I walked into the big changing marquee at Sarafand, I found all the polo experts from the Mediterranean Fleet togged out in the most beautiful breeches and riding boots. I slunk away rapidly.

We picked our horses by taking names from a hat. I had 'Palestine Gendarmerie'. I walked over to the groom who was holding this horse and asked: "What's he like?"

"Oh, he's a very fine horse indeed, but he's never once been round a course. He takes charge, and when he gets to the sharp corners he always falls down."

The course, I should explain, was one of sand.

We lined up. The Cossacks, when they ride at rest, or standing still, keep their horses' heads close in to their chests; my poor mount could hardly breathe, because I'd adopted the Cossack method. But at least I had him firmly under control. After two false starts we got away.

Well, I *thought* I had him under control. By the first bend I knew I hadn't, and what was more I realised that my ridiculous trench boots had jammed in the stirrups and if the horse came down—and the groom had assured me that he always did—I'd go down under him, something I didn't relish. So I pulled my feet out of the stirrups and let them hang down the sides, holding on by the skin of my teeth or, rather, the skin of my knees. As we went into the first bend, Palestine Gendarmerie heeled over at an angle of forty-five degrees and I thought, "Ah, here we go!" and prepared to jump.

But somehow or other we got round and were racing up the straight. I made an attempt to get my feet back into the stirrups but just couldn't manage it before we hit the next bend. I don't know how we achieved it but we got round this too, my legs swinging wide, the stirrups flapping about loosely in the most unprofessional way.

To my astonishment I found we were in the lead. I made a last attempt to get my feet back into the stirrups and so at least to pass the post with some degree of decorum, but I could hear the pounding of hooves drawing closer as the other riders, taking advantage of my pre-occupation, began to catch up.

"To hell with this!" I thought, and urged the horse on. Stirrups flapping, trench boots stuck out at angles of forty-five degrees, I passed the post—the winner. The prize—a silver cigarette box—was presented to me by His Excellency the Governor of Palestine. It was perhaps the oddest congratulatory speech ever made to a winner in history. The Governor, regarding me closely, said: "You've certainly run a very good race—but where on earth did you learn to ride a horse?"

I couldn't blame the Royal Artillery for this one; I put the blame on the poor Cossacks.

"In Russia, sir," I said, "from the Cossacks."

I thought the Governor turned pale. "Good God!" was all he said, as he handed me my prize.

We were in Malta and standing by to go on a summer cruise when a signal was received by the Captain to say that I'd been appointed to the Royal Naval Staff College at Greenwich. The news came as a complete surprise to me, for no ranker had ever been appointed before. I felt that it was possibly due to my proficiency in French, German and Latin, and perhaps to good reports sent in about me by the Captain and the Admiral commanding the Mediterranean station.

I was still far from being an affluent person; so much so that the problem of getting my wife and young daughter home posed

74

quite a difficulty. Messing expenses aboard *Ceres* had been quite high, and it had been impossible to save anything. My wife suggested that she should go and stay with her sister—a Russian refugee—who was now holidaying on the Adriatic coast. My friend, Mickey Wheelan, the Principal Medical Officer, and I managed to arrange a passage for her aboard a freighter, but where would we find the money to pay even for this?

We tried a pawnbroker. Mickey had a gold cigarette case and a gold watch, and I had a silver cigarette case. But it wasn't until Mickey threw in his gold cuff links that we managed to scrape together the proper sum. That evening after I'd seen my wife and daughter off, Mickey and I went along to the Club and ordered a gin, for I felt rather depressed at being so poor and having to borrow money.

"Sorry, sir, you can't have any more; there's enough on the slate as it is," the barman informed me courteously.

An R C Padre standing by said: "Don't be silly, Cesar, of course they must have credit!" And so we were allowed a drink apiece, but no more.

It was in this mood of gloom that we went back aboard, for neither of us could afford to stay ashore and have dinner. When we entered the wardroom, Mickey went over to the letter rack. "Hey, Sam, there's a letter here for you!"

"Take it away," I groaned. "I don't want the damn thing; it's probably only a bill!"

However, after a couple of drinks I plucked up enough courage to open it. To my utter amazement I discovered that I'd been left a legacy. The lawyers requested me to go to a firm of Maltese solicitors to make out an affidavit so that they could act for me.

The next thing, of course, was to raise some money on the strength of this letter. I consulted a Maltese solicitor who informed me that the legacy must be in excess of £500 otherwise the solicitor at home wouldn't have interested himself in the matter. From there we went to a moneylender to obtain an advance of money in the hope of being able to redeem our jewellery; but we were unlucky.

We returned to the Club and there met the R C Padre again.

"Mickey, my son," he said, "you're still looking depressed; what's your trouble now?"

Mickey explained that we couldn't raise a loan even though

I'd been left a substantial legacy. Even the moneylender wouldn't advance us a penny.

"Which one?" queried the Padre. We told him. "Well, come along with me," he said, and we followed him out of the bar.

We found the moneylender, and the Padre asked him bluntly: "Why won't you lend this money?"

"I didn't think the security good enough," stammered the moneylender.

"Well, you have my word for it," said the Padre.

Turning to me he asked: "How much do you want?"

"One hundred pounds."

"Certainly," said the moneylender with alacrity.

"What interest do you charge?" demanded the Padre.

The moneylender mentioned a fairly high figure.

"Right," said the Padre. Then addressing me he said: "You send the money direct to me—I'll pass on half the interest he's charging to him, and the rest I'll give to charities."

And then, turning again to the abashed moneylender he added: "And from now on your contribution to the Church will have to be increased, now that I know how much interest you're charging!"

I learnt some weeks later that I'd been left £1,000.

Things were rather special at the Naval Staff College when I arrived. The Admiralty had just brought in regulations to say that no naval officers were to receive a naval staff appointment of any kind unless they'd been through the college and graduated. The result was that the Second Sea Lord's department had made certain that the most brilliant officers—men who were expected in the normal way to go right to the top—were sent along immediately. I thus felt rather out of my depth.

General routine was an hour's lecture every morning, followed by a discussion. After that there was a general free-for-all with everyone encouraged to speak in turn. One of the objects of the course was to teach naval officers the art of public speaking. I'd been there some considerable time before my chance came to distinguish myself in this field, and then this only came about because I was pushed into it. Time after time I'd made attempts to rise to my feet and say something, but on each occasion I'd been so hesitant that someone had already begun to speak before I could open my mouth.

One day I was informed that the Colonel of Marines wished to see me. I duly reported.

"Bassett, you haven't been on your feet yet!" began the Colonel quite sternly.

"No, sir," I agreed reluctantly. "I didn't think there was anything I could say that would improve on what had been said."

"I know, I know," he said soothingly, "but if you don't start some time you'll never make it. I've decided that you'll open this morning's discussion."

"But, sir," I protested, "it's a lecture on economics, and I know nothing about the subject." The lecture was being delivered by a famous economist professor.

"I know," he said. "But you'll open the discussion."

Well, I listened to the speaker for about an hour and could hardly understand one word he was saying. Then to my horror, he suddenly stopped speaking, and a finger was pointed in my direction. I rose to my feet.

I began to wonder who this was who was speaking. The whole experience seemed completely unreal. After five minutes a bell rang and I sat down. Some of the others got up then and spoke quite learnedly for several minutes; I felt a complete failure.

My own view of my speech was confirmed at the end of the discussion when the director, Sir Ashley Rushton, thanking the lecturer, added: "I do hope, sir, that you won't think that the person who opened the discussion is an indication of the type of officer we get at the Staff College. We pride ourselves that we receive the cream of the Navy here. Normally, we hope for a much higher standard of opening, after such a very brilliant lecture as yours, than the one we heard today."

Naturally I thought that this spelled the end for me at the Staff College. When I went down to the bar, one of the other chaps echoed the general sentiment when he remarked: "Well, you'd better get your bowler hat ready!" However, things didn't turn out quite as badly as that. The next morning the Colonel again sent for me, and when I reported he addressed me as follows: "I've never heard such drivel in my life, Bassett. You definitely need a lot of practice, and from now on until I tell you to stop you'll get to your feet every morning."

This, in fact, didn't turn out to be quite as bad as it sounds, for a list of forthcoming lectures was always posted up and it became possible to cram up the subject in advance. After a while, in fact, I found that standing on one's feet and saying something wasn't so difficult after all.

I progressed reasonably satisfactorily until one day the discussion reverted to the Battle of Jutland. I remembered that the great criticism at the time had been our lack of intelligence about the enemy's movements. A battle fleet going to sea in those days had a screen of cruisers in front of it, called the A K line, and they were supposed to report the position and formation of the enemy fleet the moment they sighted them.

It seemed to me, from all my reading on the subject, that this was just what our Fleet at Jutland had not had, so when I stood up I said that Jutland showed that we were behind in reconnaissance matters. The army, I added, had given up cavalry and had used planes instead for reconnaissance and it seemed to me that the Navy should have done the same. Aircraft would have projected the eyes of the captain of a cruiser some fifty miles or more, and if the A K line had had even one seaplane at hand they'd have known the exact formation of the enemy battle fleet.

At the end of this speech, the Deputy Director (Captain "Bubbles" James who had sat for the well-known picture) said he thought I should have had the common courtesy to make certain of my facts before speaking as I had done, for the Director himself, Sir Ashley Rushton, had been specially promoted from Commander to Captain for the part he'd played at Jutland.

He'd been in command of a cruiser in the A K line which had sent back vital information about the German Fleet. As he was reprimanding me, the Director also sat glowering at me, and once again I thought I was in for trouble. However, nothing happened; and shortly afterwards I had, for a change, a good break.

Staff College training was well designed. We started fairly easily with lectures and discussions and then progressed to working with syndicates on war operations—on paper, of course—besides giving lectures and taking part in debates exactly as in Parliament. The course was designed so that candidates could be assessed on their ability to take the strain of a multitude of dissimilar activities.

At this particular time I was reading up on the abolition of capital punishment, for a debate; on the Russian Revolution, for a lecture; and (in a syndicate) on the defence of Singapore against a Japanese naval attack. In the syndicate, I was the officer responsible for the logistic side. I had to work out the question of oil, stores, ammunition and details of a similar nature; and I was unable to find any information in the Staff College Library which would give me a realistic picture of the consumption of oil fuel at the various speeds of the great number of different craft which made up the fictitious Singapore Fleet. The librarian did manage to get me speed trials, fuel consumption and such-like details about the various classes of vessels then either in existence or contemplated, but this wasn't of much assistance.

When I discussed the problem with my wife, who had joined me in Greenwich, she suggested that what I needed was a graph showing fuel consumption at various speeds for every one of the craft; and, if I could give her some necessary figures and a slide rule, she'd work this out for me. I knew she'd gained high honours at her Russian school in mathematics, so I produced the details and the slide rule, and she produced what is now known as a fuel-consumption curve for each type of vessel.

Armed with this I then worked out the daily normal expenditure of fuel—only to discover that the whole plan of defence, based on the size of Fleet given us by the examiners, was absolutely impossible. Only two oil carriers had been allocated for the purposes of the exercise, and I had to take into consideration the fact that they'd have to go to the Persian Gulf to refuel. By the time they'd done the double journey—Singapore and back—they would have just about enough oil for themselves. Apart from this, such were the oil storage facilities in the port that not enough could be stored to support any large Fleet action at a distance from Singapore.

When I produced my bombshell it was shown to the Directing Staff, who passed it on, in some consternation, to the Admiralty. Back came the reply that my answer was perfectly correct. Appended, too, was this comment: "As this exercise has been a part of the Staff Officer curriculum for some four years, it does seem strange that the embryo leaders of the Royal Navy have not realized before this that without extra Fleet auxiliary fuel carriers and a great increase of oil storage at Singapore and stations on the way to it, the exercise was useless."

And so my stock went up. And I have to confess that I didn't disclose that it was my wife who'd solved the problem!

I'm fairly certain that if my Colonel—afterwards Commandant-General Sir Richard Foster—had not forced me to get to my feet every day to speak, thus making me proficient, I would never have been allowed to finish the staff course. As it was, the oddest things did happen.

One day, when I was not expecting to be called upon to speak, I was playing at limericks with another Marine officer when I suddenly heard my name called.

"Captain Bassett to open discussion."

This was unusual, for one was not usually called to open the discussion unless one had become something of an expert on the subject, and the subject on this occasion was the Baltic, which was generally regarded as being outside my province.

I got to my feet, desperately seeking some way out of my predicament—I hadn't the faintest idea what the lecture had been about, apart from the general idea of the Baltic. I had a mad idea of pretending to be giddy and falling to the floor in a faint, but fortunately I was saved because at that moment one of the officers stood up and said: "Sir, it would help us very much if, before opening the discussion, Captain Bassett would tell us whether the Russian Fleet taking part in this operation actually mutinied before the operation or not." This was my first indication that the lecture had been about the Russians.

Plunging in badly, I said certainly the Russian fleet had mutinied, and went on to describe how sailors' committees had taken over control of the ships. I managed to expatiate on the theme for the required ten minutes, and then sat down; I'd done, so I thought, rather famously. It was only when I arrived home and asked my wife whether I'd been correct in what I'd said that I learned that I'd been talking the most utter rubbish. The operation I mentioned had taken place before the Revolution and had been an action against the German Fleet: and a brilliant one at that. But no one at the Staff College seemed to know the difference, and I got away with it.

In the end, too, I finished the course at the College quite honourably, and even managed to gain a good qualification.

CHAPTER IV

MY success at the Staff College opened the way to appointment as Staff Officer (Intelligence) Capetown. I was delighted at the idea of going abroad again, of course, although it meant that my wife and I were once again defeated in our attempts to get a proper home together. For most of our married life we'd been forced to live in the most ghastly "digs", suffering at the hands of a succession of landladies.

On our return from Yugoslavia my wife had managed to get an unfurnished flat at Shooter's Hill Road, and we'd bought some furniture on hire purchase. When we went to Capetown I stored this furniture in a depository, but after a while I was advised by a friend that it was deteriorating and that I'd be wise to sell it at once at whatever price I could get. I did, and lost about £100 in the process.

There was a second snag also to this wonderful appointment. Although I was given first-class travel by P & O liner to Capetown, I had so little money—and new Admiralty regulations were so stringent—that I was forced to send my wife and child by cheap emigrant ship. When the vessel arrived at Capetown I went out in the Admiral's barge to meet it. I was worried to see that the ship was flying the quarantine flag; but I was allowed on board without any trouble, and met the captain and the ship's doctor.

"Is it your wife with a little girl called Zoya?" asked the doctor, after we'd been talking for a few minutes. I nodded. "Well, Captain," said the doctor, turning to his chief, "you'll have to let this woman go ashore even if no other passengers are allowed to. She frightened me out of my life yesterday. I went down to see if the child had caught measles by any chance, and she wouldn't allow me into the cabin. She had a large knife in her hand—I think she's foreign, or something."

81

I grinned. That was my wife, all right!

As we were going ashore—the captain had waived the usual quarantine regulations—I asked my wife about the knife. She explained that she'd been terrified that the doctor would order little Zoya into an isolation ward, which would have meant that she'd have been carried on with the ship as far as its destination —Australia. Rather than let this happen, she'd decided to prevent the doctor even having a look at the child.

"Would you have stabbed the doctor?" I asked curiously.

She didn't hesitate. "Why, of course!" she answered.

My office in the Cape was in the Castle at Capetown, one of the oldest buildings in South Africa. It was some distance from the naval base at Simonstown—fifteen miles, to be exact—but I felt it was more reasonable to be situated in Capetown itself, the centre of a large commercial port.

I was only a few weeks at the Cape before I was appointed extra A D C to the Governor, the Earl of Athlone. At this time we were living in a house which had been rented by my predecessor at a place called St James, half-way between Simonstown and Capetown, but we weren't particularly happy there and I was anxious to live in Simonstown.

I'd been to see the C-in-C, whom I'd known when he was Director of Naval Information in Whitehall. He promised that he'd ask the Chief of the South African Defence Force if he could arrange for me to have a house in Simonstown, but in the meantime would I be interested in accepting the post of extra A D C to the Earl of Athlone? I was very pleased to accept, and I discovered to my joy that I was entitled to certain duty-free prerequisites.

One day, while still living at St James, my wife and I were out for a walk with our dog Jack when we heard a rustling in some nearby bushes. Jack, thinking it was a rabbit, at once went to investigate. We heard him give a tremendous howl and saw him leap into the air. When we reached him he was dead; he'd been bitten by a snake. The incident cast us into considerable gloom and made us more anxious than ever to get away from the house. It was with relief that we learned shortly afterwards that a house had been procured for us in Simonstown.

It was while I was stationed at the Cape that I passed for

promotion from Captain to Major. Arrangements had just been made that officers serving abroad could take their examinations under the supervision of the local military authorities. I asked to take the examination in Pretoria, under the Union Defence Force, which at that time included on its strength a large number of British officers, and this was agreed to.

Apart from the written side of the examination, I had to be examined on a T E W T—Tactical Exercise without Troops. This meant that we had to go into the countryside and explain how we'd deal with a given exercise. I was told to familiarise myself with the countryside, and to help me in this aim was provided with a large map. When I looked at this I saw there were a number of words I didn't understand, as they were in Afrikaans. I pointed this out, and the Colonel suggested the best thing to do would be to get on a horse and go out with a Dutch Corporal. This I did.

While we were riding over the veld, a tremendous storm broke; never have I seen such lightning in my life. The Dutch Corporal said something to me and then pointed, but I couldn't understand what he meant. He pointed again to my stirrups and I thought he was making some some comment on my method of riding, so I didn't take much notice of him. He then pointed to a farm and shouted that we should make for it, for shelter.

When we reached the place the Corporal explained that we wanted food and particularly shelter. The Boer farmer, a churlish-looking chap, looked at me with considerable distaste, and indicated that while he'd give food and drink to the Dutch Corporal, he'd refuse it to an Englishman. According to the Bible, however, he was obliged to give me water at least. So I had to be content with a basin of water. I thought this extraordinary behaviour, for, after all, the Boer war had been over for a very long time.

When I arrived back at Pretoria one of the South African officers said to me: "I hear you had a good ride; but why didn't you do as your Corporal told you?"

"What d'you mean?" I asked.

"He told you to cross your stirrups, didn't he?"

I shook my head in puzzlement.

"When he pointed to your stirrups," he went on.

"Oh," I said, "what was all that about?"

83

"We get some very fierce storms on the veld," the officer explained, "and we've discovered that a great number of people are killed by lightning hitting their stirrups. So experts advise everyone to cross their stirrups when a storm blows up."

"Well, I'm sorry," I replied. "I didn't understand. But anyway, I was lucky."

My main duty as Staff Officer (Intelligence) Capetown, was, of course, the collection of naval intelligence. Also, I worked with the Commander-in-Chief's Staff Officers, including his Staff Officer (Operations). One of our combined duties was the preparation of war plans in general, with no specific enemy in view. In accordance with this I kept a list of all the retired naval officers who were living in Africa, and in the event of war they'd be called on.

The Committee of Imperial Defence had started work in London. General outline plans were sent out to various Commanders-in-Chief, but all stations on the route to the Far East were ordered to prepare their own war plans locally, and so the Staff Officer (Operations) and myself started work.

It was obvious to us that one of the most important places, so far as the Cape station was concerned, was the island of Madagascar, as it contained one of the world's finest harbours. It could hold the combined Fleets of the world; it had wonderful natural defences, a deep-water entrance with high cliffs on both sides. The snag was that we knew very little about it.

Madagascar is a very large island, but it had never been properly surveyed, and there were vast areas in the south where even the number of rivers was not known. At one time the French had made plans to build an inland waterway. Rivers flowing to the east side of the island came down to the low-lying coastal belt and in a great number of cases, instead of breaking out to the sea, ran north and south and formed a natural inland canal. The French had considered exploiting this natural canal, deepening and strengthening it, and making it into a submarine base, with various openings to the sea. It was important for us to know the state of this canal, and also to know something more about the island, and especially to know about the naval harbour of Diego Suarez.

Our British Consul-General, who was also acting as our Naval

84

Reporting Officer, lived in the capital, which was a long way from the sea, and we heard little from him as regards the island. I wrote to him and said I'd like to pay him a visit to discuss alterations in his duties if war came. I also said that I wanted, if it were possible, some rather more up-to-date information about the island, and especially wanted to know whether the French had gone ahead with their plan for an inland waterway canal; whether they'd developed a large lake on the island as a seaplane base, and also what was the state of the naval harbour in the north. I pointed out that possibly he could obtain a great deal of this information from the French authorities.

The Consul-General replied that he would be happy to see me. But he had none of the information I was looking for, and indicated that the French themselves were just about as ignorant.

Faced with this negative reply, I decided that it was up to me to visit the place—after all, it was in my area of responsibility and I'd look silly if I was called on for information which I couldn't supply. But I realised that I'd have to do it entirely 'off my own bat' and unofficially, since neither the Admiralty nor my C-in-C would ever approve a clandestine inspection of a foreign territory, even though my interest was only in its topography.

So I applied for some of the leave that was due to me, and, with a rashness that horrifies me today, began to lay my plans.

The ordinary steamer service wouldn't touch the vital east coast. What I needed was to get aboard one of the Indian dhows which plied this coast. Luckily, I found there was a tramp leaving Lourenço Marques, bound for Singapore but calling on the way at Fort Dauphin, the most southerly small port in Madagascar.

I decided to go aboard this vessel as a deck hand, desert at Fort Dauphin and then hitchhike a ride on a dhow; or, failing this, make my way up the east coast to the port of Tamatave. Here, if I had laid my plans right, I should arrive just in time to board the regular-service steamer on which I'd have arranged to have my clothes and baggage. I could board her long enough to change my clothes and step ashore again officially as Captain Bassett, R M, as though I had travelled the whole journey in her.

I fixed the shipping arrangements nicely. Next I bought myself a camera. I managed to buy one of a good German make in Capetown and got a firm to make me special spools which contained only two exposures each instead of the normal eight. I wanted this because I hoped to post the photographs the moment I'd taken any, and should I be caught with the camera the most I could lose would be two pictures. I also asked the camera firm to fit an effective little compass. To explain my possession of what was clearly an expensive camera, I arranged for a fictitious letter, alleged to have come from my mother, mentioning that she'd sent it to me as a Christmas present. I then faked a set of fictitious paying-off papers from a ship, and got hold of £30 in golden sovereigns—which I would declare, if challenged, constituted my pay-off money. Finally, I wrote to all my five sisters and friends in England telling them that I would be sending them letters and photographs from Madagascar, and that the moment they received them they were to re-address them to me in Capetown.

With the help of a shipping agent at Beira in Portuguese East Africa, I first managed to join a tramp-steamer plying between Beira and Lourenço Marques, as supercargo. I gathered that the agent had to bribe the captain with a case of whisky. Anyhow, I was "paid-off" at Lourenço Marques, and with a proper seaman's book I had no difficulty in being taken on a ship bound for Singapore as an ordinary seaman. I showed my papers to the Master, and was then taken down to the fo'c'sle and given a bunk. The ship was due to sail at midnight.

Just before twelve the rest of the crew turned up, most of them in an advanced stage of intoxication. None were capable of recognising or bothering about me; they flung themselves— or were flung—into their bunks, and the ship sailed.

As I lay in my bunk I began to feel a tingling sensation as though I were experiencing a succession of electric shocks. I thought that, in some way, the bed had become 'alive', but I couldn't understand how this could happen. The lights were still on, however, and throwing the blankets aside to see what was causing the trouble I found to my horror that the 'electric shocks' were in fact the bites of vicious bugs. I didn't sleep much that night.

However, the next morning we ran into a severe storm and

the cargo, which consisted for the most part of cased petrol, shifted. All members of the crew were ordered down into the hold to repack it. This proved to be such an arduous task that I slept excellently that night, and indeed had no further trouble with my sleep, in spite of the bugs.

Arriving at Fort Dauphin, I set about getting ashore and deserting. I hadn't anticipated any difficulty about this, but it proved to be harder than I'd imagined. The trick was to fool the quartermaster, who rather suspected I wasn't a real seaman and was on guard to see what I was up to. My idea was to go ashore in one of the lighters which had to come alongside to discharge the cargo. I asked permission to go ashore 'just to stretch my legs'; but this was refused. Then I heard the quartermaster ask one of the crew to go ashore and get him a few bottles of Cognac. This chap returned a little later to report that he'd been unable to get any because he couldn't speak a word of French.

That was my opportunity. I pointed out that I did speak it, and what was more, had some French francs on me. I'd be happy to go ashore, I said, and get him the Cognac. This time he nodded agreement, and I went ashore in the lighter.

While we were unloading the cargo, I said to the foreman: "I'm just nipping up for a bottle of brandy for the quartermaster." He shrugged unconcernedly and off I went. I bought the brandy all right, but instead of returning to the lighter I made for the hills which rise behind the little town, and sat down to watch the ship sail away. She hung about for a while, obviously awaiting my return. Then she left.

I waited for a few hours, then took a stiff drink of the brandy, allowing some of it to spill over my clothes; then I staggered down to the port. I approached the first official I saw and gestured wildly as though asking where my ship had gone. I pretended I knew no French. I was taken before the police to whom I explained—in English—that when I'd bought the brandy I'd gone up into the hills to have a quiet drink and had fallen asleep, thus missing my ship.

I knew the French police wouldn't keep me in Fort Dauphin until the next British ship called, which might not be for another three months. They'd be anxious to get rid of me as soon as possible, and in some way or other they'd have me transported to Tamatave, two hundred miles up the east coast, where there was a regular service of ships. And, indeed, next day I was taken aboard an Indian dhow.

The trip up the east coast on the dhow proved to be ideal from my point of view. At each small port I got a chance to go ashore, helping to load or unload cargo. Then I arranged with the Master that I'd leave the dhow along the way and catch the next one coming along a few days later. This gave me a chance to reconnoitre one or two of the larger places and take photographs.

In order to throw suspicious natives or French officials off the scent, I posed as a slightly mad Englishman—not a difficult task in a part of the world where all Englishmen were popularly thought to be off their rockers. Before taking a picture, I used to make a base line and walk a brisk hundred yards, then halt and do some physical exercises. By the time I'd gone through all this elaborate pantomime the onlookers were no longer surprised by anything I decided to do, and I was able to take my photographs without arousing suspicion.

I got rid of the photographs at once by giving them, in an envelope, with a covering note, to the dhow Master and asking him to post them at the first non-French port he came to. The idea seemed to be working extremely well and I found myself roving the area well within my time-table.

As we neared Tamatave I made preparations to visit Lake Electra. Getting there, however, proved to be a bit of a problem as there were neither roads nor railway. I therefore hired a *falazan* (a sort of sedan chair) plus its crew of eight. Four men carried the *falazan* in which I sat, while the other four ran alongside singing. At the end of half an hour, they changed over.

The trip proved interesting; we passed "man-eating trees" which I learned weren't fatal to men at all, although they did trap small animals and digest them. Fording a river was a ticklish problem, however, for they were infested with crocodiles, although Madagascar is fortunate in that it has no other wild or dangerous animals and like Ireland, has no snakes.

The crew had their own peculiar method of dealing with the crocodile menace. Half of them would go a little way upstream leaving me and the rest to wait at the ford. When they'd gone a reasonable distance they'd sit down and bark like dogs. The

crocodiles, hearing the barks—and dog being their favourite diet
—would swim up to where the four crewmen were barking,
leaving the ford perfectly safe. While the crocodiles' attention
was thus diverted elsewhere, the four men carrying me would
dash into the river and ferry me across.

Travelling in this extraordinary manner it took about two
days to get to Lake Electra. The crew fed me on the way, buying
the food in local villages. I found that Lake Electra would indeed
make a wonderful seaplane base once communications were
opened up, and that the French themselves had perceived its
value in this connection, for there were signs that they'd once
contemplated opening a station there. Apparently their losses of
personnel and workers from crocodiles had caused them to
abandon the scheme.

After taking photographs and thoroughly inspecting the place,
I started back, arriving a couple of days later at another small
port farther along the coast. I asked the crew what they wanted
by way of payment—I carried my gold sovereigns in a belt round
my waist—but they said all they wanted was salt. So with a few
bags of salt—a precious commodity in that part of the world—I
paid them off happily.

I then joined another Indian dhow and travelled leisurely
towards Tamatave. Ten miles from there, the dhow put in at
another of these tiny ports which dot the coast. I intended to
slip ashore here and make my own way to Tamatave. Normally,
I reported to the French authorities at each port, but this time I
decided to by-pass them. I warned the dhow master to say, if
anyone asked him, that he was taking me on to Zanzibar; then
I went ashore. I went up into the hills and walked for some
time until eventually I was overlooking Tamatave. I was
astonished at its appearance : it looked as if something frightful
had happened to it; a lot of buildings had been knocked down
and there was an air of general desolation.

I'd already written to our shipping-reporting officer in the
place, and now I went down into the town and made my way
towards his house. I found that the town had been hit by one
of the worst cyclones in living memory. It was with great difficulty that I found our agent's house. Although he expected me,
he was anything but glad to see me.

"But you're here under false pretences," he exclaimed. "I'm

not going to have you here. The French have sent in a large contingent of troops to deal with the looting and to clear up this horrible mess; if they catch you in my house, I'll be for it. I'm sorry, but I can't be mixed up in this."

"But I'm waiting to board a ship here!" I protested.

"I doubt whether any ship'll come in here for some time," he said. "This is a lighterage port and all the lighters have been sunk. It wouldn't do a ship much good to come in here now, because it couldn't unload its cargo. Anyhow, I can't help you—I thought you'd be on an *official* visit! And for goodness' sake don't drink any of the water. There're a lot of corpses in the town and the flies are very active." He handed me a large bottle of Vichy water and a big French loaf, and left me to get on with it.

I went up into the hills again, and on the whole it wasn't too uncomfortable. The night was warm and balmy. Then I noticed a ship entering the harbour. I suspected it might be the one on which I'd booked my passage, and I was determined not to miss it. So I went down into the harbour and jumped into a small boat and pulled myself out to it. I circled the stern and found that it was indeed my ship. So I sang out and they dropped a ladder and up I went; in my cabin I rapidly transformed myself back into Captain Bassett, Royal Marines, officially on leave in Madagascar. Then I went up to have a chat with the Captain.

"I was a bit worried about you," I said. "I thought that perhaps you might not have called."

"Well, you were right to be," he said. "If I'd known what had happened I'd never have put in. But my radio broke down, and here I am. I can't get any cargo landed, though, so the sooner I get you ashore and through the Customs the better; then I can shove off."

He quickly ordered a boat and took me ashore again, this time ostensibly as a passenger aboard his ship. The French officials were very courteous and kind, and telephoned the British Consul at Tananarive. There was only one train a day to it and the Consul came down and met me, and then we both returned together. I found Tananarive a wonderful place, high up and cool in the evening but enjoying a vigorous warm climate by day. The Consul took me to see the Governor, whose first words to me were: "Where's your sun helmet?"

"I haven't got one, I'm afraid," I said. "You see I only landed yesterday morning."

"Well, you can't get very far without a sun helmet," he said, "that and quinine—you must take a spoonful every morning; otherwise you won't live long, in Madagascar!"

I couldn't tell him that I'd been in Madagascar for the past four months without either a sun helmet or quinine and had been getting along splendidly.

"Well, now," he continued in a business-like tone, "how can we help you?"

He then explained that an invading force had only two alternatives, i.e., seizing the naval harbour—strongly defended—at Diego Suarez; or, as the French had done, seizing the seat of Government at the capital, Tananarive. The capital was connected to the port of Tamatave on the east coast by the only railway in the island.

The French had landed on the west coast and had followed the course of the river Besiboka to the capital, losing hundreds of men by crocodiles and malaria. He mentioned, however, that their operations had been greatly helped by the excellent maps which had been provided by the French army. I seized on this point. "Could I get hold of those maps, by any chance?" I asked —I hope not too eagerly.

"I'm sorry," he said; "only the original ones are in existence, and they're in our museum. Perhaps the Consul could take you along and show you them."

The interview ended shortly afterwards and I went away despondent about my chances of being able to pull off anything very useful. But the next morning I was taken to see the Military Governor, and at once the whole situation changed dramatically; for the Military Governor, unlike the Civil Governor, was genuinely anxious to assist me. He said he thought it was an excellent idea to try and get topographical data about the island. He had long been pressing for it, but all his efforts had been checked by the Civil authorities, who were determined to hide the secrets of Madagascar as best they could.

"What about the original maps in the museum?" I asked. "Would it be possible to get copies?"

"Not a hope, I'm afraid," he said.

"Could anybody take photographs?" I ventured.

He scratched his chin thoughtfully. The idea seemed to impress him. "It might work," he said. "Look, I'll have a chat with one of my staff, a surveyor, and see if there's anything that could be done. I'll bring him along to lunch and we can discuss it."

He was as good as his word and brought a young officer along. This chap was quite enthusiastic about the project; he said that the museum closed at 5 p.m. and didn't reopen until 9.30 a.m.

At 6 a.m. the sun would be brilliant. It would, therefore, be an easy matter to take photographs. It didn't matter what size the original pictures were; he could enlarge them to any size I needed. However, no French officer could risk it. It would have to be done by me.

"You're a visitor and no one knows you, and you can't be expected to know about the Civil regulations," said the officer.

Anxious though I was to obtain pictures, I began making excuses. "I've no proper camera," I pointed out. "I've no knowledge of how to set about taking pictures indoors."

The officer swept aside my objections. "Oh, don't worry," he said. "I can provide you with a camera and tell you about the exposures."

"Fine," said the General approvingly, "fine. Then that's settled."

And settled it was. But I still had no idea how I was supposed to be in the museum at six o'clock in the morning!

That evening I discussed the matter with a British resident whom I'd met and who'd asked me to dinner; he wasn't too keen to be involved. However, his wife was a lady of some mettle and she said she'd help me. Her husband withdrew so that officially he should know nothing of what we were planning, and left it to his wife and me to find some means of effecting an entrance.

"I've always been surprised that no one's ever attempted to steal the valuable coins kept there," she said. "It'd be an easy matter for someone to hide themselves in the museum when it closes at five p.m., take what they wanted during the night, wait for the place to reopen in the morning, then mingle with the crowds and walk out. Now I think that's what *you* should do—stay and hide yourself, I mean, not steal the coins." She laughed.

92

"I'll come along in the morning, bringing my young son, and you can join us. The guards'll take us for a normal family."

"What about the camera?" I objected. "Won't the guards stop me?"

"Oh, no," she replied. "Cameras are permitted, there'll be no trouble there."

I went along to the museum that afternoon and entered the room where the maps were kept. There was no doubt about it, they were a wonderful set of beautifully drawn maps, showing the whole area from the coast right up to the capital. They were drawn to an excellent scale and obviously just as useful today as on the day they were made, for nothing had been done in Madagascar in the meantime to change their validity. I went away determined that I must get photographs of them, and that any risks I had to take would be well worth while. Then for a day or so I practised using my camera, with the help of the French officer, taking pictures of *La Vie Parisienne* upside down. (We put the picture upside down and then the view of it in the camera the right way up—simple.)

Our plans completed, I went along to the museum in the late afternoon and making sure there was nobody in the room at the time, hid myself in the Queen's *falazan*—an outsize sedan chair. It was curtained off and quite comfortable inside. I'd taken the precaution of depositing my camera in an ornate bowl near by so that, if I were discovered, I could claim that I'd simply fallen asleep.

Closing time was signalled by a loud ringing of bells; all visitors, and eventually the guards, left. I decided after a while to have a look round, just to make sure that everybody'd gone. I knocked at one or two doors and shouted, but there was no response; so I settled down for the night with the knowledge that I was alone in the museum.

It became very dark inside. I'd not thought to bring a torch with me and after a while I could hear the most incredible noises. It was probably only rats, but in the darkness my imagination began to run rampant. The museum was full of statues of ancient gods and idols and instruments of torture. At one time, such was the effect of the darkness and the loneliness that I even began to imagine that the gods and idols were coming towards me. Had any of the windows been unbarred at that moment I should certainly have jumped out. As it was, I decided to leave my *falazan* and make for a stone seat at the end of a passage which I'd noticed as I entered the museum.

I hurried down the passage to this seat and sat down with my back firmly against the wall behind. I still imagined things were coming near me. Then I suddenly remembered that my benefactress had thoughtfully provided me with a flask of Cognac, to help ward off the cold of the night. I opened it thankfully . . . and it was the last of anything I can remember until I awoke with the brilliant sunlight streaming through the windows.

As brave as a lion with the return of daylight, I rose from my seat and approached the wall maps. Within a short time I'd taken twenty-two very satisfactory pictures. I then walked back to the *falazan*, first putting the camera back in the bowl, climbed back inside myself, pulling the curtains across again, and waited patiently for the museum to open. I must confess that I had been tempted during those early hours to purloin one or two of the valuable exhibits, but contented myself with making faces at the idols who had so terrified me during the night.

In what seemed quite a short time visitors began to enter the museum again and shortly after ten o'clock my friend's wife, with her two boys, walked into the room. I stepped out, a little cramped by now, but otherwise none the worse for my strange adventure. Within minutes of leaving the museum the roll of films was in the hands of my French officer friend, who within a day handed me over a complete set of enlarged prints. I slipped these into an envelope and, using the ordinary mail, sent them off to myself at Capetown.

My last task on the island was to get some information about the naval base at Diego Suarez; but it began to look as though I'd have to leave without this, as I was already booked aboard a French ship calling in at Zanzibar, and it'd be difficult for me to change my plans now without inviting suspicion. I asked both my civilian acquaintance and the Military Governor who'd been so helpful over the maps to try to find out what they could about the present state of the base and let me know. Both promised to do what they could.

After a brief crocodile-hunt during which I bagged two crocodiles (which later made a delightful travelling bag for my wife),

I boarded my ship. We were due for a one-hour stop at Diego Suarez, and luck was still with me. Leaving Tamatave the ship struck a submerged object—probably something tossed into the sea by the recent cyclone—and the Captain informed us that the repairs would take at least three days. Nothing could have been better from my point of view.

We remained there, in fact, for four days. During this time I made the acquaintance of a charming French family. They took me around the harbour, but what I really wanted to see was the bay on the west side, because it was obvious that any attempt to attack the port from the sea would be impossible, owing to the deep cliffs which shielded it on either side. With a couple of guns on the cliffs, defenders could have planted shells just wherever they chose, against attacking warships. The only way to take the port, therefore, would be to land on any of the bays opening out on the west side, and attack the port from the rear.

Looking at the map, I saw that one of these bays had two hills guarding it; they looked like a woman's breasts and they were in fact called Les Menelles. I told my French friend I'd like to see this. They agreed it was a lovely place and suggested they took me on a picnic there and I could go in for a swim.

While on our picnic, I photographed the two girls of the family in their bathing suits, being careful, however, to get an excellent series of backgrounds. I was able to get all the necessary information as to beach gradient, type of sand and other details necessary for any attempt to be made to land troops there. So far as I could see, no efforts had been made to site defensive works anywhere near the beaches, which were open to any invader.

It was in a happy and satisfied mood, therefore, that I eventually said goodbye to my very kind French hosts, and boarded my ship which by now was ready to sail again. We reached Zanzibar without incident, and in due course I found myself back in Capetown, metaphorically patting myself on the back for a job well done. I kept my word to the Military Governor and sent him a complete copy of all my material. I received a charming reply saying that I'd always be welcome in Madagascar, with or without false beard!

My material and report occupied the greater part of two big packing cases which I later had shipped back to the Admiralty.

Their Lordships had not, of course, known anything of my cloak-and-dagger activities, which would certainly have earned their strong disapproval. So apart from sending back the material, I didn't draw attention to the *fait accompli*. But I must here interpose with the sad and ironic tale of what eventually happened to this material, even though I'm jumping ahead of my story.

During the Second World War, when I was running the Inter-Services Topographical Department, I attended a meeting on Operation Ironclad, which was concerned with planning the invasion of Madagascar. I was told that information about this island would be required as quickly as possible. I pointed out, confident that I could lay my hands on all the necessary information at almost literally a moment's notice, that the island was the size of France, Belgium and Holland combined, and I presumed the information they really needed was only about the port of Diego Suarez and the route that would have to be taken to seize the capital.

"If that's what you need, and I presume it is, I can provide that immediately," I said pontifically.

"Good!" said the officer in charge of the operation. "Absolutely cracking, old man! Let's have it, then."

Preening myself on my foresight, I went back to the Admiralty and told them I wanted all the information that I'd sent in from Capetown during the years I'd been Staff Officer (Intelligence) regarding the island of Madagascar. I sat down and waited, feeling enormously pleased with myself. This was one occasion, at least, on which my department could cover itself with glory.

I felt a moment's annoyance, but no more, when the officer I'd dispatched returned and said he was sorry but there was no record of any report on Madagascar.

"But damn it, man, there *must* be!" I said. "I sent it in myself. Check again."

He checked, but once again reported that he was unable to trace anything on the island. Puzzled and angry now, I approached the Director of Naval Intelligence himself. "I know it's there somewhere, sir. After all, I sent it in myself, and I'm absolutely positive that a really thorough search will turn it up."

"We'll find it, Bassett," said the Admiral. "Leave it to me."

He had the matter thoroughly investigated and eventually the

96

movements of the two big packing cases were tracked down. They'd been put in a room concerned with France and her possessions, and in the charge of a single officer. After two years he'd been replaced by another officer who, not having time to go through the cases and bring the information up to date—not that it needed bringing up to date—had the stuff sent down to a depository until he had time to deal with it. He never found the time, apparently, and the cases languished there for another two years. One day the keeper of the depository telephoned and asked what he was supposed to do with the cases—he wasn't allowed to keep them longer than that time. The officer in charge at the other end shouted hurriedly: "Oh, we haven't time to look through all that stuff now. Anyhow, probably most of it's out of date. Get rid of it!"

And so my report and all the massive documentation that had gone into its preparation had been sent off to be pulped.

My time was now coming to an end in the Cape. I'd been out there three and a half years altogether, three and a half of the most glorious and enjoyable years of my life. I'd enjoyed magnificent surf-bathing, mountain climbing and glittering social occasions as extra A D C to His Royal Highness the Earl of Athlone and his charming wife, Princess Alice. But times were now changing in South Africa and I was not sorry, on the whole, to be leaving.

For instance, an Act had been passed making it compulsory for any British officer serving on the staff of the South African Defence Force to learn Afrikaans "within six months"; and most British officers had, indeed, to retire shortly afterwards. Suddenly our relations with the South African Defence Force, which had hitherto been most cordial and intimate, became formal, if not strained.

I began to wonder who was going to relieve me. It would be a difficult and probably thankless task, but the officer would have to be good. Then I remembered my old friend, Jo Hollis, whom I'd known as a subaltern. As I believed he'd just completed the Staff course, I suggested to the C-in-C that he'd be an ideal person to relieve me. I didn't mention that both Jo and myself had been somewhat rebellious during our early days in the Corps, possessing ideas of reform which should have earned us a court martial. My suggestion was adopted, and I like to think it was of some help to Jo in his march up the ladder to the eminence he held during the war when he was Secretary of the Joint Planning Committee of the Chiefs of Staff before eventually becoming Commandant-General of the Royal Marines. Now, of course, he is General Sir Leslie Hollis, knighted both for his wonderful work during the war and also because he was Commandant-General.

CHAPTER V

On my return to England, I was appointed to the Naval Intelligence Department at the Admiralty. It was normal procedure for officers who'd spent some time abroad as Staff Officers (Intelligence) to find themselves saddled with these duties. I took over from a Major of Marines who said he wouldn't waste time telling me about the files or anything else.

"You've been three years Staff Officer at the Cape, and so I expect you know all about it, old man," he said. "Instead it will be more useful if I give you some general advice about the N I D. Don't, under any circumstances, have anything to do with the Admiralty ladies." I said I'd no intention of so doing. "Well, don't," he advised me darkly. "It'll do you no good."

Then he said he'd give me some more excellent advice. "They've got a very good library here, very good indeed. The librarian'll get you any book you like—even fiction. If you want to get away from your desk for a while you can always say you want to look up something in the library and sit down there and read a good book. What's more, if you want to read something that's been banned in this country, all you have to do is to ask our Naval Attaché in Paris to get it for you and he'll send it over in the Bag." And with this sterling advice on how to tackle my new job, the Major of Marines vanished and left me to my fate.

Shortly after this, a query came to me concerning French torpedoes. I went to the files dealing with the French Navy only to find that the drawer wouldn't open. It wasn't locked, yet it wouldn't open. Strange, I thought; these drawers are supposed to be in daily use. Finally, after I'd spent some time tugging at it I sent for an Admiralty locksmith.

"This hasn't been opened for months," he told me as he began work.

"Nonsense," I replied. "It's in use daily."

"Sorry, sir," he said, "not this one."

Eventually, he forced it open. I turned to the first file. Under "French Torpedoes" it said: "See file on French naval training". I turned up that file. This time the directions read: "School Naval Training, France. See File". Finally, after I had worked my way through at least half a dozen other files, I reached one that contained a single sheet of paper. On this was written: "Gone to lunch". My predecessor had obviously fancied his sense of humour.

When I joined the N I D, in January 1930, the country was undergoing considerable financial difficulties. The talk in the Admiralty and around the Service Clubs was that the pay of officers was to be yet further reduced. None of us realised, of course, just how serious the economic situation had become, and we were astonished when the recommendations of the May Committee, which had reported some little time before, were put into force with great promptitude. The Navy, of course, was not the only branch affected; all sections of government service, from police and teachers to the armed forces, were involved. The projected economies were not mild, either, but quite drastic, and embraced all ranks. As I had to exist on my pay only and had no other income, I never bothered to read the financial pages of the newspapers and so had no idea of the cause of the crisis, but there was no doubt that the country was going through a bad time.

Almost simultaneously with the decision to impose cuts, all units of the Home Fleet of the Royal Navy were due to leave their home ports and sail to Invergordon to take part in the annual combined exercises. Normally these combined exercises were thoroughly looked forward to by all officers and men, for they came after a spell of relative inactivity. Invergordon was an ideal base for the exercises; it possessed a large, modern canteen and plenty of excellent playing fields. The Fleet exercises also included regattas and other sporting fixtures, so that

99

there was a great deal of entertainment and social life for every-one.

At the Admiralty there was an unusual buzz of activity as officers were drafted at short notice either to fill or replace appointments in the Fleet. Yet everything moved smoothly and the general atmosphere, despite the news of pay cuts, was good.

I suppose that the Navy is used to being a kind of Aunt Sally for many politicians; we may even have taken a strange and inverse pride in being singled out yet again for spectacular economies. At any rate, the news didn't worry us greatly; worse things had happened before, and we'd survived them.

Then news came that the C-in-C, Home Fleet, had been taken seriously ill aboard his flagship just as he was preparing to leave Portsmouth for Invergordon. There was no question at this stage of appointing a relief, for it was not known yet just how ill he was or exactly what he was suffering from.

Within a few days the Combined Fleet assembled at Inver-gordon and, so far as the Admiralty knew, everything appeared to be normal with it, and there was no reason to expect trouble. Then one or two disquieting stories started to filter into White-hall about some sort of a disturbance in the canteen on the first night of the Fleet's arrival. Little notice was given to these rumours, however, until reports appeared in the Press alleging a "Serious Incident in Royal Naval Canteen", and claiming that an officer and patrol had been manhandled and thrown out. Some other reports passed off whatever happened—if anything at all had—as "a drunken brawl" involving the smashing of glasses and other hooliganism. Under a sudden barrage of Press inquiries, a signal was at once sent to the Acting C-in-C, Home Fleet, who replied that "No importance is to be attached to this incident." Feeling in the Admiralty echoed this view; it was not considered improbable that a booze-up involving thousands of men might very well lead to some incident or other.

However, better-informed heads amongst us thought other-wise, and I was sent for by my director and told that the branch of the Security Service had received very disturbing news from the local police at Invergordon. In view of this, the police had thought it wise to send one or two plain-clothes men to the base, and suggested that the Director of Naval Intelligence might con-sider sending some of his staff up from London.

"Bassett," my Director told me, "I want you to go to Invergordon immediately—in plain clothes—and render whatever help you can to the local police and security agents. I need hardly point out that it's of national importance at this particular time that we know exactly what's happening up there. An exaggerated or unfounded story might do irretrievable damage."

I was staggered by the assignment and expressed some distaste for its nature. I pointed out that I'd had no experience of this kind of work, and that senior Fleet officers might well resent an outsider being sent up from the Admiralty to investigate what would appear to be simply a domestic disciplinary affair.

The DNI listened to me patiently, and then said rather wearily: "Listen, Bassett; suppose in the last war you'd been asked to go behind the enemy lines to get some vital information, would you have gone?"

"Of course I would!" I answered, nettled.

"Well, this might prove to be just as important. Some person or persons unknown might very well be trying to cause trouble in the Royal Navy, and trouble coming at this particular time could be just as great an emergency as anything which might have happened in wartime. You once served on the lower deck, so you're in a better position to get to know the feelings of the men than anyone else I can send. So I'm ordering you to do this. You'll go at once to Invergordon, masquerading as an Admiralty fuel oil official—you know all the jargon."

And with a steely glare which betokened ill if I tried to persist in my objections, the DNI dismissed me. So I returned to my section, collected a few papers on Fleet oil requirements, UK fuel and storage facilities, and then caught a train to Invergordon.

Arriving in that damp Scottish town, I booked in at the local hotel and, after I'd freshened up and paid a quick visit to the bar, casually let drop to the proprietor that I was an Admiralty fuel official.

"I fear ye'll be wastin' y' time then," he said. "The Fleet isna putting t' sea at all!"

"Why not?" I asked sharply.

"Oh, I couldna say," he answered quickly. "But one of my pals is Superintendent o' the Oil Fuel installation, and it could be he'll know aboot it. I'll ask him to come over, if ye'd like it."

In due course the Superintendent turned up and confirmed that, if the purpose of my trip north was to go into the fuel consumption necessary for the various exercises, then I was wasting my time.

"It looks like a mutiny, with the sailors refusing to take the ships to sea," he told me.

"That's incredible!" I said. "Can you tell me any more?"

"Look, I'll tell you what I'll do," he went on. "The canteen manager's a friend of mine. I'll have him come across and meet you. He knows something of what's been happening; he can tell you what happened on that first night in the canteen."

Later we all sat down together in my room at the hotel, and I was immediately impressed by the canteen manager. "You might as well go home," he said. "The sailors are in complete control and determined the ships won't leave port."

"You're probably right," I agreed, "but I've come a long way and I don't want to go back just yet. I might as well hang on for a few days. You won't mind if I go round and talk to your staff, will you, just for something to do?"

"Not at all," said the manager, "I'll be pleased to help you if I can."

So during the next few days, with the full concurrence of the manager, I talked to as many people as I could who'd been in or near the canteen on the night of the disturbance. I suspected that there must have been outside influence at work, but all the answers to my questions appeared to discount this. The local police, too, were emphatic; although many undesirables always turned up in the town when the Fleet was in, they felt convinced that the disturbance had been a spontaneous action on the part of the Fleet personnel and had not been instigated by any outsiders. And this was the story I eventually pieced together.

Once the Fleet had assembled and anchored, shore leave was immediately granted. The vast majority of the men at once made for the canteen; there was little else for them to do in the evenings anyway. The place that night was therefore packed to capacity. Anticipating the rush, the canteen manager had engaged additional help.

When everyone had been supplied with their beer, a party of

six men sitting at a table which backed on to the long wall of the canteen began banging their beer mugs on the table. Then one of them stood up on the table and started shouting. None of the other sailors in the room paid much attention to him at first, but he kept on shouting. Finally, in what was obviously a pre-arranged move, the other men at his table began chanting in unison: "It's about your pay! It's about your pay!" until they got silence.

Then the man on the table shouted: "You poor buggers don't seem to know anything about it, or you wouldn't be so cheerful swilling pints of beer you can't afford!" This brought a hush in the canteen.

In the silence that now reigned the sailor continued: "I don't suppose any of you took the trouble to read the Admiralty Fleet Order that was put on the ships' notice boards after we'd left our home ports? Well, this was done deliberately—the officers knew that if you'd read those notices while you were in harbour with nothing to do, there might've been trouble. They waited until you were at sea and busy, and I don't suppose any of you bothered to look at it when we got here."

Some muttering greeted this, and the sailor continued: "Well, I'll tell you what the notice says. It says that everybody's pay from the Admiral down is to be cut at once. You can read it for yourself when you go back aboard.

"But I want to draw your attention to one very interesting thing. This Fleet order" . . . and he waved a copy of the order in his fist . . . "gives the present rates of pay and what the new rates are going to be. Starting at the top, we come down the list until we get to lieutenant-commanders. They get thirty bob a day —remember that—thirty bloody bob a day! Well, their cut's to be exactly *one shilling*!"

This announcement, of course, was greeted with some indignant shouts.

"But you haven't heard anything yet," the sailor went on. "Down the list we come to able seamen. Now your pay is given as four and sevenpence a day. What do you think your cut is? Hell! I can tell you: *one shilling and sevenpence*!"

There was considerable shouting and booing at this.

"Yes," said the sailor. "I thought that'd shake you. I'm going to have a drink now and then I'll tell you some more about it.

Meantime, think over what I've told you. A lieutenant-commander who gets thirty bob a day, with duty-free booze and tobacco, gets a thirtieth of his pay cut; while you poor sods get *over a quarter* of yours knocked off!"

He then sat down amid loud cheers. He was up again in a few moments, to be received this time with respectful silence and some clapping.

"Now I'm going to tell you another thing you don't know," he began, "and that is, *they can't do this to you, anyway!* I've been reading it up—and one of the things I read was a debate in the House of Commons when the First Lord last announced a rise in our pay. At that time he said this was very much overdue and wasn't in fact enough, but it was a start. At least it gave the sailors a reasonable living wage and their wives wouldn't have to take in washing or make shirts any more. He said he hoped to be able to increase the pay in the near future, but listen to this—the one thing he would promise was *that it would never be reduced!*"

These words aroused great excitement in the canteen, and there was a tremendous uproar. At last, when he could speak again, he said: "*Promise* is the word—and it's down in black and white! Well, what are we going to do about it?"

Shouts of "We won't stand for it!"—"Shame!"—and "We've been let down!" interspersed many other unprintable expressions. After a while the speaker said: "That's all I wanted to know. Now, get your mugs filled and I'll tell you what I want you to do."

The whole canteen replenished its glasses, after which the sailor climbed on the table again and announced, "All right now, canteen staff: close the bar and shove off. If you don't we'll put you out. And if any of you try to listen in to what we're saying, you'll be bloody sorry!"

Under this crude threat, the canteen staff stopped work and filed out of the canteen. When they'd gone, the speaker got up on the table again and announced: "My name's Len Wincott—I've thought all this out, and the first thing I want is that all Petty Officers leave the canteen. We don't want 'em to lose their badges, and we'll look after their interests.

"Then I want all Marines to leave—they're sworn men and might get into trouble if they break their oath. If we can arrange

104

for the cuts to be cancelled, they'll benefit along with the rest of us."

The Petty Officers got up in an orderly way and left the canteen. But a few scuffles occurred—apparently because some of the Marines refused to leave, saying they wanted to get on drinking their beer. This, it seemed, might be the foundation for the reports that there'd been fights and hooliganism in the canteen.

When Wincott was satisfied that the canteen was cleared, he launched into what was obviously a prepared harangue. He said he didn't want to hear nasty cracks about the officers; the cuts had nothing to do with them and they were probably no more in favour of them than the members of the lower deck were.

"But what you've got to get into your thick heads," he continued, "is that we're not like the officers or the leathernecks. We're not sworn men; we joined for a rate of pay which was increased with the promise that it'd never be reduced. What'd happen in civvy street, if this kind of thing was done—contracts broken? The Combined Fleets are here to do exercises at sea— well, we're not going to let the ships go to sea. And *that's all*!

"You'll obey every order that has nothing to do with preparing the ships for sea. The order 'Prepare ship for sea, hands right and left turn, double march' is your signal to double to the fo'c'sle and sit on the cables. The ships can't move with no stokers below, and the cables can't be shifted with a thousand men sitting on them. But you'll obey every other order as usual; in fact, *better* than usual. Divisions, prayers, cleaning ship, drill, exercises, fire quarters, night closing of watertight doors, boat routine and all that'll be carried out efficiently. Marks of respect and all that, especially. You've only the one thing to do—sit on the cables.

"If anybody asks you why you're doing this, be dumb. We don't want any ringleaders and we don't want any scapegoats. Luckily we've no Commander-in-Chief and there aren't any military up here, so by the time the so-and-so's down in London realise that this Fleet isn't going to sea, they'll have to do something about it. Provided you behave as though we're just registering a grievance, not against the officers"—he called them 'the naval pigs,' a term of reference reserved by the lower deck for its superiors; the wardroom, incidentally, was always referred to as the Piggery—"but against those who want our wives to take in washing and our daughters to go on the streets, you'll have the public on your side. And one last thing: don't forget they can't put sixteen thousand men in cells!"

Throughout this long speech, Wincott had been the recipient of enthusiastic encouragement. When he shouted: "Hands up for the plan!" the response was unanimous. He continued: "Right, now we haven't much time, and the first thing I want you all to do is select one man from each ship and for him to come up to this table."

Within a short time representatives had been selected and mustered at the table. Wincott then announced: "All right, you can bring the canteen staff back now. I'll talk to your representatives, who'll select a small committee from each ship and these committees'll pass on all the necessary orders."

And that, apparently, was how all the trouble started.

Wincott arranged that the various committees' orders would be passed on by canteen boats or the exchange of books from the ships' libraries; special signals would be passed by Morse signal at night or semaphore by day, if this seemed safe. It was a cleverly worked out and executed plan, but for one thing: it overlooked the canteen manager. When his staff had been turned out, the manager had imagined that some raid on his stocks was going to be planned, so he'd positioned himself beside a ventilator where he was able to see and hear everything. If there had been any disorderliness, he intended to call a patrol. But as it was, everything passed off peacefully. However, it was greatly to my benefit that he'd kept his ear to the ventilator.

The position of Wincott in the affair was naturally intriguing me. What he expected to get out of it was something of a mystery. He must have known that, despite all the precautions he'd taken, he would, in due course, be recognised as the ringleader; and that what he was proposing, despite all his talk of broken contracts and promises, was mutiny. Perhaps, indeed, he was acting purely out of consideration for the plight of his comrades; or perhaps he was disappointed that his undoubted talents had not yet been recognised by the Navy. One thing was certain—he'd never before shown any signs of being one of that special breed known as 'sea lawyers'.

What made it so easy for him to influence his fellow shipmates? In my opinion there were four important factors. First, the Commander-in-Chief was not in command at that vital moment; and, second, the Fleet had sailed just as the cuts in pay had been announced and there hadn't been an opportunity to explain them properly to the men. Third, the cuts had been inaccurately presented : it was true that Lieutenant-Commanders were to have their pay cut by only one shilling, but it was not made plain that officers' pay had been cut three times already. The cuts amounted to six shillings a day for Lieutenant-Commanders, who were now to suffer an additional cut of one shilling. The final factor was that the initial row in the canteen was not considered important enough to be reported immediately to the Admiralty, where the necessary steps could have been taken at once.

Thus, on the morning after I arrived at Invergordon, the whole Fleet was at a standstill. It was a remarkable sight. The fo'c'sles were blanketed with sailors lounging about doing absolutely nothing, with no sign of the activities one usually associates with shipboard life. I thought it would probably be unwise to attempt to board any of the vessels, but that evening I got in touch with two Marine officers in the bar of the hotel and heard their side of the story.

When some Marine rankers had first reported to them that there was something fishy going on in the canteen, they'd at once informed their captains. It appears that no action was taken, and it is indeed difficult to see what action could have been contemplated at that stage.

The morning after the row in the canteen—I believe that a patrol had in fact been thrown out when it had gone to the canteen to investigate matters, but at the time I was unable to obtain any evidence to confirm this—the crews had carried out Wincott's plan to the letter.

When the order "Prepare ship for sea" was given, all the ships' companies had trooped off to the fo'c'sles and squatted on the cables—the Marines, meanwhile, carrying on with their normal duties.

It must have been a fantastic sight, admirals and captains on the bridges and all signals made; the Marine band and detachments drawn up on the quarterdeck as usual for leaving harbour, and absolutely nothing happening. The scene was repeated again at divisions when the order "Prepare ship" was repeated. Once again the crews disobeyed orders. Finally, the Combined Exercises had to be cancelled.

What amazed me most, as I talked to various officers in the bar each evening, was their apparent acceptance of this intolerable situation.

Later, when the sailors began lounging about in groups on the fo'c'sles, one captain decided to order the Marines to clear it. He selected a Captain Cutler, an ex-boxer who liked a fight, to conduct the operation. Just before Cutler was ready to clear the fo'c'sle in the most forcible way imaginable, however, the captain ordered that there was to be no bloodshed; a terrible blow to the redoubtable Cutler, who'd been looking forward to an interesting scrap.

Cutler, knowing that he'd no alternative now but to bluff his way through, told his Marines to march up a steel ladder to the fo'c'sle with their bayonets drawn and to make a great play of sharpening them on the steel of the ladder. When his men reached the top, Cutler told them quietly, "Now fix your bayonets as if you're about to charge; but when I give the 'Charge!' put your rifles at the high-port, so that you won't injure anybody." This proved unnecessary, however, for when the sailors saw the Marines lining up on the deck with their bayonets fixed, they broke at once and cleared off the fo'c'sle.

On board Wincott's ship, the *Norfolk*, however, the committee were prepared for action by the Marines, and had worked out a plan to thwart them. As the Marines came up the gangway, one or two sailors positioned at the top were to shout: "Fall in forward!" Normally, on mustering like this, Marines automatically went aft; but the sailors guessed that a simple ruse like this would do the trick, and that the Marines, passing the word back down the lines, would all sheepishly follow the first man to go forward. Their intention was that when this manœuvre had been executed all the sailors and stokers aboard would fall in behind the Marines, hemming them in helplessly in the bows of the ship.

This is exactly what happened. Taking the words "Fall in forward" to be a command that had been passed on from their officer, the Marines made for the eyes of the ship, right in the bows. It wasn't until a number of them had foolishly gathered there that a Corporal Hill, sensing something was wrong, shouted: "Here, this is all wrong—get through the sailors and fall in on the quarterdeck!"

At this, one of the committee shouted: "If you don't shut your ruddy trap, we'll chuck you overboard!"

Hill turned to one of the Marines and said: "Hey, you take charge; I'm going down to the officer." A scuffle broke out, and whether Hill was pushed or simply fell overboard never became clear, but when he hit the water he was followed immediately by two stokers who'd jumped in after him to save him. And that ended the whole incident. Wincott, in fact, took drastic action against the two seamen who'd tussled with Hill. This was the only act of violence of which I had definite proof. It led to a suggestion that the Royal Marines had taken part in the affair, but there was not a word of truth in this. One likes to think that this was because of their discipline and the closer touch of the Marines with their commanding officer; but the fact was that Wincott had firmly laid down that no Marines or Petty Officers were to be involved!

It was certainly a strange situation to witness. There was the most powerful battle fleet in the world just lying at anchor waiting for something to happen. From my hotel bedroom window I could watch everything that was going on. My knowledge of signals here came in very handy; I was able to read all the Morse and semaphore signals which kept passing between the ships—most of them sent illegally by the mutineers—and so I was kept fully apprised of how the affair was progressing. I reported, from what I learned, that there was absolutely no evidence of outside influence; that the mutiny appeared to be a genuine expression of the sailors' feelings. I must say, indeed, that it was the most orderly mutiny I'd ever heard of.

In London, of course, the affair had become a national sensation. Foreign investors, shattered by what was happening to the British Navy—in whom, with God Almighty, they'd put their entire faith—began to withdraw their capital; indeed, the Government was forced to go off the gold standard. Finally, the First Lord of the Admiralty announced in the House of Commons that there was undoubtedly some hardship among the sailors and that their case would be investigated. In the meantime, it was essential that the ships should leave Invergordon at once and return to their home ports. There, he promised, hardship committees would be set up and any sailor in genuine need of assistance would be given immediate help. He made the proviso that this would only be done provided the ships sailed at once for their home ports. He also promised that there'd be no victimisation. But he emphasised that if there was any repetition of the misconduct once the ships had sailed for home, then the full rigour of the naval disciplinary Acts would be put into force at once.

This statement, of course, was solemnly read out to all ships' companies at Invergordon, and produced considerable discussion. Most of the sailors by now were only too willing to seize any opportunity they could to get quit of the whole business, but there was still a number of diehards working among the committees.

Wincott's own men went about the ships pleading that the First Lord's statement was only a ruse to get all the crews separated and back into their home ports where there were plenty of military and marine barracks to house them as prisoners. They insisted that there'd really be no hardship investigations and no chance of getting the pay cuts restored.

The majority of the Fleet, however, had had enough, despite this last effort by Wincott. On the morning when the signal was made: "Ships prepare for sea", there were a few anxious moments as the sailors of the Combined Fleets gazed from one ship to another to see which—if any—would be first to obey. For several minutes it appeared that no one was going to obey the order. Then one ship was at last seen to be making preparations: hoisting its boats, raising the gangway and shortening cable. It was enough. One by one the rest of the Fleet followed suit; the mutiny at Invergordon was over. There were shouts of "Blacklegs!"—"You're letting us down!"—and other slogans, but the Fleet had begun to get under way.

But the ships were not to return to their home ports without incident. Wincott and his men had still not given up the fight, and they fought tenaciously. Meeting after meeting was called; fights and scuffles broke out on board several ships, and there were many cases of intimidation. But Wincott had shot his bolt, and his power was broken.

On arrival at their home ports, twenty-four ratings—including Wincott—who'd caused trouble on the homeward journey were thrown out of the Navy immediately, without pay or gratuity. The First Lord of the Admiralty was as good as his word and hardship committees were set up at once and did some very fine work.

The authorities, of course, couldn't afford to relax vigilance for a moment. The twenty-four ratings who'd been thrown out could make themselves a considerable nuisance if they wanted to; most of them lived in the various ports. The local police at the ports, therefore, kept the men—known as S N L R (Services no longer required)—under strict surveillance, and there was some evidence that they'd been contacting sailors and trying to enlist their sympathy for another Invergordon, designed to have the cuts in pay cancelled and the S N L R reinstated.

The matter came to a head when the Intelligence officer working at Chatham, and I myself at Portsmouth, heard of a definite plot further to embarrass the Government. To my mind it smacked of the master hand of Len Wincott. The plan was that sailors at Chatham and Portsmouth, once the pubs had closed at night, were to jump into trains and buses bound for London and meet outside the Admiralty to stage a giant demonstration.

London took this threat so seriously that when I telephoned the Admiralty to report, I was told to come up to Whitehall at once. My chief said that he'd been talking to the Prime Minister, who considered the matter of such importance that he wished to see both me and the Chatham officer as quickly as possible to get first-hand information. I arrived in London at 7 a.m. and met the Chatham officer. I told him I'd been without sleep for several nights and that the last thing I was looking forward to was an interview with the Prime Minister, Ramsay MacDonald.

"Come along to my club and have a bath and some breakfast, and you'll feel a different man!" said the Chatham officer.

I went with him to his club, had a bath, and afterwards sat down to breakfast. As this consisted mainly of Pimm's No. 1 and champagne, I must say I felt a great deal better at the end of it, and in a state to tackle several Prime Ministers. We then reported to Ramsay MacDonald, and told him everything we knew.

Whether our information and views had any effect on subsequent Government action I shall, of course, never know. That evening, however, it was announced that the pay cuts—which had amounted to twenty-five per cent or more—were to be cut back to a uniform ten per cent. It was a gesture which satisfied most of the sailors, and indeed nothing more was heard of the S N L R men, with the exception of Len Wincott, to whom I'll return in a moment.

Within a few days the Home Fleet was given a new Commander-in-Chief—Admiral Sir John Kelly—a strong personality who took a quick grip on things right from the start. Although it would be wrong to suggest that there was jubilation among the sailors at the fact that the cuts had been reduced, there was no question that they felt their action at Invergordon had at least been justified by the Government's subsequent action. Things could therefore be considered to be still 'dicey', and Admiral Kelly decided to address the whole of the Portsmouth Fleet. He said he'd like me to be present to observe any reaction among the men.

The affair was staged aboard the largest aircraft carrier then at Spithead, and attended by every man in the Fleet who was not actually on duty. Kelly began by saying that it was impossible for him to get to know every man in the Fleet personally —certainly not right away—but he wanted everybody to know *him*. They could go back to their shipmates who were on duty and tell them that he was an ugly old bastard who looked like a gorilla. Having raised a laugh with this sally, the Admiral got down to business.

"Your action at Invergordon has done incalculable damage to Britain abroad; but clearly all the mistakes were not on one side, and it's no good now seeking to rake it all up again. What we have to do is to restore confidence in the country.

"I'm aware that there are still a number of disgruntled people inside the Navy, and a lot outside it, who'd like to exploit the situation if they could—a lot of people who have nothing to do with the Navy. Now, what I want you all to do is to report any activity by outsiders to your officers at once, and we'll have the bloody pants off them in no time!"

Delivered in the salty language that sailors can appreciate, this address was a roaring success. News of it spread to other vessels of the Home Fleet, and the general feeling among the men was "thank God we've someone to look after us!"

I saw a great deal of Admiral Kelly on and off in the weeks that followed, and enjoyed his direct ways and quaint language.

On one occasion I went to see him in his cabin. When I entered he was writing at his desk. I waited, but he continued writing. Finally he looked up and said: "Have you got piles, soldier?"

"No, sir!" I replied.

"Well, in that case, bring your arse to an anchor!"

This was his way of inviting me to sit down.

Reports reached me from the C I D in Portsmouth that there'd been a big influx of Communist Party members into the city, determined to exploit the situation following Invergordon. To my knowledge this was the first time the Communists had really become involved in the affair; in fact, they'd been rather slow off the mark about the whole thing. If they'd got to work at Invergordon itself, things could have turned out much more seriously. Certainly I don't believe Wincott himself was a Communist at the time of Invergordon. In fact, it was not until some weeks had elapsed that Wincott, so far as I know, came into contact with the Communists.

Following his dismissal from the Navy he'd gone into partnership with a naval deserter friend, who was operating a tea racket in the East End of London. This chap had managed to buy up enormous quantities of tea which had been rejected by the big tea firms as not being up to standard; most of it was simply dust. Wincott's friend made up this dust into quarter-pound, half-pound and one-pound packets and sold them in the poorer streets at a price considerably less than that being charged for tea in the shops. As an added selling inducement, he inserted numbers in every packet of tea and promised that whoever held the lucky number would win £2.

In this way he got rid of great quantities of tea dust at an exorbitant profit. He didn't even play square to the extent of holding a draw for the £2, but simply decamped. In the end, the racket, which was providing a lucrative enough living for Wincott, was exposed by the magazine *John Bull*, and the deserter, rather than face a charge of fraud, gave himself up to the Naval authorities.

Out of a job and drifting aimlessly, still wearing his naval uniform, Wincott found himself one Sunday afternoon listening to a Communist speaker in Hyde Park. The Communist was talking about the Invergordon mutiny and referred to the men who'd taken part in it as "heroes who would go down in history". Wincott listened for a moment and then interrupted: "I'm one of the heroes you're talking about, and I haven't even got the price of a bed in a doss-house."

The speaker closed the meeting at once and went over to talk to Wincott. When he learned that he was the actual organiser of the affair, he brought him to a party meeting then being held in the public baths off the Edgware Road. He introduced Wincott and, after a number of fiery speeches, said: "We must see that our comrade is looked after!" To start with, he suggested that Wincott's seaman's cap, with the badge of H M S *Norfolk* on it, should be auctioned.

A considerable sum was raised immediately by this method, and the cap was afterwards sent to Russia where it reposes, so far as I know to this day, in the Red Museum in Moscow. Wincott was afterwards taken to the *Daily Worker* offices, where he was given a job helping to prepare scurrilous articles about the Fleet; they were published as being 'By Our Naval Correspondent'. Copies of these articles were circulated in the Fleet, slipped inside all kinds of quite respectable periodicals—including the Salvation Army's *War Cry*.

The trouble was that some of the stories struck home as being very near the truth. There were stories of captains who had taken women on board; of women seen rushing naked around ships. Although the Admiralty at first considered asking the officers concerned to take libel actions against the C P, this idea was soon dropped when it was discovered that there was indeed some foundation for the stories, even though some of them may have been exaggerated.

The articles also called attention to apparently genuine grievances: these included the forcing of sailors to go to church daily against their wishes; depriving them of all liquor aboard, except the traditional tot of rum; and the fact that although officers were supplied with comfortable quarters, the men had no proper place to sleep and simply had to sling their hammocks where they could.

The extraordinary thing was that when civilians got into conversation with sailors in pubs and other public places, and commiserated with them on their hardships, the sailors would stagger their listeners by saying: "You don't know what you're talking about. How could any ship carry enough beer to satisfy fifteen hundred thirsty men?" Certainly the bulk of the British Navy appeared to be determined not to fall for Communist Party propaganda, whether Len Wincott had anything to do with it or not.

As for Wincott himself, he didn't stay with the C P for long. In a short time he dropped out of sight, and his next appearance on the public scene was when he turned up in the Spanish Civil War at the head of a Communist battalion. After that he went to Russia, where as late as 1958 he was reported to be still living.

But to return to the situation in Portsmouth in the weeks following Invergordon. The C I D were particularly interested in two men who were known to be in the Communist Party— two paid agitators, whose presence in the city along with other 'comrades' was indicative of the Party's continuing interest in Fleet matters.

It was reported to me that these two men were in the habit of going into a pub called the Park Hotel, off the Commercial Road. I later learned that Wincott had told the Party that if they wanted good articles about conditions in the Fleet they should contact a chap who'd served aboard H M S *Hood*, and who'd written a number of very good articles for the Fleet magazine. Wincott had said this chap was nicknamed Shorty, and that he went about with a very tall pal called Lofty. Both usually drank in the Park Hotel and were known to the barmaid there.

The two agitators had, in fact, managed to contact Shorty and Lofty. Shorty, who wasn't a writer at all but just a typesetter, although he'd contributed articles to the Mediterranean Fleet magazine, was flattered when these two strangers approached him and asked if he'd write an article on what had happened at Invergordon. He'd be well paid for it, they said.

Shorty said: "Well, I was there, and I know all that happened. I could write a story all right—so long as I don't get into trouble."

The two Communists then began to ply the sailors with whisky, but through the haze of drink Shorty slowly realised that these weren't two newspaper reporters as he had at first imagined, but two members of the Communist Party who wanted him to angle the story in a way that would suit their own propaganda purposes.

He nudged Lofty and said: "I'm off to the heads, chum; coming?" and went below. As Lofty followed him, he added: "These bloody people aren't journalists at all, they're Communists."

"What's that?" asked the dim-witted Lofty. "Some sort of religion?"

"Don't be daft!" retorted Shorty. "They want to start another Invergordon in Portsmouth!"

"Well, let's go and soak 'em!" growled Lofty.

"No," said Shorty. "We'll listen to what they've got to say, and then go back and report it."

Which is precisely what they did. The matter eventually came to the D N I, who asked me to get in touch with the sailors but to leave the agitators to the Security people.

I contacted Shorty and Lofty at once and told them they were to carry on seeing the two agitators and fall in with everything they suggested. They were also to obey all orders given to them by the Security officers. Both men were then taken from their ships and lodged in Portsmouth naval barracks. In due course they were again approached by the two agitators. This time they were told that their ex-comrade, Len Wincott, had drawn up a pamphlet detailing all the grievances suffered by Royal Navy seamen. It was intended that this pamphlet should be distributed throughout the Fleet, and that meetings to discuss it should be organised afterwards. Would Shorty and Lofty help?

"What happens if we're caught?" demanded Shorty. "We've got nine years in the Navy and we're going to stay on for our second lot. If we're nabbed doing this, we'll be chucked out!"

"Don't worry," he was assured. "You'll be well looked after. Come up to London, and you'll meet the people who'll fix it up and arrange how much you'll be paid."

In agreeing to this suggestion, the two sailors were, of course, only carrying out our instructions. After a day or so they travelled up to London, shadowed by Security men. They returned very pleased with themselves. They'd been given £50 down, with a promise that when they'd distributed the pamphlets they'd get another £500.

The next step was that they were to meet the two agitators again, when the pamphlets were to be handed over to them.

The rendezvous, however, was not to be the Park Hotel but another pub; the significance of this only became apparent after the meeting.

Shorty and Lofty duly tipped off the police, and the C I D were ready to swoop on the pub and catch the agitators in the act of passing over the pamphlets. They were disappointed, however, for when the two Communists strolled into the bar in the wake of Shorty and Lofty it was seen that they were carrying nothing at all. Clearly they'd smelt a rat. . . .

The C I D at once pounced and, acting on the orders of the Director of Public Prosecutions, who thought they had enough evidence to lodge a charge of incitement to mutiny, arrested them. On the way to Portsmouth police station, one of the men put his hand into his pocket and pulled out a handkerchief. But the detective-sergeant saw a piece of paper flutter to the ground; he picked it up and found that it was a cloakroom ticket for two parcels left at Fratton Station. After charging the two men at the police station, the detective-sergeant went along and collected two big parcels, which contained the missing pamphlets, and they were certainly a direct incitement to mutiny. They called for a mass meeting where demands were to be voiced for a redress of all grievances. The two Communists were brought before a magistrate and remanded in custody.

The case eventually came up before the Winchester Assizes. Shorty, whom I considered by far the more intelligent of the two men, didn't show up too well in the witness box; but the dim-witted Lofty behaved magnificently. When defence counsel asked a question couched in legal jargon, Lofty asked: "Cor lumme, sir! Could you put that in sailor's language?"

The judge intervened at once, saying that he'd some experience in naval language and would counsel allow *him* to put the question? When the judge asked the question Lofty replied: "That's a lot better, m'lud; I can understand *you*!" and proceeded to rattle off an answer.

When counsel asked: "When did you decide these people were Communists?" Lofty replied: "I never decided that—I don't know what a Communist is. I didn't know then and I don't know now."

"Well," demanded the exasperated counsel, "did you think there was anything unusual about these two men?"

"Yes," answered Lofty, "I thought they were insurance blokes."

"Why, in the name of heaven?" asked counsel.

"Because they offered us whisky when they knew our drink was beer. When they offered us that, I knew they wanted something off of us!"

At the end of the trial the two Communists got ten years each.

Following this affair I was asked by the head of the Security service if I'd care to join his staff. I said I'd like to very much, and so was duly transferred.

For a few weeks everything seemed quiet and it was considered unlikely that there would be any trouble among the Fleets before their big meeting at Gibraltar. Then, a week beforehand, a disturbing report was received from the Flag Office, Gib., that a number of suspicious characters were arriving on the Rock. My chief decided that I'd better go out there as quickly as possible and investigate.

There was no question, of course, of picking up a telephone and booking an air passage in those days; I knew the situation might be so serious and urgent that the delay involved in a train journey could be disastrous. Therefore I made inquiries about service planes—only to find that these went infrequently to Gib.

However, one of the chaps I mentioned my problem to said that a friend of his—an ex-R A F type—now had a job flying planes to private purchasers and was due to deliver one within a few days to La Linea—which is close to Gib. The pilot had in fact mentioned that he was prepared to give a lift to anyone who wanted to go on the trip—but only if he spoke French (a knowledge of French was vital in those days—there was no direct flight from London to La Linea). So a lunch was arranged at which I met the pilot who said he would be pleased to take me.

He was, in fact, delivering the plane to a Spanish duke. He was certainly a happy-go-lucky sort of chap. From the moment we arrived at the airfield he seemed to me a bit reckless, even for his kind of life. As we were stepping into the aircraft, a worried-looking mechanic said: "You realise your compasses haven't been swung and are completely inaccurate?"

"Oh, I don't mind that," he said cheerily. "This is my compass"—and he pulled out rosary beads.

"As long as my chum here"—and he indicated me—"can tell me when my wings are at right angles to the cliffs of Dover, I'll be all right. I've been over the Channel dozens of times."

Somewhat apprehensively, I settled myself in my seat for take-off, and as we taxied away I caught a last glimpse of the mechanic doubtfully shaking his head.

Once we were above the cliffs of Dover I looked back and down and then I tapped him on the shoulder. "I think we're all right," I shouted against the roar of the engine. The wings appeared to be at right angles to the cliffs. I was appalled to think that we were going to rely upon this kind of navigation, but what could I do about it now? We might well have been all right, of course, if it hadn't been for the sudden fog. Or as he put it: "Ground mist". To communicate we had to shout to each other—and I mean shout. The fog—or ground mist—became so bad that he finally pointed towards the ground and yelled: "I'm going down to have a look. If you sight water, shout!"

Down we went for quite a while without sighting water or anything else and then he shouted: "I've got to save petrol, you see—wouldn't do if I turned the plane out to sea without knowing."

I hung on to my seat and on we went for what seemed an interminable time, then he shouted again: "This is no good— I'll just have to go lower. Keep your eyes open."

With this admonition, he pointed the nose of the plane towards the ground. To my relief the fog—or mist—finally swirled clear.

"What I'm looking for is a river with an airfield on the left bank," he yelled again. I nodded. I could, in fact, see one just below. I had no idea, of course, just what part of France we were over. My carefree pilot indicated with his thumb that he was going to land. I sat back with a sigh when the wheels touched down. As official French interpreter on this trip, I clambered out and made for the nearby offices. I was surprised to find that the first person I met was wearing a British warm. But then, a lot of French people wore them, I remembered; a legacy of the war.

In my most impeccable French, and gesturing with my hand, I asked: "Où sommes-nous?"

The man in the British warm looked puzzled. My God, I thought, where are we—what patois does this chap understand? I'd never had this kind of trouble before. I asked in English: "Do you speak English?"—for some of these Normandy or Pas-de-Calais types had probably picked it up. The man grinned. "You're in Manston, Kent, old boy," came the answer in crisp and unmistakable British accents. We had simply flown round in a circle.

Well, we refuelled, got ourselves a weather report—which said that conditions were clear over the Channel—and took off again. This time we came down at an airfield near Paris, and decided to have coffee and something to eat. We were just finishing the meal when there was a sudden ringing of bells across the airfield. My companion jettisoned his coffee and jumped up shouting: "Rush for the plane—quick!" With that he dashed from the building and raced towards the aircraft. Wondering what was happening I sprinted after him.

"Jump in!" he cried and hauled me into my seat, perspiring and cursing. As the engines spluttered into life and we moved off I saw several people rushing towards us shouting and waving and headed by a red-faced airport policeman.

"What the hell's wrong?" I bawled.

"Fog warning," he replied against the roar of the engine. "They're closing the airport down, and it may be days before we get clear. I'll lose my bonus if I don't deliver this plane in time, so I'm taking no risks!"

I looked ahead along the runway; already the fog was closing in around us; it seemed doubtful whether we'd even get off the ground. I hung on, breathed a prayer and shut my eyes. Up into the air we soared, the cold, clammy fog beating into our faces; we hadn't even had time to put on our goggles. And then we were roaring up through a white, claustrophobic world, headed for goodness knew where.

Suddenly we were out into bright sunshine and France lay like a chequer-board beneath us. Now I even began to enjoy the trip and considered that, since I had got as far as this without losing my life, the chances were that I would arrive safely in La Linea. But I'd tempted the fates too soon. We'd cleared France and were over Spain when suddenly the engine began to splutter. I clutched my seat and again muttered a little prayer.

"We'll have to go down," cried the pilot cheerily. I wished he would show some signs of taking the matter seriously; his happy grin in the face of adversity—and possibly even death—was unnerving. Again, however, we survived. He found a field.

We made a good landing. He was still grinning, so I had to grin back as we clambered out. He was certainly an efficient mechanic; in a very little time he had unscrewed the petrol points and blown through them, clearing the blockage. This did the trick and the engine started and ran sweetly. Then he looked round—we had come down in a fairly small field—and made his usual snap judgment: "Look, I can never take off in this place with you and our suitcases. I've only got fifty yards to that row of trees and I doubt if I could clear it. See that church over there—with the steeple? You make for that with your two suitcases and climb up that steeple. I'll circle round and land in a place where I can easily get off again. You watch where I land and then make for that."

"All right," I said, "I suppose it's the only thing we can do."

I watched him take off. There's no doubt that his judgment was accurate. In fact he *just* cleared the trees—I watched leaves and a few birds' nests fluttering down in his wake. I waved after him and then set off with the suitcases to trudge to the church. Unfortunately neither he nor I knew that on the other side of the trees was a very fast-flowing stream—too wide and deep to ford. I had to search along the bank until at last I found a place where I could cross. Some time had elapsed before I reached the other side. Even then I found that I had to make a further detour around muddy fields before I could reach the church. By this time I had lost all sight of the plane. I entered the church and looked around. I was not long inside when a priest approached me; he clearly thought I was looking for spiritual guidance. I said in French that I wanted to go up the steeple; he did not understand. As I had no Spanish, and the priest knew neither French nor English, all I could do was point upwards.

This seemed to reinforce his belief that I was seeking religious consolation, because he immediately beckoned me to a confessional. As neither of us had any hope of understanding the other, I shrugged my shoulders and set off round the church, hoping to come across a door leading to the staircase up the steeple. I finally found one and up I went. When I got to the top I had a magnificent view of the surrounding countryside, but could see no sign of the plane. I took it that my pilot had simply tired of waiting for me and rather than lose his bonus had taken off. That was the last I saw of him.

So there I was, stranded in an unknown church, and with no one apparently who understood either English or French. It would have been quicker, I realised, by rail.

My troubles had, in fact, only begun. When I came down from the steeple, the priest had been joined there by a gendarme. I shouted and protested. I pointed to the sky and at my suitcases. The gendarme simply seized me by the arm and led me down the village street, past staring villagers to the local jail, where I was put in a very uncomfortable cell. I was to remain there for two hours before an interpreter came in to whom I explained my plight. When I had finished he burst out laughing: "They thought you wanted to steal the two wonderful relics which belong to the church. However, it is known that a plane came down in a field near this village, so your story is accepted. Where do you want to go now?"

"Gibraltar," I said a little shamefacedly.

"Oh, well, that will be easy. You can get a train from the local railway station."

My temper frayed by now, I carried my suitcases down to the station. Luckily the booking clerk agreed to accept English pound notes (those were the days when a pound note meant something on the Continent) and I was able to buy a ticket. Tired, dusty and exasperated, I eventually boarded a train and settled down for the long, back-breaking journey across Spain.

On arriving at Gib I booked in at the Rock Hotel. I asked whether my friend the airman had checked in at the hotel but was told that he had not—possibly for the very good reason that the French and Spanish had laid charges against him for breaking practically every flying regulation—and that there was a warrant out for his arrest. So I kept quiet and sent his suitcase to his club; I never heard from him again. I then reported to the Flag Officer Commanding and saw the local police and security personnel. I learned that there was a great deal of tension in the Fleet. The ordinary ratings were creating grievances out of incidents which normally would have been passed over as a joke, a good story to tell over a drink. One incident, for example, concerned the captain and two officers of a destroyer who had taken some girls back on board at two a.m. after a party at the Rock Hotel. The girls had moved along to the wardroom laughing and shouting, apparently bumping into the men's hammocks. The cook had then been sent for and ordered to prepare bacon and eggs.

"But the galley fire's out, sir," he had protested.

"Well, then, light the bloody thing, can't you?" he'd been told.

I found absolutely nothing to suggest that a repetition of Invergordon was likely. The men had no leader of Wincott's calibre and, so far as I could uncover, were being backed by no organisation. But the Admiral was not prepared to take risks; he cancelled combined manoeuvres. And so, after another few days, I returned to England.

One other trip I made in connection with the Invergordon affair took me to Malta to discuss with Lord Louis Mountbatten, then the Fleet Signals Officer, ways of stopping signalmen and wireless operators from sending private messages between ships. But I was ordered to call in at Rome on my way out, in order that I could investigate the mystery of a missing naval secret document. The Security authorities had received information that such a document had been seen in the Italian Admiralty in Rome.

All our ships in the Mediterranean had been contacted. None reported any missing document, yet the report from Rome was believed to be accurate. My task was to find out what the document was and where it came from. The personal number on the cover would tell me which ship it came from; all I had to do was get a look at it.

Mussolini was staging the Exhibition of Ten Years of Fascism when I arrived. I met my contact and explained that it was extremely important that I should see the document itself, if only for a second. This meant he had to bring it out of the Admiralty buildings, a dangerous business. We arranged that he'd come to the hotel where I was staying, but planned things so that he'd have no contact with me whatever.

123

At the pre-arranged time I sat in the hotel lounge casually reading a newspaper until I saw my contact walk in. Without a glance in my direction, he too sat down for a while, then rose and walked across to the lavatory. I followed and, as he came out of the first cubicle, I went in without a word passing between us. The document was there, resting on a ledge. I saw enough to identify it, and left it there for him to pick up again.

The document was indeed an Admiralty secret paper, dealing with a form of coloured-lights procedure for battle exercises. I had the information I'd been sent to collect, and when I arrived in Malta the distributing agency who'd sent out the document were soon able to identify the ship that had received it, from the number I was now able to give them. It was a destroyer. I reported to the C-in-C, who sent for the Captain of the destroyer; and the whole story came out.

The document had been lost during an exercise in which it had been needed, for reference, on the bridge. The Fleet ran into a storm and all destroyers were ordered to return to port. As they neared Malta the Captain of this vessel sent the First Lieutenant down for a rest, telling him to take the document with him and stow it away. The First Lieutenant went down to the wardroom, stretched out on a settee, and put the document under a cushion before he went to sleep. He was roused as they entered harbour and went up to anchor the ship. Later he had a bath and breakfast . . . and forgot all about the secret naval document under the cushion.

It was needed next day for a conference called by the C-in-C, but it couldn't be found so the Captain went along without it. Three days elapsed and it was still missing. The Captain thought he should report the fact, but the First Lieutenant pointed out he should have done this immediately, and said he believed it'd be found eventually. So the loss was never reported.

What had actually happened was that a Maltese mess-man had found the document under the cushion and taken it. He had to land to get provisions and he went to the Italian Consulate, who paid him thirty shillings. By 9.30 that morning the document was on its way to Rome and that same day was being inspected in their Admiralty.

This mission successfully completed, I went to see Lord Louis Mountbatten concerning the transmitting of illegal messages.

He told me he'd been considering the matter for some time. He himself had made a small interception set in his cabin, and was alarmed at the increasing amount of private wireless transmissions. Safety regulations might be ignored in sending these private messages, and there could be serious interference with official signal traffic.

He was intending to press for more interception sets to be made, and to start a system of wireless guards. I promised to report this to the Admiralty in London, and did so on my return.

With the end of the Invergordon Mutiny there was no likelihood of its repetition, but for a long time afterwards the Admiralty continued to keep a close watch on things. There is no doubt that they'd been caught out once, and as a result had had to give way to the men. The affair had wider repercussions, too, among our allies; some sailors in the Greek Navy mutinied; they attacked their officers and damaged their ships.

The attitude of our men to this was typical: why didn't the bastards follow our example? We did everything in a sensible way and achieved our ends without violence. These stupid Greeks, on the other hand, had got themselves into a lot of trouble and disgraced themselves. From the British sailors' point of view, the Invergordon affair had been entirely worth while and a completely justifiable action; the Admiralty, by giving in, had tacitly acknowledged this.

But the Admiralty kept a close watch on Fleet political activities until all the men who'd taken part in the Invergordon affair had served out their time.

The Fleet still seemed to contain a large number of Communists, Irish hotheads, pacifists and others who were liable to create difficulties, and it was decided that I should continue to work with the Security service for an indefinite time. So the security of the Navy remained my chief concern for a long time afterwards.

CHAPTER VI

I HAVE briefly mentioned my visit to the Mediterranean Fleet to see Lord Louis Mountbatten, the Fleet Signals Officer. Following that meeting with him I had many opportunities to meet and talk with him subsequently in London. After one such chat he mentioned that he'd told His Royal Highness the Prince of Wales the story of my career and that the Prince had expressed a desire to meet me.

Lord Louis said that he'd take me to St James's Palace personally and introduce me. The idea of meeting the Prince of Wales made me very nervous, of course; but Lord Louis reassured me.

"Don't worry about it, but try and realise that he's had a very different upbringing from you. You've met all sorts of types in your time. He's forced to live in a very much closed circle. You'll find him extremely easy to get on with. One thing—don't attempt to dismiss yourself—wait until he dismisses you."

I was taken along to St James's Palace, and Lord Louis introduced me to the Prince and then cleared off. I found H R H extremely easy to talk to, and I had many subsequent meetings with him. We found we had three common interests—riding, languages and music. He amazed me, however, by his knowledge of subjects which I wouldn't have thought he could know anything about.

He told me that on one occasion he'd discussed my career and the hardships of my early life in the Marines with his brothers, and they'd replied that I'd had a much easier time of it than they!

Whatever had happened to me, at least it had been left to me to make the best or worst of it. He himself had always resented being hemmed in and forbidden to find out things for himself; he hated the feeling that he had to be protected. As Prince of Wales he'd been able to do more things on his own, and by now he'd become adept in cutting out unnecessary protocol. "Not," he added wistfully, "that it often does any good, but it sometimes helps."

He told me that he found his royal isolation, and the habit of spoon-feeding him with information, particularly galling. He enjoyed telling me of an incident when he'd first moved into St James's Palace at the behest of his father, the late King George V. He walked round the whole palace, seeking a special site for his personal cloakroom.

Finally he told the Office of Works to build him one at the end of a passage-way some distance from any of the other rooms. His idea was to prevent any of his staff talking at him through the door. The Officer of Works demurred at setting up the cloak-room in that position, pointing out that the plumbing in the palace was very old and difficult to alter. H R H insisted, how-ever, saying he could visit there undisturbed and read any news-paper he wanted to without anyone raising an eyebrow.

He was extremely interested, I found, in the *Daily Worker*, principally because of its articles on Navy conditions. He told me he'd already spoken to the First Sea Lord about doing some-thing to make life aboard ship easier for the lower deck. He realised that no ship could be expected to carry enough beer aboard to satisfy all the men, but he was concerned that such a large amount of the available storage room was devoted to wine-and-spirit stores for the needs of the various admirals, cap-tains and other officers. He had suggested that it might not be a bad idea if the Royal Navy took a leaf out of the U S Navy's book and went dry.

I gathered that, upon hearing this blasphemy, the First Sea Lord had immediately downed a fortifying double brandy. Balked, H R H had returned to the attack and suggested that a canteen ship should be attached to each Fleet. And this was eventually arranged.

That H R H was extremely concerned about the plight of his fellow countrymen soon became clear to me. He was unhappy at the harsh social conditions obtaining in Great Britain in the early thirties; anxious to do something for the people he was soon to reign over; fretting constantly at his own inability to do something positive. The chronic unemployment problem parti-cularly concerned him.

"I go and speak to these men," he said angrily, "the same men I saw in the trenches now drawing the dole and trying to bring up a family. What happens then? Off I go and have a slap-up lunch with the Mayor or some other such person, every morsel of food nearly choking me. I feel so useless, Bassett—and don't you dare tell me that I give pleasure to the men by my visit, or I'll crown you with this mashie niblick!" We'd been discussing golf a little earlier.

Two of my assignments while working for the Security services involved well-known names—Mr Compton Mackenzie, the novelist, and Lieutenant Baillie-Stewart, better known to newspaper readers as "The Prisoner in the Tower". The Mackenzie case is particularly memorable to me, because as a result of it I almost found myself in jail.

At that time a number of highly placed officers and officials had been rushing into print with accounts of their experiences in various secret Government organisations. The Civil Assistant to the Director of Naval Intelligence, for instance, had written a book about cryptography which had made him extremely unpopular with the service chiefs. A Civil assistant had written a book 40 O B (Room 40, Old Block—in the Admiralty) which dealt with the early days of cryptography. And even the Director of Naval Information during the 1914-18 war, Admiral Sir Reginald Hall, was planning to write an account of his own part in that conflict, but the authorities had decided to put a stop to this, and when Mr Compton Mackenzie published his third volume of war memoirs, under the title *Greek Memories* (Cassell, 1932) it was decided to prosecute.

In the book he had, it was maintained, disclosed certain information of which he had become aware through his official wartime position. It was admitted that he had never given any pledge not to communicate this information, and it was also plain that he had not in fact done any harm by allowing it to be published. But—technically—the author had broken the law. The Security people decided that he must be convicted—in order to discourage others.

The book was withdrawn from circulation at once. Mr Mackenzie's counsel, realising that technically he had no answer and aware of his client's already considerable financial loss due to the withdrawal of the book, intimated that he would plead guilty.

Satisfied, my chief said to me: "Look, Bassett, I want you to go along and see the judge in this case, and tell him that all we want is a conviction for the record. Tell him that Mr Mackenzie has, in fact, done absolutely no damage and has lost a great deal of money owing to the book's withdrawal. We feel that a purely nominal fine would meet the case."

I strode over to the Law Courts and asked to see the judge. Innocently I explained to him that I'd been sent along to give his lordship my chief's views. The judge listened in silence. Then without a word he pressed a bell. A clerk entered and his lordship, in his sternest judicial voice, barked: "Send in the tipstaff!" This person duly arrived and the judge then uttered these words: "You are to arrest this young man for trying to influence a court of justice and suggesting that, before I've heard the opinion of learned counsel, I'm to inflict a certain punishment."

"But, sir," I protested, "I'm only obeying orders!"

"I've nothing to do with your chief!" roared the judge. "You made a certain statement to me, and you'll be tried!"

I pleaded for an opportunity to ring up my chief, and was at last allowed to do so. He had to telephone the Home Secretary himself before I could be released.

My connection with the Baillie-Stewart affair revolved around a sum of £500 in five-pound notes which he'd been given by the German Government. We'd learned about this money while compiling evidence against him before his arrest. As a further link in the case it became necessary to prove that he'd spent some of this money, and so agents were put on his trail to follow him around London and find out how he disposed of it.

The man was very careful, however; not one of these fivers whose numbers we'd recorded ever changed hands, so far as we were aware. In the end, sufficient other evidence was collected to make the charges against the spy stick, and the question of the notes ceased to matter. But after Baillie-Stewart had been sentenced and sent down to Maidstone prison, he informed the Governor that he wished to talk to the Intelligence services and tell them the whole story of what had happened.

I was sent down to interview him, the Chief emphasising to me that I must give the fellow no encouragement to believe that his sentence might be reduced, whatever he promised to reveal.

Baillie-Stewart, when I saw him, told me a number of stories, which I had to tell him we knew all about. He began by explaining that his downfall started when he met a girl in East Africa and subsequently got tangled up in a series of gay parties and big-game safaris which he couldn't afford. The girl, whom he believed to have fallen in love with him, suggested that if he did some espionage work she'd see that he was well paid for it. That's what had started it all.

"We know all this already," I pointed out, adding that it appeared there was nothing further he could tell me of any value. I hesitated, then added: "There's one thing, however, I personally was never able to find out and you might care to tell me now—how did you get rid of those fivers?"

Baillie-Stewart grinned and said: "That foxed you, didn't it?"

"Yes," I admitted. "It did—and still does."

He explained that he'd owed several large sums of money to various people, especially bookmakers. One bookie at Aldershot had threatened to go to his C O, so Baillie-Stewart had shown him the £500 in fivers, saying it was a legacy.

"If my creditors hear about this, you'll get none of it," he told the bookie. Then he suggested that the man should take from the £500 whatever was owed, and return the rest to him in one-pound notes; the fivers could easily be circulated around the various race-courses. And this was how it had been done.

We'd been watching Baillie-Stewart for some time before we actually arrested him. We'd known he was sending information over to the Germans, but as most of it was of a trivial nature it had been decided not to arrest him right away; his activities at the Tank School at Lulworth Cove soon changed this.

The Germans promised him more money if he could obtain the secrets of our latest tanks and amphibious craft, and Baillie-Stewart wangled himself a course at the school. He knew something about engines and, during a lecture on one of the latest amphibious vehicles, he piped up to say that he was not convinced that the gearbox couldn't be improved.

"We'd have to consult the blue-prints to find out," said the lecturer.

"If I could see them, I could tell you whether I'm right or not," said Baillie-Stewart. And so he managed to get hold of them, copied them and sent them on to Germany. After this, it was decided to prosecute him.

Two agents were sent down to Aldershot to arrest him. They found him in his rooms; he was already under close arrest. When they entered they saw his revolver lying on the table and decided that this would be the easiest solution. They explained to him that they'd leave the room and return in ten minutes. They looked pointedly at the revolver, left him, and waited outside, hoping that the man would do "the honourable thing" and blow out his brains. But Baillie-Stewart had no intention of ending what had so far been an exceedingly pleasant existence. In the end, they had to return to the room and take him off to the Tower.

I was amazed and delighted to wake up one morning and learn that I had been given the rank of Brevet-Major in the New Year Honours; this meant that although my pay remained as it was I now had the rank and seniority of a Major and on board a ship would rank with the Commander.

It was unusual in the Marine Corps for anybody to get more than one step up within a very short time. Promotion was painfully slow and certainly by no means sure. So that, when a few months later I was told that the Adjutant-General wanted to speak to me, the last thing I was thinking about was further promotion. I rang through and asked for the Adjutant-General, Sir Richard Ford. "Bassett speaking, sir," I said when a voice answered.

"Well, Bassett," said this voice cordially. "Let me be the first to congratulate you upon your promotion to Major."

At once I suspected that this was a leg-pull; no one ever had got or would get two steps up in their career within such a short space of time. I knew, too, that there was a hoaxer at the Admiralty who often rang people up, pretending that he was a high-ranking officer. I thought it must be this chap at work again, so I answered gaily. "Oh, you mean promotion to Colonel? I'm a Major already. Why don't you look up the Navy list before trying to pull my leg?"

The phone went dead. I sat back and wondered, and then snatched up the telephone again and rang the hoaxer I knew. "Here," I said, "did you ring me up on one of your ruddy practical jokes and tell me that I'd been promoted?"

"Good Lord, no!" he said.

"Quite honestly?"

"Absolutely, old man. After all, I don't even know your phone extension."

Fearfully, I rang up General Hunton of the Marines, the Assistant Adjutant-General, who was a great friend of mine. "Sir, by any incredible chance, have I been promoted to Substantive Major?"

"I couldn't say, Bassett—why?"

I explained about the telephone call.

"Good," he said. "I knew the Adjutant-General was going to see the First Sea Lord to ask that you be promoted—it's on account of your age, you know. There's no chance of you ever being promoted Substantive Major on the basis of seniority. The only way to get you the rank is to promote you specially. I congratulate you—the Adjutant-General must have succeeded."

Then I told him what I'd said to the Adjutant-General. His tone grew serious.

"You'd better come over right away," he said.

Conscious of storms ahead, I got my bowler hat and umbrella and walked across briskly to the Marine Office. I found General Hunton looking extremely solemn, and knew now I'd really put my foot in it.

"I've seen the Adjutant-General, Bassett," he said. "And quite honestly I've never seen him in such a temper. I can tell you this, he won't talk to you."

"But I *must* see him, sir," I insisted. "I must apologise! I've *got* to see him!"

"Very well, then," said the General. "When I take some papers in, follow me and wait in the passage. If there's no one with him, I'll let you know, and as I leave by one door you can slip in by the other."

We carried out this manœuvre without difficulty and within a few moments I found myself standing in front of Sir Richard Ford's desk. He was writing and didn't look up at once. I stood there tense and waiting, knowing that my whole career rested upon how I conducted myself within the next few moments. Finally Sir Richard looked up and saw me. "What are you doing here?" he barked angrily as I blurted out : "Sir, I've come to apologise."

Flinging a batch of papers down on his desk with a loud smack, he snapped back : "I don't want your apologies, Bassett. I'm going along at once to the First Sea Lord to have your promotion cancelled."

"I don't mind what disciplinary action you take, sir," I broke in hurriedly, "I've come over here simply to apologise. I'm terribly upset at speaking to you the way I did, I didn't know it was you." And I explained about the practical joker.

Sir Richard listened patiently to me. Then, "Get out of my office!" he said brusquely; and out I went.

His feelings were obviously deeply hurt, but I must record that he didn't cancel my promotion. His punishment was to cut me dead in the United Service Club.

My wife and Lady Ford were great friends, however, and eventually I was asked round to their house to play bridge, and here everything was settled amicably. Sir Richard told me: "Well I got you promoted—specially promoted with some difficulty—to enable you to go through the higher ranks of the Corps. But you've got to cease this Intelligence work. You've been far too long away from the Corps as it is. You've got to come back at once, and never return to Intelligence work again; is that understood?"

I nodded, quite happy to go back to the Corps, although sorry to leave Security work, which I found fascinating. The following morning I went to see my Security chief and told him: "Sir, I've got to leave Security, I'm afraid. I've been specially promoted, jumping over about twenty other officers, and my Adjutant-General insists I must now go back to the Corps and do Corps duty."

The chief was surprised, but understood, and he replied: "I'm not going to stand in your way, but you must remember that in a war—or any other emergency—you'll be recalled to us. I must say I'm sorry you're going."

Then his tone changed. "You've been given accelerated promotion, but don't think you're a very clever person. Let me tell you at once that you're not, you're just an ordinary chap who's been lucky—damned lucky! Which is ninety per cent of what makes a good security officer. Don't think you've been the finest security man ever! That's all. Goodbye."

Thoroughly deflated, I took my leave.

When I left the Security Service I was sent to Deal, then an Officers' Training and Recruit Depot, to learn something about the Corps again after having been away for so many years. Before going down to the depot I decided that I'd better kit myself out properly for my new job; I went to the best boot-maker in London, who made me the finest pair of black riding boots I've ever seen.

At Deal I was appointed Officer-in-Command of a Company and entitled to wear a most resplendent uniform complete with these wonderful boots. The trouble was that they were so tight that I had to put on a pair of my wife's silk stockings, liberally dusted with face powder, before I could struggle into them.

The first morning I wore them was a time of absolute agony. I was hearing a disciplinary offence, but all I wanted was to end it as quickly as possible and rid myself of those infernal boots, which were crippling me. I dealt so leniently and swiftly with the offender that the Company Sergeant-Major was moved to protest. I hobbled down to the High Street into the first boot shop I could find, and gasped out: "Cut these damn things off my feet!" The assistant did so with a quiet smile. Later I had them repaired and stretched to my size.

I was very pleased to be appointed Fleet Royal Marine officer to HMS *London*, then stationed in the Mediterranean—*London* was one of our larger cruisers. I loved the Mediterranean, and particularly Malta. Then, when I was all prepared to go, I was amazed to read in Divisional Orders that my appointment had been cancelled and that a Major Sandall was going in my stead.

I immediately went to see my Brigadier and asked him the reason for the cancellation. He said he knew nothing about it—but why didn't I go up to London and see General Hunton, the Adjutant-General? So I did.

"There's a very good reason, Bassett," said the General. "An important conference is to be held at Singapore. For the first time in history the three Commanders-in-Chief—East India Station, China Station and Australia—are to meet there to discuss their plans in case of war in the Far East. They want someone sent out who's had experience of different forms of Intelligence work; and you've been selected."

I explained that the previous Adjutant-General, Sir Richard Ford, had made me promise that on no account would I ever go back to Intelligence.

"I'm sorry about that, Bassett; but Sir Richard Ford is no

longer Adjutant-General. Anyhow, I've been instructed by the First Lord of the Admiralty to send you, and it's a great compliment to the Corps."

So I had to return to Deal and explain the switch of plans to my poor wife. She was very disappointed, especially after I told her that following the Singapore Conference I would almost certainly be appointed Staff Officer (Intelligence), Ceylon. I had to leave almost immediately, and there was no time even to arrange a passage for her.

My part in that conference was of course solely Intelligence work. It was soon discovered that we had little or no worthwhile information about the Dutch East Indies, particularly the island of Sabang. With its fine and lovely harbour this would certainly attract the Japanese; it was a vital communication link. So I decided to 'do a Madagascar'—in other words, to visit Sabang myself and not ask anyone's permission in advance of doing so. I knew quite well that if I *had* asked for such authority, I'd have had a very short answer indeed! I soon discovered that Sabang, among other things, is one of the most famous places in the world for orchids. What more natural than that an orchid collector should turn up on the island?

I hurried at once to the various libraries in Singapore burrowing through as many books as I could on the subject; there weren't many. But I gleaned something about this most beautiful flower—its names, peculiarities and so on. I then bought the kind of equipment I thought an orchid collector would be bound to possess, and set off for Sabang in a Dutch cattle boat. On my arrival I immediately reported to the Dutch captain of the port, giving a false name and posing as a civilian. The captain spoke excellent English and we became very friendly. He introduced me to Bols gin. "I'm going to give you some real gin," he growled.

He explained that he'd been aboard a British warship a few days previously and that they'd filled him up with English gin, which he'd found absolutely awful. So much for our national preferences! After we'd downed several glasses of the Dutch stuff, he produced a native guide who'd take me round the island and show me everything I wanted to see.

I knew, of course, exactly where I wanted to go, and I'd brought an ordnance map of the island with me. The operation went smoothly and I successfully established myself as an orchid collector. The guide and I would stop at every likely beach to swim; in this way I was able to jot down all the necessary particulars about each—the type of sand, how troops could be got off in a hurry—the kind of information that'd be necessary if a landing had to be attempted. At the same time, of course, I pursued my task of orchid-collecting. Orchids grow like fungus on the island and I had no difficulty collecting several exotic and beautiful varieties.

Back once more in the main port, I paid off my guide and booked a passage for Ceylon on an ordinary passenger ship. Once aboard I asked the purser to take charge of my orchid collection and put it in cold storage.

A few nights later the captain introduced me to another passenger who was also a collector—and well known—and he'd been working on some of the other islands. We had a long talk and I kept my end up fairly well. He said he hoped to visit Sabang himself some day, for there three of the world's rarest orchids are found. I realised after he'd been talking to me for some time that I would never have been able to find them because an expert needed an acute sense of colour, and I'm colour-blind. In fact I'd picked the worst "cover" imaginable: the first orchid authority who saw my collection could have exposed me within five minutes!

Almost certainly most of the varieties I'd gathered were quite common types, not rare specimens to be found only on Sabang. I was afraid this new acquaintance might ask to see my collection, so as to put him off I explained that I'd put the orchids in cold storage for the voyage. He approved of this.

In the end I managed to get off the boat without being discovered, and I'm happy to say that the information I'd obtained —unlike that concerning Madagascar—was not lost, and played eventually its part in the war in the Far East.

Life in Ceylon proved idyllic. My wife joined me at last and we found a house overlooking the sea. An old but luxurious American car with a Ceylonese driver was placed at my disposal and I settled down to a peaceful way of life.

No one on the island worked after 1 p.m. Everyone met at either the Grand Oriental Hotel or the Galle Face Hotel, had a few drinks, then went home and rested until about four o'clock, after which they played games. (I played golf, my wife tennis—she became so good at it that she eventually won the championship of Ceylon.)

Allowances were good and life was not too expensive. Night came down like a curtain at six o'clock and we then repaired to the Garden Club or one of the other places where we drank until it was time to go back home and have a bath and dress for dinner. Dinner was usually eaten at one of the big hotels, after which we went on to the Grand Oriental Hotel or Galle Face again where we danced until the early hours. It was considered quite out of the question to work either in the afternoons or the evenings, because of the heat and the flying insect life. (During the war, however, work was carried on throughout the whole twenty-four hours in these same offices.)

My job was to advise the C-in-C on all matters connected with Intelligence throughout the station, which involved me in a great deal of travelling; for the station extended as far as Aden on one side and took in the whole of Burma on the other. With little or no air travel in those days, it meant a considerable amount of 'getting around', and I got in a lot of overtime.

Mr Robert Buell, the US Consul, became one of my best friends on the island. He gave many excellent parties, often attended by distinguished Americans; it was at his house that I met Cole Porter. On one occasion he introduced me to two American oil executives. When I admitted that I belonged to the Naval Office, one of them said impatiently: "I've got no use for the Naval Office; *especially* the Captain-in-Charge!"

"What's all this about?" I asked. "What's wrong?"

"Look, Mr Bassett," he said, "we came to this island to build an oil installation, and we were prepared to spend almost a million dollars on the project. Now it's been turned down flat."

I said I hadn't been in the Naval Office recently, as I'd been away, but what sort of oil installation were they talking about—dangerous oil or non-dangerous oil?

"Well, thank God you *know* something about it!" said another of the Americans. "They turned down the scheme without even asking me that."

"Who turned it down?" I asked, really curious now.

137

"The Naval Captain-in-Charge and the General Officer Commanding. They said it would endanger the safety of the Port of Colombo."

"But they can't *do* that!" I exclaimed.

"Well, they have!" one of the Americans retorted. "So I and my colleague are off to Singapore in the morning. We'll put the damn thing up there, instead."

"Wait," I begged them. "Don't fly off the handle. There's been some ghastly mistake. I'm certain the Captain-in-Charge and the General haven't been put in the picture properly. I can assure you the project won't be turned down. I'll see about it to-morrow." They gave me their word to stay on the island until I'd had a chance of investigating the matter.

Next morning I went to the Naval Office bright and early and saw my Captain-in-Charge. "Well," I asked casually, "has anything interesting been happening while I've been away?"

"Nothing much," replied the Captain. "Oh, yes, two damned silly Americans came in with some idea of putting up an oil installation."

"Good!" I said. "That's great!"

"Good?" echoed the Captain. "What do you mean, *good*?"

"That's what we've been waiting for," I replied.

"Well," said the Captain-in-Charge, "we've already turned it down."

"But you *can't*!" I said. "Look up the Imperial Committee of Defence papers on the subject, and you'll see there are definite instructions to all stations *en route* to the Far East telling them to encourage people to build as many oil installations as possible! Whether they're foreigners or British doesn't matter—in the event of war everything'll be commandeered, anyway. People are even to be encouraged to build on existing Admiralty property, at no rent whatsoever!"

This deluge of information took the poor Captain by surprise; his stunned face looked up at me in consternation. Then he said weakly, "I must see those papers."

"They're in the safe," I said.

He went over to the safe, took them out and read them, then turned to me and exclaimed: "I must see the Governor right away; obviously we've made a great mistake."

I said: "I'll go and see His Excellency for you if you like; I'll tell him the Defence papers were simply overlooked, and it shouldn't be difficult to put everything right."

To my surprise the Governor took an entirely different view. "I'm sorry, Bassett, but I'm afraid my decision can't be altered now. I've been advised by military and naval people against the installation, and I've accordingly issued instructions that it's not to be built. It would endanger the safety of the Port of Colombo, to begin with. Anyway, if I changed my mind now, the Ceylonese would say: 'Ha, he was just waiting for a bigger bribe!' I'm sorry, Bassett, but it's definitely off."

"Well, sir," I said firmly, "I must warn you that I'm empowered to send code messages to London—in my capacity as Staff Officer (Intelligence), while the C-in-C's absent from the station. If you persist in your decision I shall go back at once and send a cypher message to the Admiralty saying that you're proposing to ignore the recommendations laid down by the Imperial Committee."

"Look, Bassett," said the Governor, "I can't stop you doing that if you really want to, but I have to say here and now that nothing can change my decision. I've been advised by my naval and military advisers that the project is undesirable and I've issued orders accordingly, and I don't intend to alter them now."

I returned to my office feeling very depressed. I didn't relish the idea of coming into open conflict with the Governor, with whom I was on the most friendly terms. The matter was still worrying me when I went home to lunch and told my wife about the problem. I remained undecided what to do for the rest of the afternoon. Meanwhile my wife went off to play tennis with Mr Huxham, who was then Financial Minister in the Ceylon Government. I'd been intending to go along too, but my anxiety about the installation put me off tennis

"Where's your husband?" asked Huxham, when my wife turned up alone.

"Oh, he's frightfully worried about this project to build an oil installation in Colombo; it's been turned down by the Governor," my wife replied, "and I'm afraid he doesn't feel much like playing. It seems a pity, too, as the Americans are prepared to pay a rupee a barrel for every barrel of oil shipped from Colombo."

"Good God!" exclaimed Huxham. "The Governor can't be

allowed to do that! Why, we can't even balance the budget at the moment and a thing like this would be just the very thing to put the country on its feet . . . I'm off to see the Governor at once!"

With apologies, he left my wife and rushed off to see His Excellency.

I knew nothing of this, of course, and was therefore quite surprised when I got a summons from Government House and turned up to find that the Governor had at last melted. "I've been talking to Mr Huxham, Bassett, and he tells me something which unfortunately I didn't previously know about this oil installation. He says the Americans are prepared to pay a rupee a barrel to the Government."

"Yes, sir," I answered, "that's so."

"Well, then," said the Governor a little ponderously, "on the advice of the Financial Minister, I'm prepared to reconsider my earlier decision. You can go ahead."

Joyfully I at once rang up the two American oil men and asked them to come over and see me the following morning. "The Governor's withdrawn his objections," I explained. "If you come and see me, I'll take you into the Naval dockyard and you can select any site you want."

So the following morning they turned up at my office and we all jumped into my old American car and drove off to the dockyard. "Gentlemen," I said, with a grand gesture when we'd passed through the gates, "take your pick. But I'd prefer it if you didn't ask us to knock down existing buildings."

I went off and left them to it, along with their site surveyors and engineers, and later in the day they came into the Naval Office again and said they'd put it all down on paper. If the Governor was prepared to sign it, they'd go right ahead. "By the way," said one of them, after we'd chatted for some time about the details of the scheme, "that's a very old car you've got."

"Yes, it's fairly old," I agreed, "but it suits me."

"Don't you want a better one?"

"Certainly," I said. "I'd like a Rolls-Royce, only there's no chance of my getting one."

"Well, you've saved us nearly three-quarters of a million dollars. The least we can do for you is to give you a decent car."

"No thanks," I said firmly. "It's kind of you to suggest it, but you've done a very great service to me and our Government, and I want nothing more than that."

I was very surprised, therefore, when at a party a few nights later my wife came tripping gaily back to the table after dancing and said gleefully: "When we get home to England we're going to find a lovely Rolls-Royce outside the door waiting for us."

I asked sharply: "Who said so?"

"The American," said my wife, indicating one of the oilmen.

"Well, you go right back on to the floor with him and make it clear that it's not possible; not possible at all, d'you understand?"

But I wasn't prepared for their persistence—they'd set their hearts on showing me their appreciation and they were clearly determined to do *something*. When they heard that in preparing for my return to England I'd given away my two Siamese cats—quarantine restrictions forbade my taking them into Britain—the more persistent of the two approached me and said: "Now I know what we can give you."

"What's that?" I asked, by now rather annoyed.

"Two Siamese cats," he grinned.

I shook my head and explained about the quarantine regulations.

"Oh, I can fix that," he told me. "One of our best friends is the Regent of Siam. I'm going to get him to select two of the finest cats in the country and deliver them to Paris. Another friend of ours there—the Ambassador of a South American country—will arrange for the cats to be sent over to London in the diplomatic bag."

"Well, if you can do that, it'd be lovely," I said, not believing for a moment that he really intended such an elaborate operation simply to provide me with two Siamese cats. But many months later, after our return to London, we received a letter from Paris asking us to go across, all expenses paid, to collect two Siamese cats. I couldn't go, but I sent my wife. She found two magnificent cats awaiting her and an embarrassed diplomatic official who explained that they'd made every effort to transport the cats by diplomatic bag, but the animals were too big and noisy. In the end she accepted the cats and passed them on to some Russian friends of ours in Paris.

· · · · ·

As the time drew near to quit Ceylon and return to the United Kingdom, I learned that I was to be appointed Brigade-Major at Chatham, one of the most highly-prized staff appointments in the Marine Corps.

There's a story in the Corps about a man who, receiving his discharge papers, was told by the C O, "I'm very glad you're going; you're absolutely rotten to the core!" and who replied, "That makes us all square, sir; the Corps has been absolutely rotten to me."

Happily this didn't apply to me. I reflected that many officers whose parents had spent money on their education might have reason to resent someone like myself coming from the lower ranks and being promoted over their heads. I can pay no higher tribute to the Corps than to say that from the moment I entered the Officers' Mess at Plymouth as a probationary Second-Lieutenant I never had the slightest feeling that I was being treated differently. In fact, there were many times when I thought I was being unduly favoured.

You'll remember that my prime reason for joining the Marine Corps had been my passion for horses. Now, on my return to Chatham, this new appointment entitled me to a charger. One of the Lieutenant-Colonels there—later General Sir Robert Sturgess—warned me that when I went along to the Army Remount Depot I was not to allow them to fob me off with some dud, but to wait until they brought out a beautiful chestnut which he'd seen them exercising.

His warning proved useful. When I turned up at the depot they trotted out one nag after another—all of them inferior beasts. The chaps at the depot preferred to keep the pick of the mounts for their pals in the Life Guards. Firmly I turned down each nag as it was trotted out, until six rejects stood in a row.

"Haven't you got something better than these?" I demanded.

They hesitated; then, fearing that I might lodge a complaint, they were forced to produce the chestnut. It was a magnificent animal called Baby Swallow, and I was soon to discover that he could take fences like a bird. One look at him, and I said: "That's mine!" Together with a great friend, Captain Edgar Balls (later killed in *Royal Oak*), I decided to enter Baby Swallow for point-to-point races. I wanted to prepare him for the Regimental race held annually at Cowdray Park.

Well, Baby Swallow won that race three years in succession, which made the cup my permanent property. So encouraged was I by this success that I decided to enter him for the Earl Beatty Cup, an event for which the Prince of Wales and Lord Louis Mountbatten used to enter.

I went down with my wife and Baby Swallow and my groom to Lord Digby's estate, where the race was being run, and had a quick look at the course. My groom told me gloomily that he'd been talking to Lord Digby's chief groom who prophesied that Baby Swallow had no chance against the kind of mounts being entered by the Prince and Lord Louis.

A rapid survey of the course showed me that my horse might have trouble with two big water jumps and a big ditch, especially as he'd never seen the course before, and had had no chance to practise; but otherwise he could win. I warned Edgar Balls, who was going to ride him, "Get away quickly and don't get mixed up with the rest; he's got the speed to beat 'em, if he doesn't get involved in their mistakes at the jumps."

Balls did as I'd suggested, and Baby Swallow raced home thirty yards in the lead to win the Earl Beatty Cup from several really expensive animals.

At one time I had visions of entering him for the Grand National, but unfortunately other things intervened to prevent this: one of them was the outbreak of war. Baby Swallow was taken out of my hands; one day, when being ridden at Plymouth by an inexperienced rider, he came down in a bad patch, broke his leg and had to be shot.

CHAPTER VII

EVEN with the exceptional advantages I'd been given in the Marine Corps it didn't look as if I'd ever become a Lieutenant-Colonel. Promotion was by seniority, and there were far too many officers senior to me to expect them all to die off; and anyway they seemed a very healthy lot.

The Commandant-General, on one of his visits to Chatham,

pointed this out to me. He suggested that I should accept the position of Divisional Paymaster; it was an appointment which would enable me to stay on after the normal retiring age, by which time all those senior to me should have been retired and I could then be promoted. It seemed the only sensible solution and I gratefully accepted the appointment.

This job was, of course, entirely concerned with money, a commodity about which I knew very little. I had, upon being promoted Major, naturally followed precedent and begun to pay my tailor and shoemaker, but I still had very little spare cash. My wife told me that she couldn't afford to buy an extra set of underwear even in a cheap multiple store.

However, the machinery of accounting and payment had been so perfected over the years that no one could really juggle the books. The backbone of the entire structure was, as usual, the Marine Sergeants. I myself never managed to cope with the complicated procedure, but it's part of the training and experience of a Marine officer to be able to convince himself—and, more importantly, his subordinates—that he knows all about whatever job he is called upon to do; and I don't suppose any body of men were ever called upon to perform such a diversity of tasks.

I did drop a hint to my Warrant Officer on one occasion that I'd like to do a spell at each desk, but he informed me sharply that he'd been Warrant Officer in the Pay Office for six years and—"Sir, if you think I'd allow any skimshanking, monkey business or fumkum-bunkum on the part of the staff, then I'd better hand my papers in!" So I quickly desisted.

It was not an arduous job. Each pay day I stood in the background, a swagger stick under my arm, and occasionally questioned a man as to whether he'd drawn the correct money. They never seemed to know whether they had or not, but simply trusted us to see them right. When war broke out, the job became a little more hectic, as I had to rush to the bank at all hours and draw out thousands of pounds so that the ships' companies embarking at short notice could be paid. What was more upsetting, however, was an order which arrived instructing me to release all N C Os acting as pay clerks for active duty. I was told they'd be replaced by Wrens.

The arrival of the Wrens posed many problems, and an initial one concerned their dress. At that stage of the war the clothing factories were not turning out Wren underwear in any great quantity. It was, therefore, laid down that although the girls were entitled to two sets of underwear they were to provide them themselves. The Paymaster—that was me—was authorised to credit them with the money for these, provided he satisfied himself that the girls had bought the articles. How he was to discover this was not specified. I tried to hand the task on to my Pay-Sergeants, but they pointed out that the order specifically stated that it was the Paymaster's *direct* responsibility. They were kind enough to proffer several suggestions as to how it might be carried out.

I grew rapidly more restless in this cushy berth, however, especially as I saw older officers being recalled and given active service appointments. I asked my Commandant if I could volunteer for more active duty, but he put me off by saying that with my peacetime experiences in Intelligence I was certain to be given a job in that field very shortly. Sure enough, I was called over to his office a few days later and told that I was to report to N I D within the next forty-eight hours.

Next day I travelled up to London and went to see the Marine Commandant-General to find out if he could fill me in on my new duties. What, in fact, was I supposed to be doing in N I D?

"Oh, I imagine you're going back to this false beard, foreign countesses and secret ink business," he said casually. "But anyhow, go and see the Director of Naval Intelligence."

I reported to the Admiralty. The Director himself was not available, so I saw his deputy, a Marine Colonel. I asked him what I was supposed to be doing.

"I haven't the slightest idea, Bassett. The D N I keeps nearly everything to himself. Retired officers and civilians are arriving here every minute and the whole place is like a madhouse. Personally, I'm going bonkers!"

"Is it security work?" I persisted, feeling a little desperate.

"I don't know, I just don't know," he repeated almost savagely. "I think the D N I is worried about some of the Naval Intelligence reports which are out of date, and possibly you're to revise these. But look, there's an Oxford don with an enormous beard working farther down the passage, in a disused lavatory.

Why don't you go along and join him, and wait there until the D N I's free?"

So I quitted the D N I's office none the wiser, and made my way along this passageway until I came to the disused lavatory. Inside was no venerable professor with an enormous beard, but an extremely youthful-looking chap who turned out to be Frederick Wells, an Oxford Classics don.

"I've been expecting you," he announced, rather surprisingly. "I'm your assistant."

"Oh?" I said, a little shattered. Then, after I'd recovered my composure a little, I asked: "What are you working on, anyway?"

"The coast of Norway," he said.

"Is that because you speak Norwegian?"

"Oh, not at all," he said. "I speak German, French, Latin and Greek quite well, but I don't know a word of Norwegian."

Taken a little aback by all this, I was afraid to ask him for more precise details, principally because I didn't like to admit that I personally had no idea what *I* was supposed to be doing. Glancing surreptitiously over his shoulder, however, I saw that he appeared to be working on topographical details of the Norwegian coast. From then on, I managed to play it all by ear.

I soon found out that Frederick Wells had a most wonderful brain. He'd been in the office for only a few days, but had already collected a great deal of information concerning Norway, simply by visiting shipping firms and map-makers. He'd also got hold of some photographs.

A long time afterwards an abortive attempt was made to put down in some sort of chronological order just how this apparently haphazard attachment of an Oxford don and a Royal Marine officer to Naval Intelligence Division was to develop into one of the largest inter-service and inter-Allied Intelligence organisations, employing, finally, almost six thousand people. But in the beginning we had no clearly defined task, and indeed little idea as to why we'd been called in at all.

Wells and I started by working on hundreds of small jobs which were so varied that it was difficult to discern any pattern, or even end-product. Such end-products as we did turn out were, in fact, only made possible by the most haphazard of phone calls or a lucky contact. The reports themselves were drawn up on scraps of paper. It was all a very hit-and-miss, make-do-and-mend affair.

Office hours and routine were chaotic. We ate and slept when and where we could, and for half the time neither Wells nor I had any idea what the other might be doing. We only began to keep a formal diary when we were allocated a Mrs Pipon as our clerical assistant.

Looking back over that diary now, I realise it wouldn't have been much use to an enemy agent if he'd been trying to find out what we were up to. What could he have made of the following entry, for instance: "Mr X, a sandy-haired Boer gave information about harbour works at Regensburg. Superintended building of stretch of Rhine and Main-Danube canal. Air Ministry want to know (two gins and one pint of beer). Can seaplanes land on Irish loughs? Frederick Wells went to firm selling fishing tackle to get some information."

The fact is that in those early days I thought I was only marking time until I could be transferred to security work. For a long time I had no idea that the D N I had personally anticipated a demand made a little later by Winston Churchill, and had decided to set up the nucleus of an Inter-Services Topographical Department within the Admiralty on his own initiative, selecting me to head it because apparently, apart from my general qualifications and my fourteen years in Intelligence, he'd been impressed by my report on Madagascar. Although Wells and I continued from day to day to supply certain topographical information to the various departments, it was a long time before I woke up to the fact that this was precisely the job I'd been called to the Admiralty to do.

I found myself appalled at the magnitude of the task, because the information available couldn't have been more scanty. Discussing the matter one day with my old friend—General Jo Hollis, then Secretary of the Joint Planning Committee of the Chiefs of Staff (he had to sit in on all the important meetings of the War Cabinet)—I told him that the situation was impossible. For instance, when the Chief of Naval Staff had asked me for a report on Petsamo, all that we'd been able to produce were two old newspaper cuttings. When the Chiefs of Staff had asked for information on the Cape Verde Islands, all I could find in the files was a report starting with the prophecy: "The importance of these islands will be greatly enhanced when the Panama Canal is completed."

Wells and I had laboured for several hours in an effort to help the War Office over "the port of Turalia" in the Canary Islands. We'd consulted dozens of maps and gazetteers but had been unable to discover a darned thing. When we told the War Office that in our opinion no such place existed, they replied that the report about the place had come from a very experienced agent —a man unlikely to make an error.

It wasn't until I asked to see the original report myself and noticed that the agent had used the remark "inter alia" which had been rendered "in Turalia" by some girl typist, that I was able to clear the matter up. This, I pointed out with some emphasis, was a ridiculous way to conduct affairs.

Jo told me that Churchill himself was much aware of this gap in our Intelligence. When the Force Commander had returned to London after the failure of the Norwegian campaign, he'd complained bitterly, not so much at the scanty nature of the intelligence, but at its sheer unreliability. In some cases, the Commander protested, he'd been forced to base his plans on woodcuts dated 1890. One of his parties had had to go ashore carrying a *Baedeker* for 1912. Going by Intelligence information, ships had tried to off-load cargoes expecting to find cranes or jetties where none existed.

Churchill, who had just become Prime Minister, had been so concerned by all this that he'd immediately set up a committee under Mr Attlee to go into the whole question. The committee had begun its task by asking Service planners to submit a list of all countries with which they were likely to be concerned, and under such headings as Defence, Topography, Air, Naval and so on, to describe the state of Intelligence available about it.

Within a few days Churchill, impatient as usual to get things moving, was inquiring about these reports, and Jo had to tell him that while the Admiralty and the Air Ministry had come through promptly enough with their material, the War Office had not yet put in a report.

"If the others can do it, so can the War Office," Churchill had barked. "Tell them to send it over immediately."

Thereupon Jo had telephoned the War Office explaining that the Prime Minister wanted to see them at once.

"But some of the remarks are in pencil," he was told. "We'd like time to polish it up."

"Never mind that," said Hollis. "I'll do all the polishing up that's needed."

Even Jo, however, had not been prepared for the 'rough' nature of this War Office document. A glance showed him that they'd been treating the whole matter as something of a joke. Underneath Topographical Intelligence someone had scribbled the word "lousy". Under one heading there was this facetious comment: "In possession of 1864 *Baedeker*, believed to be out of date." Another section bore the entry "F A". Joe had started erasing this, when the bell rang and Churchill asked: "Have you got that report yet?"

"Yes, sir, but I'm afraid some of the remarks are in pencil and not very—er—"

"Never mind," Churchill snapped testily. "Bring it here at once. No doubt I can understand it just as well as you can."

Jo hurried in with the report and placed it gingerly in front of the Prime Minister. Pointing to the scribbled "F A", he murmured, "Of course, this, sir, means 'Fanny Adams'—that is, nothing."

Churchill looked up, and grinned. "I hope you're not suggesting, my dear General, that I could have placed any other interpretation on those initials?"

It was as a result of these disastrous reports that Churchill had ordered an Inter-Services Topographical Department to be formed at once. The D N I had already formed the nucleus—Wells and I.

I first began to realise this one day in May 1940, at the height of the Battle of France. Freddie and I were sitting at the bare table, which, with two chairs, was all the furniture we had in the disused lavatory. We'd just dealt with, of all things, a message contained in a bottle. We'd been asked to find out where this had been dropped into the sea, working out tides and sets, starting from the date on the message, and we'd managed to find an approximate answer. I'd just remarked to Freddie that this job was getting to be a real joke, when the phone rang. I picked it up and a voice barked: "Is that the topographical section?"

Well, it seemed as good a description as any of our department. So I said "Yes."

"Can I speak to the Chairman?"

Assuming responsibility, I said: "Yes—er—speaking."

"An important conference is being held at the Air Ministry at 2.30 this afternoon, chaired by the Air Chief of Staff, and you're required to come over and receive instructions," the voice said crisply, then rang off.

I turned to Freddie. "Well, this is a new one. Ever been to a conference before?"

"No," said Freddie.

"Well, we'd better go, I suppose. No sense in dodging the issue. Heaven knows what it's all about."

As the voice had said that this was to be an 'important' conference, I thought that Freddie and I had better go along at least looking the part.

"We ought to dress up for it," I said. "What we need are a couple of those terribly efficient-looking briefcase things. Doesn't matter that we've nothing to put in them."

"Good idea," Freddie agreed. "Let's go down and see the Civil Assistant."

So we went down the stairs to the C A and told him we had to have black attaché-cases.

"Haven't got any," he said shortly. "There's been a big run on 'em. Everybody wants the damn things."

But even as he was talking, I noticed three or four attaché-cases lying in the corner.

"Those would do," I said, pointing.

"Oh, they're no good," said the C A. "The locks are broken. You can't open or shut them."

"That doesn't matter," I said, "we haven't anything to put in them, anyway."

Armed with this business-like equipment we went over to the Air Ministry and were ushered into a room already crowded with high-ranking Air Force officers. The Chief of Staff then swept in and took his seat at the head of the table.

"Gentlemen," he began briskly. "I must apologise for calling you all to this meeting at such short notice. However, the Prime Minister has instructed me that I'm to bomb the Dortmund-Ems canal. It's to be done at once, regardless of cost!

"This canal, I need hardly tell you, is a vital section of the route along which supplies are brought up to the German Army,

150

and, if we can manage it, we might give the French army a chance to reorganise and hold together. Because of the limited number of aircraft we have available and the limited power of our bombs, we have first to find out the most vital part of the canal where those bombs'll do the most damage.

"My Intelligence Officer has told me that no such information exists in any of the Ministries, and so I've asked the chairman of the Topographical Department to come across. I've instructions as to the precise nature of the information we require. He will, of course, at once turn the whole resources of his department over to this task."

And with this the Air Marshal called upon his Intelligence Officer to list the requirements. When the I O had finished speaking the A M turned to me and said, "Well, you see what's required, Colonel Bassett. I'll excuse you now, as we want this information urgently. The Prime Minister insists that the operation should take place almost immediately."

With that, Frederick and I looked across at each other, rose from our places and, bowing to all present, took our leave. Once outside the door, however, I turned to Freddie and said: "What the hell was he talking about? *Put the whole of your department to work on this!* We haven't *got* a department! Someone's made a hell of a mistake: surely there's a department in some Ministry somewhere whose job it is to dig up this kind of stuff? I think we'd better wait until Sir Charles comes out, and then explain to him that we're not the people he wants. Eh?"

Freddie shook his head doubtfully. I asked him, "Where the devil *is* the Dortmund-Ems canal, anyway?"

"It's a canal system linking Belgium, Germany and France," said Freddie thoughtfully. "But really, I think I ought to warn you, Sam, that I believe this *is* our job. In any case, it's no good trying to find out if the Ministries know anything about it— clearly none of them does."

He hesitated, eyed the sky for inspiration, and then said: "I know of a chap who was up at my college in Oxford who may be able to help."

I looked at him for a moment with terrible misgivings. Then, realising that I was clearly in for it, I said: "All right then, let's go." We waited on the steps of the Air Ministry in Aldwych (now Television House) until a taxi came along. From Paddington we took a train to Oxford where Freddie took me along to University College and introduced me to his friend. He was extremely helpful, but his knowledge didn't answer a lot of the questions on our list.

However, it was something to go on with, and I told Frederick to return to London and try to build something from this material. In the meantime I'd see Professor Mason at the School of Geography, and find out if I could get any other information. Here I learned that there was an engineering chap at one of the Cardiff colleges who might know more. It was thought that he'd taken some part in the planning or construction of the canal.

Professor Mason said that he'd telephone this college. I warned him that the conversation must be guarded and that on no account should the place be mentioned.

In those days the effort of making a trunk call was like something out of a nightmare. Delays could easily amount to twelve hours or more. The operator, when I tried to put in this call, said that all lines to Cardiff were in use and that it was impossible to say when I might get through.

"But this is urgent," I said. "It's of national importance!"

"Have you a priority?" asked the operator.

"Yes," I lied.

"Well, that's no good either," said the operator happily. "You have to have a No. 1 priority if you want to get through immediately."

"I *have* a No. 1 priority," I exclaimed, ignoring the fact that I could be flung into jail for simply saying that. Within seconds I'd been connected to Mason's friend in Cardiff, and I explained guardedly what I needed. He sounded a decent chap on the phone, and said he'd do what he could; he had a number of blueprints, maps and photographs which he'd be delighted to let me have. I put down the receiver triumphantly. The next thing was for me to get to Cardiff.

But I had to reckon with those extraordinary wartime difficulties which made it practically impossible to do anything in a hurry. How the devil was I to get there? By train would take hours. The obvious way was by car, but to hire a taxi for a journey like that you needed petrol coupons.

"We've no blasted coupons," I said bitterly. "We're sunk."

"Don't worry," said Professor Mason, as interested as I was in the success of the operation. "Oxford to the rescue again! I think I can lend you some." He produced a small bundle from what was obviously a precious hoard, and telephoned a local taxi-driver. At first the man was reluctant to undertake such a journey, even when the Professor produced a fistful of coupons. But I impressed upon him the nature of his patriotic responsibilities and in the end prevailed upon him to take me.

I crackled off through the night slumped in the back of an old Austin and finally reached Cardiff at 2 a.m. After the weariest of drives through the black-out, our headlights merely two pin-holes of light, I was exhausted when I finally tottered into the engineer's study in Cardiff. There, spread out on the table, were the blue-prints and photographs we wanted—precious information that could easily change the course of history, that could play a vital part in saving the French army and Europe. I knew that nothing must prevent my getting this information back to London at once.

Bundling up the maps and photographs and hastily shouting my thanks to the engineer, I raced down the steps, and yelled at the taxi-driver who had been patiently waiting outside: "London! And step on it!"

In any film script, the man would have banged the door shut, pressed his foot on the accelerator and practically shattered his windscreen with his fierce getaway. But this was England, where even in wartime the cautious nature of the people, bedded in a realistic appreciation of the verities of existence, still remained uppermost.

"I can't do *that*!" exclaimed the taxi-driver, as though I'd asked him to murder his grandmother. "I haven't got enough coupons!"

"Good God, man, don't you understand this is no time to worry about coupons?"

"That's all right for you, guv, you haven't got your living to worry about," he persisted morosely.

"Hell, man, this is life and death!" I insisted. "If you find Hitler on your doorstep some morning, you'll understand!"

"Can't do it without coupons, guv—Hitler or no bloody Hitler!"

"Look," I said desperately, "take me to London, and I swear

you'll get whatever coupons you want. And twenty quid on top of that."

"Hop in," he said, and I flung myself thankfully into the back.

It was just after 6 a.m. when I arrived back in London, unshaven and red-eyed from my cross-country journey. Tired and hungry though I was, I went straight to the office to find Freddie Wells.

"You can't type, by any chance?"—I'd noticed he usually made notes in shorthand.

"As a matter of fact, I can," admitted Freddie.

"Good," I said. "Let's find a typewriter."

I shot out and into the nearest office. To my dismay I found that the typewriter there was clamped firmly to the desk. Hastily I went next door, only to find similar security arrangements. Every damned typewriter in the building, in fact, was chained to its desk. There was nothing for it but to indulge in a little strong arm stuff.

With an iron bar I found lying about, Freddie and I managed to prise one loose. We carted this back to Room 30—our disused lavatory—and then I scrounged around further until I unearthed some brown paper and a pot of glue. By noon, we were able to stand back and contemplate the results of our efforts. Rough and ready though it was, the report included impressive cross-sections, details of the sectional construction of the canal and its geological formation, certain engineering data about the lock gates, and a number of photographs. I rang up the Air Ministry and told them the report was ready.

"Good show, old boy! I'll tell the Air Marshal right away. There'll be a meeting very shortly."

And that night, acting on our information, the R A F struck at the Dortmund-Ems canal in one of the first big British air operations of the war. It destroyed one of the German army's lines of supply and also proved to the world that Britain had the capacity to strike back at Hitler's Reich, despite Hermann Goering's boast, "Not one bomb will fall on German soil."

Needless to say, Freddie and I felt very pleased at the way our infant department had conducted itself, and I considered, frankly, that the warm congratulations we received were heartily deserved.

Despite this and subsequent bombing of the Dortmund-Ems canal—it was attacked no less than sixteen times in all by the R A F—the Battle of France continued to go against us. A few weeks after this hectic affair of the canal I was summoned to the office of the First Sea Lord, who told me that the Chiefs of Staff had decided that nothing could now save the French army; its collapse was imminent.

The Chiefs of Staff considered that it had become vitally necessary to evacuate the B E F and as much of its equipment as possible. In order to do this, however, the C I G S needed information for his field commanders indicating the easiest routes to the coast. The proposed evacuation area was the region around Dunkirk.

A staff officer, the First Sea Lord continued, would be coming across from the War Office almost immediately with the latest dispositions of the B E F, and the information which I was to provide should be in the hands of the C I G S within a matter of hours. Routes, he advised, should obviously avoid large towns or villages or river crossings, and should eschew the coast itself except in places where there was easy access to the beaches.

"And that," said the First Sea Lord, "is only the first part of your task. Secondly—and possibly more important—you must secure a complete description of every beach in the area where even rowing boats could go in and take troops off. And that's *really urgent!*" he barked.

I quitted the presence immediately, and returned to the disused lavatory to inform Freddie that we'd been given the most hellish job imaginable. By now our staff had grown to four people— we'd been reinforced by Mrs Pipon and a naval surveyor, a Captain J. B. Law. I told Freddie that I'd take Law and go out and try to discover something about the ports and small beaches near Dunkirk; meanwhile would he get on with the first part of the task discovering the easiest ways for the British army to get to the French coast.

"In that case I'd better arm myself with some French maps," said Freddie philosophically—he'd already made contact with the Michelin people in London and knew where to go.

I nodded and set off with Law into the streets of London to see what I could dig up about the French beaches. Within half an hour I realised that I was engaged on a hopeless task; shipping companies, tourist agencies and the like could tell us plenty about the big holiday beaches and large ports on the French coast—places like Le Touquet. But they had absolutely no information about the small beaches around Dunkirk. I decided that we could spend days hunting around like this to no purpose, and told Law that we'd better go back to the Admiralty at once.

I reported to the D N I that I'd failed to get the necessary information. But just as he was about to pick up the inkstand and hurl it at me, I broke in hurriedly to say that I had a scheme to propose.

"What is it?" the D N I demanded fiercely.

"I suggest that we organise two or three teams, each consisting of a naval surveying officer, a Royal Engineer and a Marine officer, and dispatch them to France immediately," I said, speaking as rapidly as I could. "You could arrange to have three destroyers waiting at Dover with steam up. The teams could land on the beaches near Dunkirk and obtain the precise information we need, not something based on guess-work and sheer hope. One destroyer could sweep as far west as possible, another as far east, while the third could concentrate on the region in between. As each team completes its investigations, the destroyers could then race back to Dover where we can have fast cars waiting to pick the men up."

The D N I was well ahead of me, for by the time I'd finished speaking bells were already ringing on his desk and his office was suddenly filled with alert, efficient looking officers.

"Ring up the Hydrographers—ring up the Royal Marine office—get the War Office," barked the D N I. "Get cameras, French money and equipment."

He hurled orders at them with tremendous zest, and within less than half an hour three teams of officers had been assembled in my office. I gave each a quick briefing. I emphasised that they were to look for beaches where rowing boats could go in and take men out to larger vessels waiting offshore. In addition, they were to take as many photographs and gain as much other information as possible—anything which they thought might be of use in evacuation.

The scheme worked beautifully. As each team completed its task, it re-boarded a destroyer and raced back to Dover. As information began piling up on my desk, Freddie and I started

156

writing our report, even before all the teams had returned. When everything had been completed and sent over to the CIGS, I could see that the First Sea Lord was impressed. Thoughtfully he congratulated me on our success.

"There was only one little thing wrong with it," he added, "but it was quite excusable, in view of the haste with which you prepared your report."

"What was that, sir?" I asked, taken aback.

"One of the destroyers went into a small place called St Vaast —but the clearances you gave were incorrect, and she ran aground. However, don't worry, she was able to get off and go into another place."

Nettled at this reflection on our efficiency I checked up and found that there were *two* St Vaasts; and the skipper of the destroyer had chosen the wrong one! The department itself had been 100 per cent right, but I thought it better not to get into an argument with the First Sea Lord about it, so we let the matter drop.

The report was not only useful in getting the British Army off the beaches of France in 1940, but in getting them back on again some four years later.

It is of interest to me, looking back, to note that in those teams one of the Royal Marines became a famous Commando and, more important to me, my son-in-law, Colonel Peter Hellings, DSC, MC. Another Marine is now General Douglas Drysdale; one of the Naval surveyors became the Hydrographer to the Admiralty; and another surveyor his assistant.

By now Frederick Wells and I had begun to feel our way into the business of Topographical Intelligence with growing confidence. Private firms and learned societies, we found, were our only really satisfactory sources of information; Intelligence reports from the various Ministries generally proved utterly inadequate—a legacy of the twenty years of Intelligence starvation between the wars.

The financial neglect and administrative indifference during that time had been reflected in the type of officer put to this work. Only sheer incompetence could have produced a report in 1940 listing as "a modern installation" a battery of guns first installed back in 1908. Why were officers who knew little or nothing of the countries about which they were supposed to be compiling information appointed to the jobs in the first place? I came across some of the most extraordinary howlers.

For instance, when I turned to a file dealing with the port plan of Savona in Italy, I found that some well-intentioned person had indicated that a sewage farm was situated on the front. This struck me as being so unlikely that I consulted the original Italian chart and discovered that the area was, in fact, marked *Convento delle suore della purificazione*—the Convent of the Sisters of the Purification! The trouble was that officers were appointed to N I D only on a short-term basis—and therefore with no incentive to make a decent job of what they were asked to do—and given posts for which they had no aptitude.

If the same lack of even elementary preparedness obtained in other branches of the Services, it's no wonder to me that Hitler almost defeated us. The miracle is that Britain's hour of need produced men like Churchill, with his inspiring leadership—and Beaverbrook who cut through incompetence and mediocrity to provide us with the means to win the Battle of Britain—to come to our rescue and save us from disaster.

The Battle of France had been lost; Dunkirk had been achieved, and such were the depths into which the nation had been plunged by these sudden and inexplicable disasters that even this humiliating rout was held up as a shining triumph of our arms. Seldom can national self-deception have gone farther.

Then the nation, immune to the thought of permanent defeat, began to stir from its lethargy and realise that at long last it had to get down to work. But first it had to endure; the bombs began to fall.

The D N I, in accordance with general Government policy, thought it advisable to disperse some of his staff immediately, and suggested that I should take myself and my people to an Admiralty building several miles up the Edgware Road. This didn't seem a very good idea, because the area was close to two big railway junctions, and the Welsh Harp provided the Luft-waffe with an excellent landmark; but the D N I explained that underground offices had been prepared there for the Board of Admiralty in case the bombing should become too intensive.

Frederick and I therefore moved all our records out of the

centre of London, and by scrounging some of the excellent furniture which had already been installed in anticipation of the arrival of My Lords Commissioners, we proceeded to provide ourselves with comfortable quarters for the first time.

Only one tiny discomfort arose to mar the luxury of our new estate; as fast as we found an excellent pub at which to eat, the wretched Luftwaffe would come over and bomb it. We were reduced to travelling farther and farther afield in an often fruitless search to find sandwiches; lunch or dinner all too often turned out to be a pub-crawl, much to the growing alarm of Frederick Wells, who didn't consider ale-quaffing at all his *métier*.

One day the D N I sent for me, and when I reported to Whitehall said he was taking me over to see Admiral Sir John Cunningham (now Lord Cunningham of Hyndhope), who was to command an important operation at Dakar. Admiral Cunningham, a brisk, tough, Nelson-style man told me he wanted to know all there was to know about the defences of Dakar, with specific reference to the kind of guns possessed by the fort; for their size would determine the type of warship he'd send in. "We don't know whether they're six-inch or nine-point-two. That's what I want you to find out."

I decided that my first step must be to secure all available photographs of Dakar. The Ministries, I knew, would have absolutely nothing; the best place to find anything would be one of the big Fleet Street photographic agencies. I therefore hopped on a bus and drove through the morning sunshine, getting off just beyond Temple Bar. London was already showing her scars from the ruthless bomb attacks, but on that day I felt almost cheerful. With operations such as Dakar being planned, we were at last on the move and the picture was not quite so black as it seemed.

Briskly I strode into the agency and asked to see the editor. I was ushered into his office and explained that I'd come to borrow all the photographs he could produce of the whole North African coast.

"Oh, I know what *you* want—Dakar!" he said, grinning.

"No, not necessarily." I hedged, wondering how the hell he knew. "I want pictures of Dakar, of course, but I've really come for the whole coastline."

"Well, play it your way, old chap," he said cheerfully, "but I know it's Dakar. Anyway, you can't have them—not until this afternoon, anyway. You see, the Air Ministry has them, and after that the War Office wants them."

"Well, I've no idea why they should want Dakar particularly. But so far as I'm concerned what I want is the whole coast. And I want it as soon as possible."

"Anything you say, old man," replied the editor. "But I can't let you have them until I get them back, can I?"

I returned to the Admiralty for the time being empty-handed and asked to see Admiral Cunningham at once. I was quickly admitted and Cunningham could see from my expression that something serious had happened. Rapidly I told him about my trip to Fleet Street.

"Clearly there's a lot of useless duplication going on," I said. "But what's far more important—our security's being endangered. It's a hell of a mess—to be able to walk down Fleet Street and discover that our impending operations at Dakar are a matter of common gossip!"

Sir John was equally perturbed. He said decisively : "It's time that one central intelligence agency was left to handle these matters entirely." As I left, he picked up a telephone.

As a result of this disconcerting example of the danger to security in allowing each Ministry to have its own topographical department, our still small section was finally made responsible for the sending of all photographs and for taking the necessary security measures. In a nutshell, this incident put the department really on the map.

Not that the photographs yielded any great results in the case of Dakar. It wasn't until I discovered a merchant captain just returned from there and on forty-eight hours' leave at his home in Weybridge that we managed to get really useful information. With the aid of a bottle of whisky to compensate the captain for taking up so much of his precious leave, Captain Law and I were able to extract the essential information. Our performance was duly noted and the importance of a really responsible and expert department further underlined. But the battle was not yet entirely won.

For a while things continued to be a bit chaotic with ourselves and the various Ministries uselessly striving against each other for the available sources of information. Photographs from Fleet Street agencies, from private firms, from illustrated magazines, were often competed for as though they were precious prizes. It seemed a ridiculous way to run a war, although I personally was terribly lucky. Frederick Wells, with his brilliant academic mind and training, knew a number of obscure learned societies to which the officers from other Ministries had no access. Captain Law was an expert on maps, charts and town plans, soon exposing the weakness of our existing information on foreign places. The general attitude until then had been that anything was better than nothing, but I set my face against this philosophy from the first.

I once received an example of how easy it was to be fed unwittingly with wrong information, without allowing oneself to be careless. I'd been sifting through certain pictures in a Fleet Street agency one day, when I came across a picture which was wrongly captioned.

"I say," I said to the editor, "you've got a wrong caption on this one. This isn't Ceylon."

He looked at it. "Oh, perhaps it isn't," he said easily. "What does it matter? We don't bother much about these foreign places. If somebody asks for a picture of Ceylon, I ask one of my boys to go through the stuff and dig out some place with coconut trees and white buildings. Who cares whether it's really Kamchatka or Woolloomooloo? It's quite different with film stars or politicians—we've got to be dead accurate on *that* lot!"

It was exactly this kind of thinking, of course, which made matters more difficult sometimes than they needed to be for Topographical Intelligence. I remember once being asked to supply some information on Casablanca, with a deadline so tight that it was obvious after a few hours' work that the job simply couldn't be completed in time. That was the way with most things in those days—everything was wanted the day before yesterday. I decided to see General Hollis and ask for a forty-eight hours' extension. But when I explained what I wanted, he said: "Oh, you needn't worry about that, Sam. One of the Majors from the War Office who knows the place well has just provided me with an excellent report. I'm just about to take it in to the Prime Minister."

I guessed the Major he was referring to was one of our friendly rivals in the War Office. "Look, Jo," I said, "if it's him, I know he's probably gone to exactly the same places for his information as I have. But I've checked these sources and I'm not satisfied with their accuracy. Could I have a look at what he's written?"

"Well, all right, Sam, but it's a bit irregular, you know."

He handed me this War Office report—a really big affair neatly pasted up on brown paper—quite impressive-looking. It started off with some excellent photographs of what purported to be the city of Casablanca.

"This isn't Casablanca at all," I said to Hollis triumphantly. "It's Toulon!" I flicked through a few more pages. "Look here!" I exclaimed. "He's marked a sandy beach on this map. Yet I know for a fact that there's been a dry dock there for years. The whole thing's wrong—absolutely misleading."

Hollis was incredulous. "Are you certain, Sam?"

"Well, I'm certain about those two things at least; I haven't had time to look at the rest."

"You'd better be," warned Hollis. "I've got to take this report in at once. I'm going to warn the Prime Minister that you say at least two of these facts are wrong and that there might be more for all you know. But you'd better be certain of your facts. If you're wrong, God help you!"

"I'm certain about those two things," I said doggedly. And Jo, who knew me of old, took the report in without another word. He came out again within a few moments. "The Prime Minister wants to see you. Now, Sam, before you go in I want to make this quite clear to you—you've got to be quite definite in your reply. If you say these pictures and map are quite wrong you've got to stand by that. It's no good saying, 'I think it's so-and-so', or 'To the best of my knowledge'. The Prime Minister won't stand for any wavering. You've got to be firm and accurate."

"Very good, Jo," I said. And he ushered me in. Winston Churchill wasted no time on preliminaries. "I understand you say that this report is completely inaccurate," he growled, thumping the brown paper paste-up on his desk.

"No, sir." I said quickly, "I didn't say that. I had only a few moments to look at the report, but I did notice that the picture on the first page was not of Casablanca, and the map on another page is completely out of date. If two important things like that are wrong, then possibly the rest of the information is equally inaccurate."

"You were asked to get this information inside forty-eight hours, and you produced absolutely nothing," said the Prime Minister, taking a deep breath and glaring at me from beneath his bushy brows. "This officer has produced a very fine report, well within that time."

"Yes, Prime Minister, I know. But what good is it if it's in-accurate? There seems to be an idea among senior officers that all we need to do to collect information is ring up some secret service or other who'll tell us everything we want to know. Well, sir, it's not like that at all. If you only give someone forty-eight hours in which to work, then you'll only get forty-eight hours' worth of information. This thing grows like a snowball. You go to a place and ask for information and they say, no, we haven't got it, and suggest a shipping company. So you go there, and they say they're sorry they can't help but Lloyd's might be able to. . . ."

I noticed then that the Prime Minister was glowering and gasping as though he had difficulty with his breathing. I decided to stop talking at once.

"How dare you try to teach me the elementary facts about Intelligence!" he roared, when he'd recovered his voice. "I knew all about it before you were born; do you understand? Get out of my sight at once!"

Terrified out of my life, I didn't stop to argue. I bolted. As I went out through the inner office like a runaway horse I shouted out to General Hollis: "I'm afraid I've had it, Jo!"

"Stop!" shouted Jo. "What's the matter, Sam?"

I halted in my headlong rush to exclaim in despair, "The Prime Minister told me to get out!"

"Oh, don't pay any attention to *that*," said Jo sharply.

"What?" I cried unbelievingly. "You don't understand, Jo! He lost his temper and bawled at me to get out! I tell you I've had it!"

"Nonsense, Sam; calm down. If you'd had it, bells would be ringing all over the place by now, and I'd be rushing in there to be told to get rid of you immediately, and that you were never to show your face again on the staff of this or any other Intelligence organisation. I bet you if I took in some papers now, I'd find him sitting there grinning like a cat. He's only enjoying himself. I tell you, you're absolutely all right."

And, to my utter surprise, I was; certainly I heard no more about the incident.

But for some time afterwards I lived in fear that the Prime Minister's wrath was about to strike me down. Eventually, Jo Hollis sent a message over to say that the Casablanca operation had been cancelled, but he thought that I should get out my report anyway, so that he could show it to the old boy.

I set Captain Law, Freddie Wells, Mrs Pipon and myself to work to prepare a report that would outshine any Intelligence report ever written. As there were no longer any security restrictions involved, I decided to get the Admiralty's hydrographic department to print it properly. I had transparent overlays made so that the main map of Casablanca was free from any confusing details. It seemed such a pity at the time that this *de luxe* job was not actually to be used : nevertheless, it made the department feel good just to produce it.

We felt a great deal better when we learned that it had been given a good reception by the Prime Minister himself and lodged in a place of honour in the War Cabinet's map room, where it was to remain for some time. There's no doubt that the effect of the Dakar and Casablanca incidents did finally lead to a complete change in our status.

Orders were given that indiscriminate and haphazard collecting of topographical intelligence was to cease forthwith, and that the work was in future to be carried out solely by my department. In my moment of triumph I even thought of asking that the Major who'd produced the first report be allotted to me, but Hollis warned me against any such action. "The Prime Minister hates eye-washing above everything," he said. "He won't stand for it at any price."

Jo told me how, when the War Planning Room was nearly ready for occupation, the P M went over to see it. There was a very impressive array of pneumatic tubes set up for receiving and transmitting messages, but the installation hadn't yet been connected up. However, a retired officer who'd been brought back to take charge of it had arranged for two Marine orderlies to keep pushing phoney messages through it from the passageway just outside the room. This chap then went through the drill of pretending to read the messages and redirect them on their journey.

The Prime Minister watched this performance for a while. Then he was introduced to this officer with the words: "Here's an old soldier who's been recalled to help us all." To this, Churchill replied brusquely: "He's certainly a typical old soldier. Let's have one who hasn't learned these foolish tricks. Get a younger man at once."

"No, he won't have eye-wash at any price!" concluded Hollis.

Now, from a tiny group answering *ad hoc* questions and collecting scraps of information piecemeal, my section grew rapidly into an organised department with set programmes of work to be accomplished against stated times, schedules and a list of priorities. This, at any rate, was the theory; in practice, of course, most things fell short of that ideal. Requests demanding immediate attention continued to flood in, thus putting back the long-term programme.

A new high-level service section—the Operations Planning Staff and the Joint Planning Staff—reiterated the demand for a Combined Services Topographical Department which would act as the clearing house for all knowledge of this kind. I was then formally appointed chairman—a post I'd more or less assumed since rejoining the Admiralty. It's extremely difficult for me, looking back, even with a good memory and my various papers to advise me, to recall exactly how the department, so tiny and insignificant to begin with, grew into the colossus it eventually became; although the need for such an organisation had been quite clear from the beginning to anybody who'd thought for a moment about the problem.

The Prime Minister's own directive at the end of the Norwegian campaign had also been quite specific. And yet the Chiefs of Staff and Joint Intelligence Committee meetings waffled on and on without issuing precise directions or delegating responsibilities, and without allocating more resources or personnel.

In the end the Directors of Intelligence of the other two Services—the Army and the Air Force—did appear to come round to an appreciation of the need for a department charged with collecting topographical intelligence not only for the Navy, but for all the Services; something which my own D N I had been pressing for from the very outset.

Even when the department had begun to function with something like reasonable purpose and efficiency, I think many senior officers were still very vague about what our purpose really was, or indeed why we existed. I remember being sent for one day by the Director of Intelligence at the War Office; he asked me, "Why on earth do you want Royal Engineers officers, Bassett, when all you're concerned with are things like trees, mountains, hills and so on, which anybody can get from a map?"

I had to give him a kindergarten lecture: we were an island nation; any operation we undertook would have to be of an amphibious nature—the most difficult of all military operations is the actual landing of men and stores over a beach. Naval charts —which he presumably thought adequate to our purpose—were quite useless for such operations.

"They simply tell *ships* how to stay *off* beaches," I explained. "Topography, however, means drawing up a detailed picture of any area, city, town, manor, parish, or what-have-you; and everything that exists in that area must be recorded, natural or artificial. From a military point of view, this means knowing a great deal more than the fact that a beach exists somewhere.

"We've got to find out the nature of the approaches to that beach so that we can land on it; what the beach itself consists of—what kind of mud, sand, pebbles compose it—how troops can be moved inland after a landing. Then we have to know all about what is beyond that beach—the roads, railways, ports, harbours, cities, towns."

I didn't have to go much farther; from the stunned look on my listener's face, I realised that I'd rammed my point well home.

"And only a Royal Engineers officer, preferably one who's an expert in transportation problems, can assess the real usefulness of piers, jetties, wharf cranes and lifting gear; pronounce authoritatively on beaches and bridges, rail gauges, tunnel clearance and the whole control of a railway system," I went on.

"Why do we try to capture some ports and leave others alone? Primarily, because of their discharge and clearance capacity. And that's the sort of information the Topographical Department has to dig out."

I then took a deep breath and flung the following set of

facts at him: "To produce a small ten-page brochure for one operation recently, our small team had to consult over three hundred books, magazines and technical journals, some eighty maps and charts, and thousands of photographs—both aerial and ground pictures. It took us hours to understand and explain a technical matter which could've been dealt with in a few minutes by a specialist."

At which, the Director of Intelligence threw in the towel; I got my R E officers.

Meanwhile, the continual air raids on London were causing havoc with the department's work. It was heartbreaking to race up to the City from Edgware Road only to find that the place we'd hoped could give us certain information had been bombed. The D N I had obviously been giving some thought to our situation. He sent for me one day and without any warning said: "Bassett, I want you to remove yourself and your whole section, lock stock and barrel, to Oxford. Tomorrow."

"But, sir!" I cried in horror. "Oxford! Why Oxford? Heavens, sir, we won't be able to carry on our work from there—it'll take hours just to get up to London, to see the Ministries, and other people we have to consult . . ."

(Not a particular telling point, really; for it had taken me more than three hours to reach Whitehall from Edgware Road that morning, because of the bombing near Marble Arch. But the D N I was in no mood to listen, anyway.)

"You've been sent for to take orders, not give advice, Bassett," he said sharply. "You're to transfer to Oxford tomorrow morning. You'll report to Professor Mason at the School of Geography at 0800 hours. And it's up to you to make your own transport arrangements."

The D N I was blunt and direct, and clearly didn't intend to waste any time giving me tedious explanations for the move. I'd certainly have appreciated such an explanation, but I realised that the D N I regarded the department—which in my mind loomed very large indeed—as just another cog in the wheel. He had too much to do to offer explanations for every move he had to make, and therefore dispensed with them.

It was only when we'd settled in at Oxford that I realised what an excellent choice he'd made. The place was entirely free

from bombing or other interference; there were wonderful libraries all around us and societies who could answer questions on
practically every conceivable subject; and there was the Oxford
University Press where we could have our reports printed with
the utmost security.

There was one slip-up during the move, which brought
domestic disaster. We'd left all the moving arrangements to
Frederick Wells, and that was the big mistake. I mentioned that
we'd acquired certain pieces of extremely comfortable furniture
earmarked for the First Sea Lord and Board of Admiralty. Strictly
speaking, only naval Captains of at least six years seniority and
full Colonels of the Marines were entitled to a carpet—and then
only a small square. We'd been using wall-to-wall stuff, to which
only Admirals of the Fleet were legitimately entitled.

We'd deliberately put Wells in charge of the removal, because
if anyone complained about our splendid furnishings we could
say that an Oxford don could hardly be expected to know that
the square yardage of the carpet to which we might be entitled
depended on how many gold stripes you had. But the scheme
backfired on us. Freddie was certainly unskilled in the arts of
service scrounging. Finding some difficulty in removing one of
the very fine roll-top desks which we'd intended to make our
own, he rang up the Office Keeper for assistance. That was the
end of our dream of living in state at Oxford; the two lorries
already loaded had to be unloaded while Freddie stood in the
street with an expression of unconcealed dismay on his face.

The move to Oxford really dates the formation of Inter-Service
Topographical Department (I S T D) as it came to be called.

Although there were still some students at the School of Geography when we arrived there, most of the tutors had joined up.
We were received with the greatest kindness by Professor
Mason, but a pacifist on his staff seemed very upset. He said it
was disgraceful that the School of Geography, known all over the
world as the foremost geographical institution, should be put to
such a use. I was very tired at the time, and replied : "Nonsense!
One of our lorry drivers asked a policeman on Magdalen Bridge
the way to the school, and the policeman said he knew of no
such place in Oxford. He said he thought there might be one in
Cambridge!" That quietened the pacifist for a while.

Professor Mason kindly allowed us to select several large

rooms which were no longer in full use. Law and I commandeered two rooms for ourselves and put our two typists in the Anthropological Library. They had no typewriters. I told them to carry on with their knitting or whatever they liked until the Admiralty provided us with the equipment to do the job.

Perhaps the Anthropological Library was not quite the place for young ladies, but the thought had never crossed my mind that they might be tempted to explore the books on the shelves. One day, as I approached the door, I heard girlish giggles inside. My entrance was greeted by hushed silence. I thought their faces looked a little flushed, but I ignored this and handed them some work.

When they were absent from the library having lunch, I returned to investigate the bookshelves, and as I moved round the room, glancing up at the forbidding titles, I noticed two or three books lying on the typists' desks. I opened one of them and realised why the girls had been giggling: the book investigated in detail the sex life of the Zulus.

Nearly all the books in the library dealt with abstruse and involved sex problems. I found another with the enticing title of *Strange Marriage Customs*. Others were copiously illustrated and left nothing to the imagination. I decided to have these extremely interesting books cleared out, otherwise even when the typewriters arrived I felt there'd be little typing done.

The following morning we had a visit from the D N I himself, who wanted to see how we'd been fixed up. I took him round the rooms and he seemed pleased. But when we came to the typists' room and he saw the two girls sitting there doing nothing, he almost lost his temper.

"What the devil's going on here, Bassett?" he demanded. "Why aren't the girls typing?"

"I'm afraid we haven't got any typewriters, sir, it's as simple as that. They wouldn't let us take the ones we were using out at Edgware Road—said they'd been earmarked for the Board of Admiralty, and that sort of thing. But the Civil Assistant has promised to send down a couple as soon as he can."

The D N I then proceeded to give me one of the biggest roastings of my career. "Look, Bassett. I selected you for this job because I thought you could think big—and *act* big. You're as bad as that other Marine Colonel I have at the Admiralty—

you're afraid to take a risk! Here we are spending twelve million pounds a day on the war, and you worry about two typewriters! I passed a shop in the High where the window was absolutely full of the things. Go along there right away and get as many as you need. I suggest you start with twelve to begin with, and two duplicating machines; obviously your section's going to expand rapidly."

"Should I ring up the Civil Assistant and arrange for him to pay for them, sir?" I asked.

This only enraged him further.

"*Certainly not!*" he roared. "I'm giving you an order to go out into this town at once and get twelve typewriters and two duplicating machines, and I'm not concerned about who's going to pay for them. You've got to get it into your head, Bassett, that you must forget about this petty administrative work. We're fighting a war against an enemy who's determined to win it by every means at his disposal, by fair means or foul, and that's what we've got to compete with. Now that you're down here at Oxford away from my central control, you'll have to act independently. You've simply got to *act* big and *think* big!" And he finished up by telling me that he'd be around again in the morning to make certain that I'd carried out his orders.

It's one thing for an Admiral to bark out that he doesn't care who's going to pay for things; it's another for a humble Lieutenant-Colonel of Marines to assume that, if the Admiral said it, then it's all right. In one way or another the can would some day have come back to me; so I conceived a small strategy.

I know it may seem strange that this should be necessary in wartime, but wars are lubricated by money, and, contrary to popular opinion, a great deal of care is generally taken about how the stuff is spent. I didn't intend rushing out and ordering hundreds of pounds' worth of equipment without having a proper order for it; long association with the Admiralty had told me that nobody just bought typewriters by walking into a shop and saying, "I'll have that one, and that!" So I rang up the Civil Assistant in Whitehall. Over a very bad line I shouted: "About those two typewriters I asked you to send down to Oxford . . ."

"Typewriters are in very short supply," he interrupted, giving me no chance to finish.

"Well, don't bother about them," I went on. "The Admiral's just ordered me to go out and buy myself twelve new ones, along with two duplicating machines."

That did it! Unintelligible splutterings shocked my ear. I shouted back: "I can't help whether you've got the money or not, or what your arrangements are—all I know is that the Admiral has *ordered* me to have twelve typewriters and two duplicating machines by tomorrow morning. And that's that. That is, unless you care to help."

He seized this alternative at once. He'd been declaring for days that it was impossible to supply even two typewriters, but now he promised to find twelve from somewhere and have them delivered by special lorry that night. I warned him that I'd stand for no monkey business; that if he didn't give me his solemn word the typewriters were on their way from London by the time the shop in Oxford was preparing to shut, I'd tell them to send along the machines at once and charge them to him.

He didn't fail me. The typewriters were there in the Anthropological Library the following morning, their covers off, the two girls typing away, when the D N I appeared in all his stern splendour. He took one look at the impressive array of machinery and said, with enormous satisfaction: "Now, you see, Bassett, what comes of thinking in a big way?"

I replied: "Yes, sir. Indeed I do."

I think the first Intelligence brochure the Department was asked to produce was one on the Atlantic Islands, the Cape Verdes, Azores and Canaries. For this I had two Naval officers who'd been seconded to me, and also the invaluable help of Professor Mason and some of his geographers. Frederick Wells acted as editor.

"What is the difference between a pier and a jetty?" Freddie asked me one day.

I answered, "What does it matter? Every naval man knows."

"But many of the people reading our reports aren't naval people," he objected. "Where can I get a dictionary of these terms?"

I told him that the Naval Hydrographer in London should be able to help. So he went up to see him but returned to tell me that the Hydrographer had said there was no such thing, that no exact definition existed for many nautical expressions. And

Freddie began compiling a dictionary which to this day is a standard work in the Hydrographic Service.

One day a complaint arrived from the Admiralty that there'd been no one on duty at the School of Geography on the previous night when an urgent call had been put through. Following this, I arranged to sleep in a camp bed on the spot. Professor Mason discovered me one morning brewing some tea over a spirit stove. "Good gracious! What *are* you doing, Colonel?"

I explained. The result was that he suggested I should bring all my own furniture up from Chatham, take over some rooms in the school for my personal use, have a bath installed in a disused cloakroom, put in a stove and settle down properly. And that is what I did. When everything was ready, my wife quitted her job in the Censorship Department and came down to join me. For the magnificent accommodation I now enjoyed, the University authorities charged me the sum of twelve shillings a week.

Mason was always splendid when extra room had to be found. When I mentioned a difficulty we had in copying photographs, it was at his suggestion that we set up a dark room in a small lavatory on the ground floor. An old professor poked his head in one day, only to find a photographer and two girl assistants working there. "Oh, excuse me!" he said hurriedly. "I can see the old place isn't what it used to be."

The staff, too, had begun to grow. Yet it was not until after the Crete operation in 1941 that the War Office seconded some army officers to the department. The Prime Minister himself initiated this development. He'd been supplied with some inaccurate information about Crete, and asked about my department—how was it? What was the state of it?

The War Office, suddenly conscious that it had neglected to send any Army officers along to me, picked out a couple at random and dispatched them to Oxford. One of these officers was an expert pig-sticker—and little else. He was hopeless, and I got rid of him immediately.

The Air Ministry weighed in about this time with two valuable additions, however, a geographer and a geologist. The War Office tried again with two more Army men. Then the Admiralty sent me someone whom they described as a naval surveyor. I was told that he'd lost a leg, had now been fitted with an artificial one, and that he'd have to attend the Orthopædic Hospital for treatment. I agreed to this, of course; I'd been asking for an additional surveyor for a long time. A few days after this officer had joined us, however, Commander Hughes, the surveyor in charge of this section, came to me and said: "Colonel, who's this new chap supposed to be?"

I told him that he was a surveyor.

"Well," said Hughes grimly, "I gave him a little job to do on Stavanger, and he came over and asked me what the tiny marks on the map were. I must say that shook me a little. 'They're the depths,' I said, 'in fathoms.' And all he said was, 'Oh, I've never seen those before.' A bit odd, isn't it?"

"Perhaps he's a *land* surveyor," I suggested. "Anyway, send him along to me."

While I was waiting for this young man to turn up, I looked up his papers. There was no doubt about it; there it was in black and white: 'Naval Surveyor'.

"It says here you're a naval surveyor," I began at once when he entered my room, "but you don't seem to understand depth markings."

"Naval surveyor!" he laughed. "I'm not a naval surveyor—I'm a cavalry officer!"

"But," I spluttered. "You're in naval uniform."

"Oh, I know," he said. "There's a story behind that. Would you like to hear it?"

I nodded grimly. It turned out to be a strange and wonderful tale. He'd been a cavalry officer on the reserve, and his hobby was playing about with speedboats. When the Russians invaded Finland he'd immediately volunteered to help the Finns, but was told no Army personnel were being sent to fight. The Navy, however, were sending some river gunboats and other small craft. As he knew something about speedboats, perhaps he'd like to try them? When he saw the Admiralty, they were quite interested, and said they'd contact him later. The Finnish expedition failed to materialise, and he forgot all about his interview. That was until he reported to his old unit upon the outbreak of the war with Germany, when he was informed that he'd been earmarked for the R N V R.

"Which was absolute nonsense," he said. "I know nothing about the Navy, and I marched over to the Admiralty to tell 'em so." Apparently he found himself directed to the Second Sea Lord's office, where there was a terrific number of people. He waited for his turn, then approached an officer dealing with some papers, gave his name, and before he could say anything else was told, "Oh, yes, you're in batch 'C'. There's a charabanc outside the Admiralty; get into that, and your uniform'll be supplied eventually."

"But I've nothing to *do* with the Navy," he'd again protested. "I'm a cavalry officer, and I want to rejoin my unit!"

"Look, for goodness sake don't waste our time!" the officer had barked at him. "We're trying to evacuate the whole British Expeditionary Force and we've got to get everyone away as quickly as possible to man the various ships and small craft."

Before he knew what was really happening he was in naval uniform and on board a destroyer. He went at once to the Captain, but as he began to explain what a terrible mistake had been made, the Captain cut him short and hustled him away, yelling: "I can't be bothered with all this rigmarole now, man! For Heaven's sake get up for'ard and keep a lookout for torpedoes!"

The look on the Captain's face stopped any further discussion. As he reached the prow of the ship a German aircraft had landed a bomb plumb on the deck, and the next thing he knew he was sitting up in hospital—minus a leg. After his discharge the Admiralty had given him some odd jobs to do until this one at Oxford had come up. Because he wanted treatment for his leg at the hospital he'd been glad to accept. "But I know nothing about naval surveying," he finished lamely.

"Well," I said, "it obviously isn't your fault. But what *can* you do?"

It appeared he couldn't offer much to the department; he didn't think he could help on the Army or Air Force; he knew nothing about the geographic side, and less than nothing about industrial research. In desperation I mentioned that I was thinking of starting a model-making section.

His face lit up at once. "Why that's just up my street!" he exclaimed. And so I kept him, with very useful results.

At Oxford we were now away from the seemingly lunatic confusion of Whitehall. By this period of the war our Chief Planners could visualise a scheme of further action, and a directive by the Prime Minister that from now on planning should be devoted to offensive action with the ultimate idea of re-invading the Continent helped my department considerably. We were able really to organise our work; to decide which operations were likely to be more urgent; to schedule certain jobs and fulfil them by a stated date. There were system and method in our work. The end-product too, became more worthwhile.

Originally, it had been a matter of sticking a few photographs on pieces of brown paper, which had to serve perhaps a bearded Commando on a French beach, or several higher officers in Whitehall trying to work out a plan for blocking the Corinth Canal. Now we'd begun to print and bind volumes which would satisfy the needs not only of the actual fighting units but also of the large technical—and later scientific—staffs who contribute to the planning of any modern operation of war.

With the influx of staff, more accommodation was needed. On the advice of the registrar of the university, now Sir Douglas Veale, I served notice of requisition on the principal of Manchester College, which was right opposite the School of Geography, and in a very short time we moved in there, too.

With the registrar's assistance, accommodation was provided in the New Bodleian for our growing library of ground photographs, and we took over part of the Ashmolean for our draughtsmen and map-makers. Section after section was added rapidly to the Department. A Contacts Registry was also set up in the New Bodleian, whose job it was to list the names of all persons, British, Colonial or refugee whom we knew of or could contact, who might provide expert knowledge of foreign parts. A feeder organisation was established in London, with the job of collecting photographs and technical information; over eighty technical publications were received in the capital from abroad every month. Our attempts to set up a liaison with the R A F air photographic libraries continued, but I'm afraid they didn't show any enthusiasm.

The D N I rang me one day to say that he was bringing a "Mr Smith" down to see me. He warned me that, whether I recognised the person or not, I was to call him "Mr Smith" under all circumstances. Intrigued, I awaited the arrival of the visitor with some impatience. He duly arrived, and quietly the Director said: "This, Sam, is the famous Colonel Bill Donovan—known as Big Bill—a personal friend of the President of the United States. He's over here to find out what we're doing about the gathering of topographical material, because obviously the United States is coming into the war shortly. Take him around and show him everything you've got."

Mr Smith appeared suitably impressed with our efforts. So much so that he asked if I could travel back to the United States with him to help in the setting up of something similar there The D N I demurred, however, saying I couldn't be spared at that time, and Commander Hughes went instead. A little later Colonel Donovan again asked if I could go over, and this time the D N I agreed. I crossed in the *Queen Mary*, accompanied by a U S Marine Major called Cam-Judge.

I enjoyed the trip until I reached New York, where an embarrassing thing happened; I passed out cold at a Broadway show, from an overdose of alcohol! It happened like this. On our first night in New York, Cam-Judge phoned some friends and we were both invited to a cocktail party. Anxious to cement Anglo-American relationships, the hostess arranged for three seats at one of those terrific musical shows for which it's almost always impossible to get reservations. But she was a friend of the leading actress in the show, and managed to fix it.

After the party—at which I had drunk, as I thought, with moderation—we went on to the theatre. That was a show about which I remember nothing. To me the chorus girls began dancing in triplicate, and soon I had to close my eyes. How I got back to the hotel, and what happened afterwards, I don't remember. I only know that in the morning I found myself lying on my bed still fully dressed. As the train rolled down towards Washington later that day, I felt quite ill. Then an attendant came along with a luscious-coloured drink. Without asking who'd sent it, I gratefully gulped it down and felt much better. When I asked for another one, however, the attendant said I'd have to go to the club car. I tottered along and found Cam-Judge sitting there, grinning like a cat.

"How're you feeling, old boy?" he asked.

"Terrible! Awful! I think I'm dying!" I said. "I must apologise for passing out like that last night. And after our hostess had gone to such trouble to get those tickets."

"Never mind, old chap," he said soothingly. "Wasn't your fault really. Y'know, the trouble is those small war tots of gin you've been drinking in Oxford. That stuff you were at last night was over ninety per cent proof—and the tots were king-size. That's the trouble with an Old-Fashioned—packs a kick! I'd advise you to keep off cocktails and stick to the straight stuff, the rest of your time in America." I took his advice.

In Washington I was taken to see the U S Chiefs of Staff, to whom I delivered a lecture on I S T D. I stressed our difficulties and mistakes and gave them a detailed account of how we overcame them and how the organisation now worked.

Big Bill later took me to a Service club where he introduced me to some of the men who were going to work in the American counterpart of I S T D. The Colonel asked me to give them a brief outline of my talk to the Chiefs of Staff, which I was happy to do. When I'd finished the Colonel asked, "Any questions?"

A young officer stood up, and to my astonishment, asked: "I'd like to know what you're doing about your colour problem in England, sir."

"That's a damn fool question!" roared Big Bill. "Let's have a few more *sensible* questions. Then"—and he directed a pointing finger at the culprit—"perhaps *you* can tell Colonel Bassett how *we're* dealing with *our* coloured problem."

One of the important and immediate results of my visit to America was the attachment to I S T D of several United States officers. First to join were six geographers. They were followed quickly by Army, Air Force and Marine officers, and several other ranks, among whom were photographic experts. By then, too, I had Dutch and Norwegians working with me, and several University dons who were invaluable when it came to the complicated job of editing material.

The complete reports were always sent to the Oxford University Press for printing and binding. This involved contact with Dr Johnston, printer to the University, a really impressive personage. Trying to see him was as difficult and frightening as seeking audience with Royalty.

I remember once, when we were worried about possible leakages, that he took me round the plant to show me how all printing plates were accounted for at every stage and that no unauthorised persons could possibly have access to them. I had to agree that a leakage while the actual printing operation was in progress was highly unlikely. "But," I said, desperate to justify my investigation somehow, "what happens to the plates before and after printing?"

Dr Johnston was quite capable of handling that one. "I sleep on them, of course," he replied shortly, and I really think he did.

On another occasion the D N I had the temerity to send a young R N V R officer down to Oxford to deal with the question of layout, pagination and titling. At once the D N I received a tersely-worded letter from Dr Johnston, which brought him post-haste down to Oxford.

"We've got to go and eat humble pie, Sam," said the D N I. "It's about that young fellow I sent down to help with the layout."

We were met at the gates of the Oxford University Press by Mr Batey, the assistant printer, and ushered into the presence. Batey then left, although I knew quite well he was staying within earshot. Dr Johnston proceeded to list for the Admiral the shortcomings of the young man he'd sent down. The Admiral didn't have the chance to say a word. Then as he finished and the Admiral leaned forward to try and explain, the doctor quickly rang his bell: his secretary answered: she called Mr Batey: and the assistant printer returned.

Very formally, Dr Johnston then asked him : "Mr Batey, how long have you been in the Press?"

"Thirty-five years, sir."

"Do you think you know all about printing?"

"Oh no, sir, I'm *learning*. Under your guidance I've learned a certain amount, but I've a long way to go."

"Well, now, do you think we could produce this book that Colonel Bassett wants done? Do you think our printers could understand it? Do you consider that our proof readers would, perhaps, make some mistakes?"

"Well, sir," said Batey. "They've dealt with Bibles printed in every language of the world. They've dealt with rare manuscripts, with musical scores, with mathematical treatises and with industrial and scientific material of all descriptions. All in all, I think they could, sir."

"Thank you, Mr Batey. That will be all."

And with a nod of the head, Dr Johnston dismissed his assistant. Then turning to the D N I, he said courteously : "What do you think, Admiral? Do you think perhaps we could handle the Colonel's brochure?"

"Why, of course, Dr Johnston, of course," replied the DNI hastily, and I've never seen a man look less comfortable. The young RNVR genius swiftly vanished from Oxford.

Additions to the staff sometimes came about in the most haphazard and accidental way. I was attending a garden party one sunny Saturday afternoon when Mrs Haldane came up to me and said she wanted to introduce a friend of hers, a Mr Rodney Slessor. She explained that he was very depressed. He'd been working on the photographic side of an advertising agency and on the outbreak of war had immediately tried to join the RAF in which his brother was an Air Marshal.

Unfortunately he'd been turned down on health grounds and he was now looking for some kind of war work; she wondered if I could use him. I interviewed Slessor and found that he knew a great deal about photography and photographic reproduction; as I was looking just then for someone to run the library, I took him on.

Then there was Gerald Andrews, one of my daughter's discoveries. At the cinema in Oxford one evening she noticed a Royal Marine officer sitting just in front of her. When he left she noticed that he appeared to be wounded, for he was walking with obvious difficulty. He had been wounded at Narvik, Norway. She got in touch with him shortly afterwards and told him that her father was a Marine Colonel; that he'd formed a little club in Oxford for the members of his department, and that any Marine officer would be very welcome to come along some evening.

He accepted her invitation and to my delight I found that before joining the Marines with a wartime commission he'd been on the staff of *The Economist*. I knew that I had to get an industrial section going soon, so I suggested he might like to run it. He said he'd be most happy to do so, and that was how one of our most important sections came to be started.

By now sections dealing with one country or groups of countries had been organised on an inter-service and even an inter-allied basis, each with its own editor and specialists such as geographers and geologists, feeder unit, contact registry, tech-

179

nical research unit and map-making, drawing and model-making subsections.

The work had really become a matter of searching for information, reducing this information to its military value, and then producing books complete with every graphic and technical aid. We had no passionate foreign countesses, I'm sorry to say; and although bearded persons did sometimes come up to see us, the beards were their own. The main problem was to find out how to get on to a certain beach, and then how to get off again. But occasionally we were asked to produce something out of the ordinary; and then the department became involved in operations which later received a great deal of publicity in books and films.

The raid on the German ships at Bordeaux by a party of British canoeists carrying limpet mines proved to be one of the most spectacular, heroic and certainly most publicised.

Our part in this operation was to make sure that the canoeists could find their way, once they'd left their submarines, into the mouth of the River Garonne, and then in their trip up-river to Bordeaux itself some eighty miles from the sea. Here they were to place their limpet mines under some German ships which were preparing to sail for Japan carrying vital radar equipment, which at that time was something of a mystery to the Japanese.

We had to pinpoint safe hiding-places for the men along the river bank, where they could lurk during the day, for the actual travelling would be done during darkness. It was imperative that just before dawn each morning the canoeists should find themselves within reach of a place where they could take cover and rest. Such hide-outs had, of course, to be away from towns or villages. We therefore had to find stretches of river which were quiet but also near easily identifiable landmarks, without being able to see for ourselves what the areas were like.

Our naval and tidal experts set to work at once to discover everything they could about currents and the sets of the river from Bordeaux to the sea. I'm certain no report has ever been so assiduously prepared so far as tides, sets, eddies, currents, curves, etc., are concerned.

Currents differed considerably, of course, according to the width of river, the depth of water, the curvature of banks and such factors. We had to study more than two thousand ground and aerial photographs of the region and make more than six hundred silhouettes to enable the canoeists to identify their position in darkness; we even studied the distinct smells of the region —such as those of a brewery and a chemical factory. The model-making department helped with the silhouettes by working out the heights of various landmarks and natural features along the river banks.

Then we had to establish what distance the canoeists might be expected to cover during the course of a night. To do this we borrowed a canoe ourselves, loaded it with all the equipment it would carry during the attack, and, with the assistance of Royal Marine officers in training units throughout the country, arranged a series of tests on different rivers, including the Leam and in the upper reaches of the Thames.

Our tidal and mathematical experts translated these findings into equivalent distances on the River Garonne, making allowances for increasing fatigue. With these figures we then went back to the map of the river and worked out both the maximum distances the canoeists might be expected to cover in a night, and the minimum; somewhere in between these two marks we had to find the nightly hide-out. Ideally, we decided these should be among thick reeds or bushes with a smooth surface where the crews could rest.

For more precise details than the photographs we possessed could yield, we interrogated hundreds of people whose names were on our Contacts Registry. We were careful to conduct these inquiries in a casual fashion; the contact was invited for a drink to a club where he or she was told that we were simply trying to caption some photographs. Over a Scotch or two we'd bring the conversation around to the nature of the country near the River Garonne; had they ever gone on picnics along its banks? What about lovers' walks and other secluded places? And so on. In this way we managed to build up a detailed picture of both banks.

The operation was a spectacular success, although it resulted in the loss of all the canoeists with the exception of an old friend of mine, Colonel 'Blondie' Hazard, and his batman, Marine Sparks.

All set off knowing that even if they succeeded in making

the long journey through enemy-held territory, and even if they managed to blow up the German ships, we had no means of bringing them safely back to England.

We couldn't arrange a rendezvous for a plane to fetch them, for we didn't know how long it would take each of the canoeists to get there, or how they might be scattered after the operation. Nor could we give them the names of French contacts who could put them on the 'conveyor belt'; there was always the possibility that they might be forced by torture to reveal the identity of such persons. All we could do was advise them to use their own initiative in seeking out friendly French people; and this, in fact, is exactly what Blondie did.

It was some time before I had a chance to interrogate my friend after his return to England, and as usual I found him most reticent about his exploits. Marine Sparks, however, was more talkative, and I was able to piece together the story of Blondie's daring.

His journey up the Garonne went smoothly. He reached the last river hide-out before the others, and rested up to wait for them; the plan was that all were to go in together. Only one other canoe made it, however. Blondie decided that there was no point in waiting around for the others—anything might have happened—and that the attack would have to take place as scheduled. Dressed as French fishermen, they worked their way into the harbour and manœuvred alongside one of the German ships. They made no attempt to conceal themselves—audacity was the keynote of the plan—and right under the eyes of hundreds of German soldiers on the deck above they pretended to handle their craft in such a clumsy fashion that they bumped against the ship's side. Blondie started roasting his companions in execrable French—which the Germans presumably took to be a local patois.

Gesticulating wildly and excitedly as a French fisherman might do in these circumstances, he yelled abuse at the unfortunate Sparks as he lunged desperately with his oars in an attempt to push the canoe off. To the soldiers on deck the whole thing seemed an uproarious pantomime. Even as Blondie—under the pretence of trying to untangle the ship's ropes—planted his limpet mines, the German soldiers jeered and pelted them with potatoes. At last Blondie indicated to Sparks that they should

182

shove off, and away they went to a further shower of potatoes and peelings and continued jeers.

Slowly Blondie moved around the harbour, planting his bombs under the other ships. Then he and Sparks made for the shore and sank their canoe. They waited for a while hoping that the other canoeists would turn up, but when a series of explosions indicated that their work was done they decided to walk into Bordeaux—Blondie claiming that he was going to give himself up to the first honest-looking Frenchman he saw.

The plan, quite astoundingly, worked successfully. Near the centre of the town, Blondie spoke to a young Frenchman, explaining that he was an English officer and had something to do with the bangs which they'd just heard. The Frenchman said nothing, but took a look around and then led the way to some tables outside a café and ordered coffee.

In slow French, he explained that he would have to leave them, but they were to wait there until someone turned up; he would be holding a French newspaper in a particular way, and by this they would identify him. The Frenchman went away then and Blondie and Sparks, wondering what was to happen next, calmly sat down to enjoy the coffee and smoke cigarettes. They hadn't long to wait before a second Frenchman approached, holding the newspaper as they'd been told to expect. He was an older man, cool but more cautious than the other one.

"When I've gone about two hundred metres down the road, get up and follow me," he said. "Keep your eyes open and, if you think anybody's following you, duck down a side street and get away as best you can—we'll find you again, don't fear!"

They did as they were told and very soon found themselves among friends who put them on the 'conveyor belt'. And in this way they reached England safely.

"What about our information, Blondie?" I asked. "Was it any good? Did it prove helpful?"

"It was absolutely wonderful, Sam, except for one thing."

"Oh, what was that?" I asked sharply.

"You didn't tell us anything about inquisitive cows." He chuckled. "One morning we'd settled down quietly by a river bank and just opened our self-heating soup when we heard a rustling behind us. We all grabbed our revolvers and prepared

183

for a fight. Then we looked up to see a cow gazing down at us
—what a relief!

"We shooed it away and settled back again. A few seconds
later there was another rustling, and there wasn't much we could
do about it this time. There were no less than six cows standing
around there in a gaping circle. We realised we'd have to clear
off. Six cows standing in a semi-circle gazing at a clump of reeds
was bound to attract someone's attention soon. Luckily, we
found another place to hide."

Our success with the Bordeaux raid was due in great measure
to what I always call "My B B C stunt".

Lord Louis Mountbatten had made it clear to me that he
wanted as much information as possible about the small beaches
of Europe—those well away from the holiday centres—for the
Commando raids he was planning. The photographic library,
under Rodney Slessor, had been growing, but it still didn't have
a great deal on these beaches—and had little hope of getting
more. In this quandary, I called a conference—it consisted of
Wells, Slessor and myself—to see what we could do about it.

A chance remark during the conference about cyclists and
hikers set me thinking on the right lines.

"Listen," I said. "There must be millions of photographs in
this country taken by amateurs who've visited France and other
places on the Continent. Probably a lot of these hikers and
cyclists haven't had enough money to put up at the more expensive tourist centres. There's a good chance that many out-of-the-
way spots are known to them and that they've got pictures of
'em. The point is—how to get at them?"

"You can't put an ad. in the papers," Freddie said. "The
security risk's too big."

"But if we asked for photographs of places all over the world,"
said Rodney triumphantly, "we wouldn't be giving away a
thing!"

This was the answer, of course. Then either Wells or Slessor
added : "We could use the B B C."

"Good idea," I said. "We'll try and do that."

So I went up to London immediately and saw the D N I to get
his permission to go ahead with the scheme. My idea was that
the B B C should broadcast an appeal for holiday snapshots, not
limiting the entries to any one country. The D N I received the

scheme enthusiastically and so I went off to Broadcasting House in a good mood. The B B C said there'd be no difficulty, and they agreed to let Rodney Slessor make the actual broadcast.

"What kind of a response can we expect, do you think?" I asked.

"Oh, it depends," I was told. "It depends on what day the broadcast's made and at what time—whether at midday or after the nine o'clock news. It depends on the war news—if it's bad, people tend to be depressed and switch off their sets immediately. If it's good, they sometimes go out to the pubs and celebrate. On our last appeal of this kind—an appeal to people to send foreign phone directories and guide books to the Ministry of Economic Warfare—there were ten thousand replies!"

Well, there didn't appear to be anything to worry about in this. So I reported back to the D N I and told him that we could probably expect something up to ten thousand answers, and he was quite satisfied. The broadcast on a Sunday night was given just after the nine o'clock news, and the B B C arranged for a commercial firm to handle the replies when they came in.

Early on Monday morning I had a frantic call from the B B C to say that Broadcasting House had been snowed under with letters; nearly thirty thousand had arrived in the morning posts alone. I was delighted. But my pleasure didn't last long. At about eleven o'clock the D N I turned up at Oxford. I must say I'd expected him to come into my office and to start passing congratulations all round. Instead he rasped out: "Bassett, have you heard what the result of this broadcast is?"

"Yes, sir," I said, beaming at him hopefully, "isn't it marvellous?"

"Oh, is it?" he shouted angrily, "well—who's going to pay for it?"

"I don't quite understand, sir," I stammered.

"Well, think it over, Bassett," he said, "who's going to pay for it?"

And off he went, promising to return in an hour's time, and I sent at once for Slessor and Wells. I explained that the D N I seemed to be in a terrible state about the broadcast and wanted to know who was going to pay for it.

"I suppose we'd better offer to pay for it, then," said Slessor.

When the D N I returned I said to him at once: "Sir, Slessor,

Wells and I have decided that, as the broadcast was our idea, then we're prepared to pay for it."

The D N I then surprised me. He broke into a roar of laughter and clapped me on the back: "Oh, don't be silly, Sam! Of course there's no question of you paying anything. I just wanted you to realise that I haven't got inexhaustible funds at my command!"

"But the financial side has all been taken care of by the Director of Naval Contracts, sir," I pointed out. "I got his approval to everything and a proper contract was drawn up before we began."

The D N I looked at me in silence for a moment. "Well, bless my soul, Sam! That's excellent!"

The letters continued to flood in. It was a remarkable performance by the people of Britain, for everybody, apparently, wanted to help; even those who possessed no photographs. One man wrote in to say that although he had no pictures to offer us, we could have a pair of binoculars. Someone else sent along three pairs of skis. A variety of shotguns turned up—in fact a whole lorry-load of stuff which was of no use to us had to be taken away from the B B C.

The generosity of people with their private photographs proved to be quite extraordinary—they cheerfully sent along all their family albums, some quite rare and expensive. We had a terrible job trying to reproduce some of the photographs without destroying these beautiful albums—which we'd promised to return intact.

The total response to the B B C appeal was some sixty thousand replies and more than four million photographs. This was only a beginning. Fleet Street took up the appeal at once and, as a result of many articles and cartoons, thousands more photographs came in. One lorry turned up at Oxford loaded with tins of cine-film—the result of several travel series. In this consignment alone we estimated that there were over *three million* single pictures. By the time the effects of the appeal had died away, we'd been inundated with *ten million* photographs.

Of course, until we'd perfected our reproduction plant, we were unable to deal with coloured prints or pictures. Cine-films presented a separate difficulty, because it was almost impossible sometimes to identify single frames. But eventually this cine-film helped us enormously, especially in building up panoramic pictures of whole stretches of coastline, such as were needed for D-Day.

Sorting through the millions of photographs was a monumental job, for the whole process, from the time of the broadcast to the time when a picture was finally filed away in the New Bodleian, involved over sixty separate operations. Another problem was that few people had bothered to caption their pictures accurately. Planters returning home after years abroad had simply stuck a picture in an album and labelled it 'Up Country'. A view of a French beach with a figure beside a boat in the foreground would bear the legend 'Phil's yacht'.

In order to cope with the tremendous task of sorting out all these pictures and returning those we didn't want, I had to engage extra staff. The local Labour Exchange sent us as many girls as they could manage, but their standard of intelligence was not always of the highest. We didn't have enough gazetteers to hand round for them to be able to consult something authoritative, so we had to rely for the most part on the girls' own knowledge of geography. This was not often extensive.

One girl was found labouring for hours in search of a town called "Bivouac in the Desert". Another was fixed by the caption "Land of the Midnight Sun". Yet another had discarded a picture of East London, South Africa. When asked why, she answered: "We don't want pictures of our own country, do we?" When it had been pointed out to her that there were no beaches in the East End of London, England, she retorted "Of course there are —I've often bathed at them! They call them Southend or Southsea or something."

Slessor soon realised that at the rate we were then progressing it'd take us some sixty years to get through the job; so we decided to try and speed things up a bit. The Americans at once came to our assistance. Big Bill Donovan, who was as anxious as anyone to take advantage of the appeal's success, arranged for fifty U S Service girls to be flown over from Washington. An empty college was placed at their disposal, but turned down by their Commander on the grounds that it didn't have enough showers, lavatories, baths and other facilities. The college authorities agreed to the conversion of the place on a temporary basis, but insisted that it would have to be restored to its original state of decrepitude once hostilities were over. This was something the Americans couldn't stomach, and eventually the girls were put up in a big country house just outside Oxford. They proved to be of enormous help until in the end they were replaced by British and Allied Wrens who'd been picked by the Commandant of Wrens for their special interest in the subject.

Typical of the invaluable assistance we received at this time from the Americans was a gadget devised for blowing-up or reducing the size of any print to make copies suitable for filing. The inventor was a U S officer attached to our library, one Jimmy Phillips. The device had a plate-glass top with a series of springs underneath which pushed the selected photograph up to the glass without in any way damaging the spine of a book or the binding of an album, no matter whether it was the first page, the centre or the last; this was important not only because we'd promised not to damage these wonderful albums, but, more important, because we didn't want to give any indication of which photographs we'd selected.

The diagram of this apparatus was sent to America by air mail and within three days the first machine was on its way by bomber, to be followed by a great many more. I asked the R A F photographic research department at Farnborough how long they'd take to make such a machine, and was told that if all the material were available—which was doubtful—it would take up to three or four months. So much for American hustle, which played a part in the war that is all too often overlooked by some short-sighted British people.

In the end, we had to abandon our idea of filing our vast library of photographs in a grid reference system based on degrees of latitude and longitude. The geographical system we finally adopted worked very well, and it became the proud boast of the library that no matter what place was asked for, it could be produced within a matter of minutes. When the King of Norway visited us on one occasion, he was asked to test out the library.

"Please make it difficult, Your Majesty," pleaded Rodney Slessor.

"All right, then," said King Haakon. "I've a small shooting box situated not far from Oslo. Can you find that?"

Within two minutes a picture of the shooting box and the

country round about it was produced for him; His Majesty was properly impressed.

It was around this time, so far as I can remember, that I suddenly noticed a grave deficiency in another important direction—there was a tremendous shortage of beer in Oxford. So I thought: I've a big room in the School of Geography going begging—why don't I turn it into a club? For by this time the staff of ISTD had grown considerably, and they'd no proper place in which to relax and chat together during the evenings, free from the possibility of being overheard and perhaps infringing security. I told Rodney Slessor of my idea and he said: "Good-oh, splendid!" But I added that there appeared to be a snag.

"What's that, old chap?"

"Where are we going to get enough beer?" I asked.

"Oh, don't worry about that," he replied. "A relation of mine runs a brewery near here—he'll supply us with as much as we want."

It was while we were celebrating the opening of the club that a messenger came to me and whispered: "Your daughter has just arrived in a car with Captain Hellings—who wants to see you." Hellings was one of the young men I'd sent across to gather information on the beaches of Dunkirk.

"Send them up!" I said briskly, thinking that it was about this task that he wished to see me.

My daughter was in a state of great agitation. "Peter wants to speak to you privately, Daddy," she said.

I nodded. "Well, I can't talk to him here—send him over to my office."

She attempted to say something, but I swept past in a very convivial mood. Thus I was quite unprepared for the surprise that awaited me. As young Hellings entered I was all ready to discuss beaches with him. Instead, he began nervously, "Colonel, sir, can I have your permission to marry your daughter?"

I was so taken aback that I completely forgot to ask him the usual questions—whether he could support the girl, keep me in comfort and so on. All I managed to say—and weakly at that—was: "Tell me, Peter, can you put a tap in a new barrel of beer?"

"Oh yes, sir!" he said eagerly.

189

"Well, go and do it," I said. "You'd find a half-hogshead in there somewhere, and we've a crowd of Dutch, Norwegians and Americans arriving at any moment to deal with it. So be off with you at once!"

And leaving me there to reflect sadly on the encroachments of advancing age, my future son-in-law went off to broach the barrel. He made an excellent job of it.

One of the first occasions on which the department produced what were then called Isis books—Inter-Service Information Series books—was for the Commando raid on Dieppe in 1942. In this book we drew particular attention to the peculiar softness of the sand on the Dieppe beaches—a type of sand which can be very easily scoured or wind-blown. The local wind often blows up suddenly because of the heat of the day, sweeping the sand from one part of the beach and building it up in great drifts elsewhere. Its behaviour depends upon local conditions, of course, and is not predictable.

This capricious wind played a very great part in the failure of the Dieppe operation. Aerial photographs taken just before the landings showed no signs of a formidable sea wall which ran for some distance just behind the beach. The wind had blown the sand into drifts which completely obscured this wall; but by the time the Canadian tanks arrived on the beach, it had been up to its tricks and had cleared away the sand, exposing the wall again. This was to prove an almost impassable obstacle for most of the tanks; only one or two managed to surmount it. It was one of the primary causes of the failure of the operation.

My own interest in Dieppe centred around Peter Hellings, who by now had become my son-in-law (he and my daughter were married on a forty-eight hour pass). Peter and his party of Commandos had been handed an almost suicidal job. They were aboard a destroyer which was to ram the lock gates with explosive charges. Once this had been accomplished they were to jump off the ship and attack and destroy the harbour installations.

I followed all the battle reports with a sinking heart, as the situation grew more and more depressing. I learned that the Marines had been wiped out almost to a man. Then I heard that Peter's destroyer had been damaged before it could reach the lock, and that the Commandos aboard it had been transferred to landing craft and sent in to reinforce the men storming the beaches.

As my daughter was then expecting her first baby, I went to Combined Operations and saw the Chief of Staff and explained that my son-in-law was in the raid, and asked whether I could be told first if he became a casualty. The Chief of Staff, in the most kindly way, said he'd be pleased to arrange this.

My daughter, reading of the raid in the newspapers, was extremely worried of course, for she knew Peter might be involved. I pooh-poohed this, saying that so far as I knew his Commandos were being kept in reserve. But meantime I'd given my staff instructions that if the phone rang for me at any hour during the evening, they were not on any account to allow my daughter to answer it. Towards midnight I heard the telephone ring. It was the Adjutant, Portsmouth, calling to say that Peter was all right.

"He's fast asleep now with his face in a plate of bacon and eggs," said the Adjutant. "He's got some superficial injuries, but he's all right."

My heart full of gratitude to Providence, I went in to tell my daughter that her husband had indeed been in the raid—but that he was now safe. A few hours afterwards, my grand-daughter was born.

I've referred once or twice already to our model-making section, which had been set up following the urgings of Lord Louis Mountbatten, shortly after he'd taken over command of Combined Operations. "The R A F have a very large model-making department, but they're completely obsessed with their own requirements," he told me. "What we need is our own topographical model-making section."

I had the temerity to say that I thought models could sometimes be misleading. "The vertical interval has, in some cases, to be altered, sir, and this gives a false impression of slopes. In my opinion, contour maps would give a far more accurate picture," I pointed out primly.

"My dear Colonel Bassett," said Lord Louis patiently. "Our Commando units now under training have to know everything there is to know about land and sea operations; they have to be taught all about our weapons and those of the enemy. If you think there's also time to teach them map-reading, then you'd better think again!"

And with this admonishment ringing in my ears, I sat down and shut up.

Charged with setting up the section then, I managed to contact a retired Marine Colonel called Hicks who I knew was a contributor to *Punch*, and interested in model-making. He said that he'd be delighted to help, and I at once put him in charge of the section.

As usual, we turned to America for the tools to do the job and, as usual, they turned up trumps. The necessary materials were provided in very quick time, and we were in fact able to produce a model in time for the Dieppe raid. In connection with this I told Hicks to go across to Combined Operations and get all the necessary details. When he returned he seemed worried about something.

"What's biting you?" I asked.

"It's Lord Louis," complained Hicks, a morose note in his voice. "He wanted me to give some indication of the natural features of the beach against the figure of a man, so that proportions could be judged. Then he said he supposed it would be too difficult for me to make models of soldiers, and that bits of sticks would do. I don't think Lord Louis realises," went on Hicks plaintively, "that I've been model-maker to His Majesty the King. But I intend to get my own back on him. As he's just been made a general, an admiral and an air marshal, I'm going to make a model of him in each of these uniforms and place all three on the beach."

And Hicks was as good as his word. I should add that Lord Louis, instead of being angry, saw the joke at once, and has in fact retained the three models to this day.

Not long after this I was sent for by the First Sea Lord and told that he wanted me to make a model of one of the Norwegian fjords—the Longhi.

His Lordship was full of suppressed excitement as he gave me this instruction.

"I'll let you into a little secret, Sam"—and his eyes gleamed with triumph—"we've discovered that the *Tirpitz* is there."

My own reaction to this news must have given him satisfaction. The *Tirpitz* was one of the most formidable weapons in Hitler's naval armament, a giant battleship that constituted the pride of the German Navy. If ever she sailed out into the Atlantic, her massive guns might well swing the Atlantic supremacy in Hitler's favour; at the least she could wreak untold havoc among the great convoys which were then struggling to keep Britain's life-line open. Her destruction or immobilisation was of paramount importance and one of the Royal Navy's principal objectives.

The First Sea Lord explained: "The model must be sufficiently large-scale to show the *Tirpitz* in detail, and must also take in a considerable area of the country in the vicinity of the fjord. We intend to bomb her with planes dispatched from an aircraft carrier. To do this, however, it'll be necessary for the planes to leave the carrier some distance from the fjord, and fly inland until they come to its source and then swing round and come down right on top of the *Tirpitz*.

"Unfortunately we can't determine the precise spot from which the planes will take off and cross the coast until the actual day of operations. That's why it's absolutely essential—and I mean *essential*, Sam—for the model to give sufficient detail so that wherever the planes cross the coast they can find their way to the head of the Longhi fjord. And that's no cakewalk, as you probably know—for those damned fjords all look alike from the air."

And with that, the First Sea Lord sent me on my way.

My first task was to find every map and chart of the region and to blow them up to the same scale as the intended model. After we'd done that, I realised that the model would be so vast that it would have to be constructed in at least four sections. With the aid of two U S officers, George Staempfli and Sidney Freedberg, who volunteered to paint the scenery, the giant model was completed on time and taken up bit by bit in large boxes to the Admiralty; but after a lengthy wait the lorry driver was told to take the model straight back to Oxford—which he did, to my considerable astonishment. I patiently sat down to await developments, certain that I would be told in due course what was wrong with the model—and I didn't anticipate having long to wait. Nothing happened, however, and I thought that the operation must have been called off. Then the scrambler phone rang one morning and I was told that everything was still on—but five full-scale models of Longhi fjord were needed as five aircraft were to take part.

"We also want you to find a loch in Scotland or somewhere, with surrounding country similar to that around Longhi; we intend to send some pilots up there to practise run-ins."

I put down the scrambler and stared blankly at the wall. This was a heck of a job to be handled within a few days of the operation. Not for the first time, nor certainly the last, I condemned to perdition those upper-echelon officers who seemed to think everything could be turned out at a snap of the fingers.

Finding a loch similar to the Longhi fjord in Scotland provided some difficulty, but was a comparatively simple part of the job. What really floored us was the problem of providing four more full-scale models of the *Tirpitz* in its fjord with a reasonable facsimile of the surrounding countryside. When I put it to the experts they said it couldn't be done. Four extra models meant sixteen new sections, and as a job of carpentry alone it would be impossible to turn them out in time.

In sheer despair I said: "Well, chaps, let's go over to the club, then, if no one has anything else to suggest. It's no good sitting around here moping. We're just as likely to find inspiration there as anywhere else."

And I couldn't have picked a better course. Sitting in the club sipping a gin was one of our Norwegian officers who'd just returned from a Commando raid. He'd been wounded and had his right leg encased in plaster bandages. He it was who produced the brainwave. We discussed our problem, moaning about the planners who seemed to think we could mass-produce models as if we were Henry Fords. The Norwegian listened sympathetically. Then suddenly he slapped me on the shoulder.

"Look," he broke in eagerly, "why don't you get some plaster bandages like these on my leg, lay them over the model you've already made, and take a plaster cast?"

"Olav," I shouted delightedly, "you're a genius! Now why didn't *we* think of that?" And I jumped up at once to get the operation under way. In a matter of minutes I had my staff out in every available car visiting all the hospitals in the Oxford area, collecting all the bandages they could. Within a half hour, the first of the cars was back, and we began at once to create

194

a plaster cast. But when all the cars had reported back, we found we were still short of bandages.

"Find out how they're made!" I shouted, and someone telephoned a local hospital.

"Lint and plaster of Paris," he bawled over at me as he put down the receiver.

"Good! Try the hospitals again!"

And once again our small fleet of cars dashed out into the Oxford night seeking the precious bits of material upon which the destinies of Britain might very well depend. This time they returned with enough plaster of Paris and lint to build a dozen models.

We set to work immediately. Within a matter of a few hours, we had sixteen moulds ready. We scattered them about the college buildings in any room which had an electric fire, to dry them out as quickly as possible. Once they'd dried, we tested them and found that they were, if anything, even stronger than the original, and really excellent copies. Now the artists set to work painting in buildings, trees, piers and other features. They were well forward with the work when I had a sudden thought.

"By the way," I asked one of the Norwegians, "what are conditions like over there just now?"

"Oh, there's ice and snow," he said.

"I thought so," I murmured. "That creates a bit of a problem, doesn't it?"

The problem was this. The most important landmark for our pilots going in would be a large lake situated at the head of the fjord; it provided a perfect signpost. In shape it was like a cross, from any height quite unmistakable and easily spotted miles away. Once sighted it led in directly to the Longhi fjord; and the *Tirpitz*. It was imperative that on the model it should be instantly recognisable to the pilots. There'd have been no difficulty about this if the attack had been scheduled for one of the summer months. But with Norway in the grip of ice and snow we'd have to paint the countryside on the models white—including the lake. I called in some of the Norwegian experts who knew the fjords well. "Is there any difference between ice, snow and snow-covered ice, so far as colour's concerned?" I asked them.

They thought the matter over. Then all shook their heads. There was no difference, so far as they were aware. But of course they could only speak from knowledge of what things looked like at ground level. All the artists and model-makers expressed themselves similarly baffled.

"Well, we'd better ask the Polar Institute at Cambridge—perhaps *they* can help," I suggested.

But it was no use; they could give no idea of what a pilot might see from a height of ten- or twenty-thousand feet.

That night in the club, while I still wrestled with the problem, I remarked aloud: "I suppose the only thing we can do is to send a reconnaissance plane over to find out!"

At once Colonel Hicks, the chief model-maker, jumped in to object. "It seems useless to me to send a pilot over by himself—he couldn't possibly assess the problem with an artist's eye. It needs an artist to have a look and get the right impression, and to know how to translate that impression on to the model."

"Could you do it, Hicks?" I shot back.

"Of course," he said abruptly, "one glance would be enough."

"All right then, you'll get that glance," I said. "Jump into some warm clothing and I'll have a car waiting to take you to Benson airfield in half an hour."

Poor Hicks, he looked horrified! "But I'm nearly seventy," he spluttered, "and I've never been in a plane in my life! I don't think my heart could take it!"

"Well, then," I said, knowing that I couldn't force him to go, "what about one of the young American artists, then?"

"Listen!" said Hicks, his patriotic instincts aroused, "this is a British operation, so let's keep it that way. I'll go, damn you!"

And off we went. He was, in fact, probably the best man we could have sent, because of his enormous experience. He came back about six a.m. and, after my wife had revived him with coffee and brandy, he'd recovered sufficiently to tell us that he had enjoyed the experience.

"It was wonderful," he said. "The night was beautiful and the lake stood out like a jewelled cross."

The pilot had varied the height as they circled round, and he was certain he'd be able to reproduce it quite accurately. However, he needed a rest now. And with that we allowed him to go off to bed.

When he rose just before noon he said to me: "I must go to Birmingham, Colonel. There's a firm up there which specialises in model-makers' equipment. I want to see them." So off he went by car, returning that same evening with about thirty different varieties of marble—some crushed to powder, others in quite large grains. He worked these materials into the tiny spaces left for the lake on the models. Then he stood back and observed his handiwork. "Yes, that'll just about do it," he said, with justified pride. "That'll *just* about do it."

The rest is history. Pilots of the R A F and Fleet Air Arm bombed the *Tirpitz* and inflicted such damage that she was never able to take part in operations again. (Afterwards we provided the intelligence for the X craft, but that was simple because we had Norwegians who knew everything about the place from ground level.) As the pilots returned from their very successful mission, my interrogators questioned them about the value of the models we'd prepared.

"Absolutely first-class, old boy," they were told. "The bally lake looked just as it did on the model—no chance of making a mistake."

Which was all we wanted to hear.

Although by this time I S T D was sitting in on all planning projects ranging from small commando raids to immense operations such as Torch (the North African landings) there were still some Service organisations which continued to work on their own—possibly because they didn't know of our existence.

One example of this comes to my mind. A raid was made in Italy by British paratroops; its aim was to destroy an important railway viaduct. The party was provided with extension ladders, and explosives which they were to plant in the four piers supporting the viaduct. They were given an exact height for these piers and were told that their ladders would reach comfortably to the top.

Their tragic experience showed otherwise, however, for their Intelligence was inaccurate. They discovered that there were in fact six piers, not four. The ladders did *not* reach the vital places for the charges, and the construction of the viaduct was entirely different from what they'd been led to expect. As a consequence the raid failed and all the party were either killed or captured. The tragedy was that Oxford had complete engineering drawings of the bridge, cross-sections of its construction, photographs—

and indeed the services of an Italian railway engineer who'd actually worked on it.

The Norwegians attached to I S T D were magnificent characters—intelligent and daring. Many took time off from their duties with the department to carry out hazardous raids on their Nazi-occupied homeland.

A party of them came to me one day to explain that although several commando raids had been carried out on a large factory which was being operated by the Germans, none had succeeded in putting it out of action permanently. The Germans always managed to replace the damaged parts by bringing in machinery from Germany or some of the occupied countries. Clearly the Germans considered this factory to be of the highest importance.

"Yet there is an easy way to knock it out," said Finn Dall, one of the Norwegians. He explained that power for the factory was provided by an immense hydro-electric works situated some ten or fifteen miles away, which had pipes running down a steep cliff. These works were probably the most impressive in all Norway, and had taken more than ten years to build. "Yet it would be a simple operation to destroy or damage them so badly that the Germans could not repair them for years. And they are not so well defended as the factory."

I thought the idea a magnificent one, and got in touch with Combined Operations and Norwegian headquarters. As a result, a raid was planned and my gallant Norwegians were seconded to take part in it.

It proved to be an immense success—the hydro works were rendered useless, and the factory thus deprived of its power; it had been engaged in heavy-water experiments which the Germans had hoped would lead to the secrets of the atom-bomb. Indeed, I understand that, although we discovered a more efficient and easier way of making them, the German experiments there would eventually have yielded results, possibly in time to allow Hitler to use the weapon against London.

Yet the thing that remains vividly in my mind about the raid is of a far more trivial nature. Before going off on this hazardous operation, Finn Dall asked me: "If I do have to escape through Sweden and get to Copenhagen, is there anything you'd like me to bring you?"

"Well, as a matter of fact there is," I said with mock serious-ness. "Could you get me some Acidol—it's a hydrochloric acid preparation that helps people like me who suffer from a deficiency of acid. I used to get it before the war from Germany—but I can't get it anywhere now."

"Right," he grinned. "Only too happy to oblige."

Of course I forgot all about the request until the party returned from the raid. I saw that Finn Dall was not among them. I asked what had happened to him.

"Oh, Colonel, don't you remember you gave him another assignment? He went off on his own after we'd done the job."

"Good heavens!" I exclaimed; "I did mention something about a medical thing I wanted—but surely he didn't go off just to get that?"

They only grinned and nodded.

Three weeks later Finn Dall turned up again in Oxford.

"What on earth happened to you?" I demanded, when he reported to me.

"Hell, Colonel! Remember you asked me to get some tablets for you? It seemed such a simple thing to get to Copenhagen, so I made my way there and managed to get three bottles."

Solemnly he laid the three bottles down on my desk. I could only thank him for his great kindness and make it quite clear that I'd never intended he should take a risk of this sort for me. What I didn't tell him was that one bottle would have been quite sufficient. I needed only one tablet every two or three months—and he'd brought me back a stock sufficient to last for at least two hundred and fifty years!

Shortly after this, the Admiralty asked me to provide an accurate fix of a certain church on the Norwegian coast. This church had been built after all the Norwegian maps then in our possession were printed. As an outstanding landmark, it was of the greatest importance to commandos or warships engaged in shore bombardment. I asked my Norwegian section C O to come and see me, and explained the problem.

"That shouldn't be too difficult, Colonel. The easiest thing would be to send one of my surveying officers over with another naval officer. They could probably find someone in the town to provide them with an up-to-date map. At the worst, they could make a fix themselves."

"But I don't want them to take surveying instruments," I said. "Too clumsy. They can take a prismatic compass, perhaps—that can be carried in the pocket and easily thrown away if necessary."

"Certainly, Colonel, whatever you say. I shall arrange it."

He saluted and left the office. Within a week he reported back to me. After another solemn salute he laid a map on my desk with the exact position of the church. A quick glance showed me that it was a really professional job.

"But they couldn't have done all this with just a prismatic compass?" I exclaimed.

My Norwegian broke into a great laugh. "No, Colonel—they couldn't." Then he called in one of the Norwegians who'd taken part in the raid. Grinning widely, this chap explained how he had got the map.

"We reached a place overlooking the town," he began. "It was wooded country hereabouts and as we came out of the woods we saw a German officer and an N C O busy with a theodolite and levelling equipment upon the road. We crept down very quietly behind them, and then"—he drew his finger across his throat—"disposed of them very easily. We hauled the bodies up into the woods; we exchanged clothes. Then we took their instruments and made a complete survey. We had no trouble—none, that is, until we got down to the beach where the submarine was waiting to take us off. The captain appeared a bit upset when he saw two Germans approaching, but we shouted until he understood. He took us aboard all right, but he made us land in Scotland in handcuffs."

The Norwegian laughed. " 'Think of the effect on the local population if they see us fraternising with two Jerries,' the Captain told us. 'The best thing to do is pretend you're prisoners.' "

CHAPTER VIII

EARLY in 1943 I was sent for by the D N I and told that I was needed for a very special job. "This is top-secret stuff, Sam; only four or five people are in the know." He then explained that I was to go at once to Weybridge and see Dr Barnes Wallis, who'd been told that I was coming.

I drove down to Weybridge in a special Admiralty car, and was ushered in to see the man who has since come to be regarded as one of our greatest wartime brains. After we'd settled down in two comfortable chairs, Dr Barnes Wallis explained what all the mystery was about.

"I have perfected a special type of bomb, with which we intend to destroy the Moehne and Eder dams in North Germany," he began. I showed surprise; those dams, vital to German industry and their war effort, were heavily defended; the problem had always been to find a method of bombing them which would justify the great risks involved. Conventional bombs were of little use; the chances of hitting the dam wall and causing any serious breach with them seemed remote.

"My bomb will literally bounce on the water at the base of the dam," explained Dr Wallis. "If it's successful, a vast area of war factories and other installations will be inundated, and the damage will be almost impossible to repair. But the bomb can only take maximum effect under certain conditions."

He hesitated, then emphasised the following words: "Those conditions exist when the dam is full and the pressure of water on the dam wall on the other side—the lake side—is at its lowest. In short, we need to know the moment when the dam contains its maximum amount of water just before spilling over. Once it starts spilling, it spills rapidly—the level of water in the lake rises and builds up a counter pressure to the water on the dam side. That, Colonel Bassett, is where *you* come in!"

The matter was clearly urgent, and I wasn't inclined to waste time. I telephoned Oxford and warned my staff to be on duty when I returned. Then I told the Admiralty driver to take me there.

"Certainly, sir—though it's been some time since I did that journey," he said.

I jumped into the car, my mind already working on the problem of the dam. But the pleasant rocking of the car and the rushing darkness outside soon made me drowsy and I must have fallen asleep. When I awoke, we were driving smoothly along an excellent, broad road, but one which I failed to recognise.

"Are we all right?" I asked the driver, a trifle uneasily.

"Oh yes, sir. I must say I don't know the road myself. but we're probably on the new by-pass I've heard about."

I nodded and settled back in my seat. Then I noticed several figures rushing excitedly towards us, waving their arms frantically and shouting.

"Better pull up, driver," I said, "something seems to be wrong." I had no idea *how* wrong!

"Where the ruddy hell are you going?" shouted an irate figure, sticking his head inside, when we pulled to a stop. "Don't you ruddy well know you're driving along a runway? Don't you know the ruddy bombers are just about to ruddy well take off?" And with that we heard an enormous roaring sound somewhere in the darkness.

"Duck!" shouted the angry man, and dived headlong into a ditch.

"Better follow him!" I shouted to the driver, who needed no urging. He twisted the car around and drove towards the dark outline of a hedge a little distance away. The car scudded across the tarmac, hit an enormous bump, and plopped down into soft mud. At that moment the first of the night bombers roared past us down the runway and rose into the air—two seconds after we'd quitted the spot.

There was a terrible uproar when the last of the bombers had taken to the air. We were led shamefaced before the C O, who ticked us off in no uncertain terms, roaring out that we might easily have wrecked a whole night's operations against Germany.

I thought that this was a little far-fetched, but I saw his point. However, after I'd explained that we'd lost our way in the darkness and were really not to blame, we were treated to a few reviving drinks and sent on our way. It was the early hours of the morning before I finally arrived at Oxford to find my staff anxiously awaiting me. Naturally I hadn't been able to say a word about the problem of the dam over the telephone. But after I'd explained the details, they decided it shouldn't be difficult to provide the answer.

They changed this opinion the following day, however, when they discovered what information we had to work on. The task would have been easy if we could have taken a series of aerial photographs from reconnaissance aircraft. Daily pictures would have shown the steady rise of water, and it would have been a simple task to calculate the moment when the dam was full to its maximum. But such photographs were unobtainable. The Prime Minister himself had ordered that no reconnaissance was to be carried out over the area of the Moehne-Eder dams—or within 150 miles of them—for several months before the raid. If the Germans were to suspect an intended attack on the dams, they'd increase their anti-aircraft defences. These were considered formidable enough already.

To the credit of I S T D, we did have an impressive mass of information about the dams. The Germans had, quite rightly, considered them among their greatest engineering feats, and had published a great deal of technical details about the dams themselves and the countryside around them, before the war. We had details of the construction work at all stages. Statistics gave the rate of filling season by season from the time of the dams' completion until just before the war. Rainfall and other vital figures were also tabulated. But this was not sufficient to indicate the present capacity of the dams or their present rate of filling. My technical staff decided it was absolutely vital that they should be given some idea of the state of the feeder rivers and streams.

To this end I made another trip up to London and saw our aerial reconnaissance men, who said they'd do what they could. They promised to take pictures some distance from the area to include portions of all or some of the feeder rivers. And with this I had to be satisfied.

Within a few days, photographs arrived at Oxford from the Air Ministry, and my experts got to work. From these prints they were able to work out the height of the water in the feeder rivers and compare them with the pre-war statistics. These were useful data but still did nothing to answer the vital question of when the dam would fill to capacity and overflow. What we wanted was some indication of how fast the water rose on the concrete structure, and on what dates.

"What exactly do the pictures say?" I asked.

Carefully we started sifting through the hundreds of photographs of the area in our library. We were fortunate that this had always been a popular tourist area because of the spectacular dams themselves and the forest in the countryside around them. We found we had plenty of coloured souvenir albums; these showed the dams at almost every stage of filling. But the old problem always baffled us; we didn't know the dates when the pictures were taken.

It was one of our hydraulic experts who finally came up with an inspiration. "I wonder," he said slowly, "I wonder if a botanist could help us?"

"How?" I asked, eager to clutch at any straw.

The hydraulics expert pointed to a set of pictures lying on one of the tables. The hundreds of photographs of the dams and surrounding countryside had been laid out like the pieces of a giant jig-saw puzzle.

"This is a nice set," he said. "The photographs show the dam at various stages of filling. We don't know when they were taken but they do show differences in the state of vegetation and tree foliage. It now amounts to this: we know all the technical details concerning the construction of the dam and the improvements made to the feeder sources since the beginning of the war. We also know the amount of water going to the industrial plants using the dam. We have accurate rainfall statistics up to the beginning of the war, and comparative figures since. If we could get just one set of pictures dated even *approximately* by the botanists, it'd give us something to start with."

So off I went to London to find a botanical expert. This proved to be easy. Certain botanists were being employed by the Government at that time on experiments connected with the use of explosives and incendiaries in jungle or tropical areas, and the officer in charge said he'd go down to Kew and consult his contacts. He phoned me later in the day to say that he'd found a botanist who had not only visited the dam but had written a thesis on the flora surrounding it. He'd be up to see me at Oxford very shortly.

The botanist duly arrived and sat down to go through the

hundreds of pictures we had of the dam. After more than nine hours of sifting and checking, he'd picked out a complete set, most of which he could date accurately.

Some pictures had to be loosely captioned "end of June, beginning July"; but for others he was able to give precise dates. This was enough for my staff to go on, and at 3 a.m. one morning I was woken with great excitement to be given the results of their calculations. They'd produced the exact time and day when the the dam would start to spill. I found it difficult to accept their conclusions at first, despite the complex explanations they gave me; the task had seemed impossible.

This botanist had also discovered another important point. Reconnaissance pictures taken some time earlier had shown a large affair on the dam wall believed by the experts to be a camouflaged anti-aircraft post.

"No, it's only tree branches set up there for shade," said the botanist. "There's nothing hidden."

Well, the result of our researches is well known. The famous dam-busters led by Wing Commander Guy Gibson, v c, bounced Barnes Wallis's bomb with such success that the dam was destroyed and vast areas of German industrial plant knocked out completely. It proved to be one of the most daring and successful raids carried out by the R A F during the entire course of the war.

Mention of botanists reminds me of a short-lived scheme put forward by someone to burn the German harvest; our botanists actually made a report on all the wheat, barley and corn-growing areas of Germany. But when Winston Churchill heard of this he was horrified. The suggestion that Britons could even conceive such an idea disgusted him. He made it plain that the people who were prepared to have him go down in history as the man who was prepared to starve German women and children should resign their staff appointments immediately.

All the sections and feeder organisations mentioned were formed by ourselves because of sheer necessity, which we are told is the mother of invention. However, there was one section which was wished on us; it was called the Fire Vulnerability Section.

As we became properly organised we used to send the Prime Minister photographic albums beautifully produced by the

Oxford University Press and which showed the P M ground and air pictures of areas of projected operations. We were told that the P M had been concerned with the discrepancies in the information in our albums and the reports given out by the Air Ministry. Places razed to the ground were shown to be quite normal in our books. Marshalling yards from which flames could be seen sixty miles away were working without any evidence of such damage.

We heard that the P M had seen the Bomber chiefs and had been told that with the great loss of bombers it was expedient to announce the success of operations. A loss of some forty bombers, with the news that they were off their main target, anyway, would cause a great drop in morale. The P M then insisted that he must have the true picture; and a special section under the skilled leadership of Basil Ward, an architect (now Professor B. Ward and famous for Hammersmith Hospital and skyscrapers at Oxford University) was sent to my organisation at Oxford.

We had maps and photographs, etc. It soon became obvious to this section of English and American architects, fire insurance experts, and engineers that our bombing was not selective enough. Incendiary bombs were being dropped on areas where the fire risk was low, block-busters were wasted on areas where fire bombs would be more effective and economical. Industrial area damage was being assessed purely from aerial photographs which could only show external damage. This section then set about producing zonal maps, with fire-risk areas shown in red, etc. These were eventually produced for every city and town in every country where bombing was taking place or likely to take place. Professor Basil Ward was sent to India to advise Lord Louis Mountbatten when S E A C was set up.

Not only were the maps of immense value to Bomber Command, they were also of extreme value to our advancing armies; H Q, and vulnerable war material etc., could be stored in areas of low fire risk.

With the advent of 1944, planning for D-Day intensified, and I S T D were right in the thick of it.

Some time earlier, we'd discovered the need to mass-produce copies of some of the prints in our enormous library of photographs. When we prepared our I S I S books, we discovered that it was impossible to reproduce pictures satisfactorily by the ordinary block-making process used by all printers. During the process, vital information was frequently blurred or lost.

It was essential that our books, which were to be studied by the Prime Minister, by the Chiefs of Staff, and by the Commanders in the field, should provide them with the most accurate information possible. We had therefore to devise a way of reproducing prints which would retain all the essential detail. This was particularly so in relation to aerial photographs; a tiny speck sometimes yielded information of the highest importance. (The classic case was when a Wren studying a photograph of Peenemünde, the German research station, hit upon the secret of the V2.)

Rodney Slessor came up with the answer. Before the war he'd worked with an advertising agency and had learned something about photographic reproduction. He remembered an extraordinary photo-reproducer machine invented by a Swiss named Graber. This had been widely used in the heyday of glossy picture postcards, but had apparently gone out of fashion in more recent years. Slessor came to me one day and said, "Colonel, I believe if I could locate Graber and get one of his machines it might solve the problem."

As this was one of our major headaches I told him to go ahead. Within a few days, using our facilities, Rodney managed to track Graber down and discovered that three of the machines were still in existence. Although they'd not been in use for years, Graber thought they could still be made to work. Within twenty-four hours, the three machines were delivered to the New Bodleian.

The various tanks connected to these machines had once contained chemicals and were now badly rusted. But we eventually had one working and discovered it to be invaluable. We simply set the machine for one thousand or ten thousand, or whatever number of prints we required, and then went away and left it to do the rest.

It worked by passing a roll of photographic paper over a glass frame behind which were a negative and a high-powered lamp. The roll then went through into developing tanks, fixing tanks and then washing tanks. After the final washing, it passed over

electrically-heated drums, and when it came off it was guillo-
tined to the required size and number of prints. In no time at
all we had the three machines working at full speed and all
our problems over the clarity of our pictures appeared to be
solved.

But few things are destined to run smoothly in this world!
Although we'd taken over the whole of the New Bodleian, we'd
been asked by the University authorities not to use one room
which had been set aside for the new library. This was a magnificent room, beautifully decorated and inlaid with the most
precious woods gathered from all parts of the world. One day
I got a frantic call from Dr Veale, the registrar.

"For goodness' sake, Colonel, come over here at once! Something *dreadful* has happened!"

I ran across to the New Bodleian and entered the library. Dr
Veale was standing there in a state of great agitation . . . and
no wonder! Twisted strips of the most lovely woods were hanging from the beautiful ceiling like party streamers. I ran outside,
mounted the stairs and burst into the room above, where the
Graber machines were busy churning out prints. My misgivings
were confirmed; despite our precautions, the rusty tanks had
let us down and were steadily leaking. The dripping water had
seeped under the floorboards to the exquisite veneers of the
library ceiling below.

I am glad to say that, although the damage was extensive and
repairs involved a great deal of time and patience, the Office of
Works, after consulting the original artists and craftsmen, managed to make good the damage to the ceiling; and we fixed the
leaks in the Graber machines, which were to play an important
role in the D-Day preparations.

It would be wrong to suppose that I S T D had been doing
nothing about D-Day before 1944. A large and special section
had been working on this project exclusively since early in 1942,
and we'd already built up an enormous dossier of topographical
intelligence for the day when we'd return to Europe.

Early in 1944, however, I was given the approximate date of
D-Day, and decided to carry out a special reconnaissance over
the beaches where Allied troops were to land. I disguised exactly
which beaches by taking in the whole of the north coast of
France. I arranged for a special squadron of Spitfires to take zero-

height obliques of the whole coastline. The pilots called this mission 'Dicing for I S T D', for it was an extremely risky job.

They had to skim over the surface of the channel at zero height and swing in along the coast, getting as near to the shore as possible without being hit. Most of our photographs subsequently showed great splashes of water all around the aircraft, demonstrating just how dangerous it was. We lost several excellent pilots and aircraft on this mission; but we obtained valuable obliques of the whole zone in which the landings were to be made.

They were exceptionally fine photographs; one could easily read the inscriptions on hotels and shops—sometimes see right through the windows into the rooms. These pictures made an entire panorama of every beach involved; I joined each strip with a piece of Scotch tape, then took a complete set up to S H A E F headquarters and saw Admiral Ramsey. I explained that if he'd tell me how many copies he wanted I'd have the sets sent to the Oxford University Press to be properly hinged.

"Well, Bassett, I'd better consult some of my staff. Please wait."

I waited while the Admiral went away to consult his experts. He came back and said: "The feeling is that as these pictures show the actual beaches for the D-Day landings, we should keep the number down to a minimum—in which case, only the planners involved and the Force Commanders should have a copy. Let's see what that adds up to."

He made a quick calculation, then looked up and said: "I make it forty."

Back at Oxford I arranged with Dr Johnston to have forty copies of these panoramic views hinged and they came to me in beautiful order, really magnificent productions. I forwarded them at once to the Admiralty. A few days later the scrambler phone rang and I answered it; Admiral Ramsey wished to speak to me personally. His first words were: "Those silhouettes of the beaches, Colonel. We want forty thousand!"

I couldn't speak for a moment. I could hear the Admiral calling down the phone: "Bassett? Are you there, Bassett?"

"I'm here, sir," I said faintly. I recovered sufficiently to say: "You've made a mistake, sir, haven't you?"

"Mistake?"

"You've got too many noughts, sir," I said.

"Yes, yes, I know what you're getting at, Colonel," said the Admiral. "But when I showed these silhouettes of yours to the planners at a meeting of the Force Commanders the other day, they went down so well that it's been decided the gunnery staffs are to make a grid for the pictures—a transparent thing to go over each one.

"The various naval commanders'll be able to call for fire by just giving the grid number. So every ship taking part in the bombardment's got to have a copy, and they'll also be used by every landing craft—be a lot more valuable than any other navigational aids. Anyway, we need forty thousand."

"But that's absolutely impossible, sir!" I exploded. "We haven't got the paper, and we haven't enough time!"

"Well, it's a requirement, Colonel," said the Admiral sharply.

"I don't think it can be done, sir," I said stolidly. And that, so far as I was concerned, was that.

The next day a top-priority message arrived at Oxford from the Admiralty, addressed to me personally. It said bluntly that the First Sea Lord had received a complaint from General Eisenhower to the effect that Colonel Bassett had been told to carry out a vital task and had refused to do it on the grounds that it was impossible. He was, said General Eisenhower, to be told that the task was utterly vital, that he was holding up the war effort, and that he was to get on with it at once. If anything was needed from America, it would be sent immediately. The work was to have the highest priority.

There was absolutely nothing I could do then but try and comply with this command, but I still didn't see how it could be done. I went round to consult Jimmy Phillips, the American officer whom we regarded as the statistical expert in the library.

"Look, Jimmy, I know it's ridiculous, but just say supposing we were asked to provide forty thousand copies of our panoramas, what would that mean in actual material?"

"You must be off your head," said Jimmy. "It'd be a *heck* of a lot. But let's see."

Within a matter of moments, he had the answer: "Well, we'd need two million photographs to begin with, which means seven hundred and thirty miles of photographic paper. In addition we'd want ten tons of chemicals every second day. And that's only to *begin* with."

"Thanks," I said. "I knew the damn thing was impossible."

Armed with these precise figures I went up to the Admiralty at once and put the situation squarely before them. I'd already checked with the Ministry of Supply and had been told there wasn't ten miles of photographic material available in the country—let alone seven hundred and thirty!

"It just can't be done, on the basis of the available materials alone," I pointed out. "I haven't even bothered to work out the time factor yet. But there just aren't the materials."

I was told to hold on and a call was put through at once to General Eisenhower himself. I could hear Eisenhower's metallic mid-Western tones rasp over the scrambler as he answered: "Tell Bassett to list his exact requirements and I'll have bombers fly the stuff over from the States."

Within three days, the first of the bombers touched down with the supplies of photographic paper and some of the necessary chemicals. From then on, until the job was completed, they were landing every third day, ferrying in fresh supplies. Meanwhile, however, I'd been forced to face up to the problem of the time factor involved.

Slessor and Phillips came to me and asked when exactly would these panoramas be required. I'd no alternative but to tell them the approximate date of D-Day. They made some calculations, then Slessor turned to me and said: "It's impossible, all right. Working all out, twenty-four hours a day without stopping for a moment, the job still couldn't be completed until at least a fortnight after that. The machines have to stop for a few seconds every time they make a print, and there's no way of speeding 'em up. In any case, they just can't be run continuously. They're fairly old and decrepit and need constant maintenance and overhaul. They'd seize up within a few days."

"Can't you think of some way round the problem?" I asked. "I just can't face Eisenhower now and tell him that the job's impossible, after he's flown all this stuff over from America."

The two men sat down. I don't know how long we all sat silent there in that lovely room, looking out over the sunlit grass of a beautiful Oxford lawn; but at last Jimmy Phillips looked up. "We have to convert these machines to cut out those two- or three-second stops for each print."

Another silence, then: *"That's it!"* shouted Slessor. "I've *got*

211

it! The R A F people down at Farnborough were experimenting some months ago with a continuous-process machine. Instead of having a glass plate with the negative, they just use a slit. And there's no delay whatsoever. The only thing is, I *don't* know how they've been progressing with it."

"Well, we'd better get down to Farnborough at once," I said. "That's the only way to find out."

We raced down to the R A F experimental station as fast as our car would take us, and saw the C O there.

"I wondered at what stage this continuous-process photographic machine was?" I inquired, keeping the excitement out of my voice.

"Oh, it's very well advanced," he said. "As a matter of fact we tried it out a couple of days ago, and it worked perfectly."

"Could we see it?" I asked, glancing gleefully at my colleagues.

"I don't think so. I'm sorry, but it's not actually working at the moment. But you can have a chat with the people working on it—no doubt they can explain it all to you."

And he led the way to where some of his assistants were working. The machine had apparently performed quite excellently; better even than they'd hoped for. The men said they were having one or two teething troubles with it, of course, but they thought they'd be able to iron these out fairly soon.

"Could we have it?" I asked bluntly.

"Lord, no, old chap! This is only a prototype!" they said, with shocked faces. "It'll be some time before the modifications are completed and it's in full working order."

"Look," I turned to the C O. "We have to print two million photographs." And I explained our need to cut out the pause in the Graber machines.

"I'm sorry, Colonel, but it's quite impossible," said the C O.

But I had a trump card up my sleeve. Now that my persuasions had failed I produced a piece of paper signed by the Supreme Allied Commander himself.

"This," I said, fixing the C O with my eye, "is a priority No. 1, signed by Eisenhower himself. It orders everyone to give me anything I need . . . *And, sir, I need that machine!*"

The C O read the message gravely. "Well, Colonel, you'd better have it."

Within a very short time the machine had been loaded on to a lorry. I'd arranged for the technicians working on it to come along—we didn't think we could operate the thing ourselves—and we set off over the countryside, rocking and jolting at top speed as though all the devils of hell were after us. By that evening the machine was installed in the big room in the New Bodleian and we'd begun our work.

Before we began the job, however, I called a conference of all members of the staff who were likely to be involved in this gigantic operation. Even with the new machine, everybody who was not engaged on a top-priority job had to be put to work on the D-Day photographs. Teams would have to work day and night shifts until the job was complete.

This involved a matter of security. Anyone who even glanced at some of the pictures we were going to work on would know at once what they were connected with; all the world was waiting for D-Day. The secret of the actual landing places would therefore be known to everyone who took part in the operation, including the civilian technicians I'd brought along from Farnborough. Two courses were open to me. I could either turn the New Bodleian into a kind of fortress, locking everyone up until after D-Day—which meant keeping almost a thousand people behind locked doors for several weeks. Or I could give them all a jolly good talking-to on the question of security. I chose the latter course.

Then we started work. The machine ran beautifully and, after it had been in operation for about an hour, Rodney Slessor came to tell me that, provided we had no mishaps, he'd calculated that we could turn out the two million photographs well within the time limit which had been set. He pointed out, however, that the Graber machines were likely to present a little difficulty, which would have to be solved. Before we could have a smooth run on them—that is, until the prints matched the negatives exactly—they were inclined to use up a great deal of photographic paper. And as we intended running some hundreds of miles of material through them, this would shortly add up to a tremendous amount of waste. We couldn't store it anywhere, and it would have to be disposed of somehow, not only because it would be in the way, but also because if it were seen lying around in such quantities an enemy agent might discover what we were doing. So we arranged to make a bonfire four times a day on the tennis ground attached to Manchester College.

I liked to think, as I watched those fires, that they were symbolic of Hitler's Reich—going up in flames in the very near future.

CHAPTER IX

SOMETIMES I don't think that the English Channel likes me very much. I've already told how I nearly drowned in it during the 1914–18 war, when a French destroyer crashed into the Naval Examination Service yacht.

In the Second World War it made at least two other attempts to finish me. I'd taken to flying across it when possible; but just before D-Day I had to trust myself again to its treacherous embraces.

When ISTD had completed forty thousand panoramic albums and thousands of other brochures and reports for the Allied attack on Europe, its work was by no means done. Demands for additional information continued to flood into my headquarters in Oxford: areas suitable for gliders; for parachutists; bombing targets for D-Day itself; targets for demolition work to be carried out by the French Resistance—the requests seemed endless.

But once the basic information had been sent forward to S H A E F Headquarters, the question arose as to how we should dispose of the thousands of reference books which we'd accumulated over the years of planning. I told Wing-Commander Dan Ion, the section's librarian, that the only thing to be done was to return them to their original owners where possible; generally the individual or learned society who'd sent them in had put a name on the flyleaf. The Wing-Commander went away to organise this.

He came back to me a few days later in a state of some agitation. "Colonel," he said, "there's something here I think I should draw your attention to—it might be important."

"Yes? What is it?"

"Well, as I was sorting through the reference books, I glanced at an old copy of the *Guide Bleu*, and I noticed *this*." He read out a few words of French which at first didn't seem very important. They said that one of the chief industries of Normandy was peat-digging—the peat being sold for fuel on a large scale. The Wing-Commander had been a geologist with the Anglo-Iranian Oil Company before the war, and clearly he saw some significance here which escaped me.

"Well, what about it?" I asked.

"Well! If there was peat-digging there once, then some peat must still exist now. I've gone through dozens of more modern copies of *Guide Bleu*, but I can't find any mention of peat. I can only conclude that when some of the French Channel ports began importing coal, the peat industry just died."

"So what?" I said. And then a light dawned. "Of *course*!" I exclaimed. "The tanks!"

I should have understood immediately. What would happen to the armour the Allies were planning to land on the Normandy beaches if the ground proved unable to bear their weight? It was a paralysing thought.

The previous safety margin for tanks or armoured vehicles landing on soft sandy beaches had been put at one foot depth of pure primary sand surface. For D-Day it had been decided that at least three feet would be essential, because of the immense weight of armour being landed and the way the surface of the sand would be scoured.

If the sand now proved to be a mixture of mud, buttery clay or peat particles, then the more the top surface was scoured by tank tracks the more it would act as a lubricant—and the tanks and tracked vehicles would be unable to manœuvre. On the wet sections of the beaches the tanks would simply go round and round in circles without making a yard of progress.

The probable result was too awful to contemplate: the whole Allied attack, which depended to a great degree on hammering the enemy's coastal defences with the largest assemblage of armoured fire-power the world had yet seen, would be bogged down on the slippery beaches of Normandy: the Allied armies would be hurled back in disorder and Hitler would be left master of Europe.

I jumped at once to the scrambler and got through to S H A E F headquarters. I explained that we'd come across something which seemed quite serious.

"We'll send somebody down at once!" I was told. "Oh, boy, is this a lulu!"

The Supreme Commander's chief geologist, Professor J. D. Bernal, raced down to Oxford immediately and proceeded quite understandably to berate me for not discovering this difficulty earlier.

"And now what are you going to do about it?" he demanded belligerently.

"If it hadn't been for my foresight years ago, we still wouldn't know anything about it," I replied, nettled. In fact, some years before when my staff had advised me to discard old and outdated books, I had refused, feeling that we would be throwing away valuable material; now this decision of mine had paid a dividend —and *what* a dividend!

There was no point in recriminations. I said I'd try and find out where the peat had been dug and the extent of the strata— and that was all I could do. Professor Bernal returned to London.

We had nothing on our files which would indicate the position of the peat, so I decided on a bold step; in fact, there was no alternative. I dispatched two Free French geologists to Paris with instructions to secure either geological maps of the region, or information about it. This move seemed to satisfy the professor; but what I wanted were results—not satisfaction for the professor.

The Free French raiders did a magnificent job. They entered a Paris swarming with Germans, went straight to the Geological Institute, and came away with four large volumes of geological maps which they brought back safely to Oxford. Unfortunately, although these showed beyond doubt that peat did exist in Normandy, the scale of the maps was such that we couldn't find out whether the peat strata came within miles of the beaches. The only answer appeared to be personal investigation, and the problem was passed over to S H A E F.

French Resistance men and Coppists—Combined Operations Pilotage Parties—were sent across to bring back samples of the sand. For some reason I've never been able to discover they were told that aerial photographs had shown dark streaks along the beaches; that these were thought to be peat deposits and that, if they were, then all the Allied armour would be useless—and that this was the reason for their trip. When the Coppists got there they found that the 'dark streaks' shown up on aerial photographs were simply rocks, apparent to the most inexpert eye.

What was more important, however, was that the Coppists confirmed there was peat on the beaches. I should have been satisfied with this, perhaps, but I wasn't. Possibly I was needled by the criticisms of Professor Bernal. I hope I was solely concerned with ensuring the success of the invasion. Certainly, the latter motive prompted my subsequent actions.

I went to S H A E F—although time was now getting very short, and there were only a few weeks to go to D-Day—and pointed out that despite this last operation I still didn't know *where* the peat was on the beaches. I was very sharply told that Admiral Ramsey was quite satisfied with the information, and in fact was rather disgruntled with my organisation. "So you'd better take it up with *him*."

I saw Ramsey—Admiral "Black" Ramsey as he was called for some reason—one of the finest senior officers with whom I've ever had to deal. Although up to his eyebrows in problems, he could still find time to discuss mine.

"Look, sir," I began. "In my opinion my geologist was quite right in drawing attention to the fact that there were peat deposits in Normandy. Even though it was rather late in the day, surely it's better late than never?"

Admiral Ramsey looked thoughtfully vague.

"But how much further have the Coppists got us?" I went on determinedly. "All they've done is confirm that there are peat strata—which we already knew. But whereabouts on the beaches is the peat?"

Ramsey said patiently : "My dear Bassett, the Coppists have given us similar information about a great number of beaches, and their information has always been satisfactory."

"But, sir," I protested, "their work—until now—has always been concerned with theatres of war where there was nothing like the weight of armour involved. What we need is an expert analysis of practically every inch of the beaches. If the peat deposits, for instance, are under the dry sand, then it doesn't matter, the tracks'll still grip. But if it's mixed with the wet sand up to high-water mark, then we're sunk. There's still just time to carry out a proper reconnaissance."

"How would this be different from the reconnaissances already carried out, Bassett?" The Admiral's tone was impatient.

I explained in detail the techniques of taking and testing soil samples, delicately using geological augers or rubber tubes called sand containers, and what could be learned from the tests. But I went on to point out how unsatisfactory these methods could be sometimes—when the soil, removed from its natural environment, lost many of its properties, and when only a limited number of samples could be taken for testing. Then these had to go to a soil scientist to be analysed. I quoted the classic example of a test made in North Wales where as many as five hundred samples were taken and yet clay present in the soil was not detected.

I paused to gain breath and make my main point: "Sir, I S T D gained experience in this work following reconnaissances carried out on the beaches of Norway. We discovered that samples brought back from the beaches were sometimes useless for testing two days later. So we devised our own practical method of soil-testing—carried out on the spot. We mixed samples of sand, peat, clay and mud in boxes and taught ourselves to recognise each of these by feeling it with our fingers."

This method, I pointed out, was just as effective in the dark as in daylight. All the operator needed was a wet towel to clean his hands after each 'dig'. And the supreme advantage was that whole beaches could be covered.

"Can *you* do this?" asked Ramsey, when I'd finished.

"Yes." I couldn't resist boasting a little. "In fact I've won several free drinks by doing the test in a dark room with over thirty boxes of mixed and unmixed sand."

"Right you are, then," he said briefly, "you're the chap to go."

My daughter had often told me that I talked too much. I'd certainly talked myself into this one, and there was no way out!

I lunched with Admiral Ramsey while his staff made the necessary arrangements for me—including a cover passport, as issued to all our tourists. And that night, after a farewell pep talk from the Admiral, I went down to Portsmouth and was there kitted out in a special rig. Then I boarded a submarine. It was the first time I'd ever travelled in one, and I don't mind admitting that I was more scared inside that thing than I was at the thought of stepping ashore on a German-occupied beach.

I arranged with the Captain to return to the same place on the shore the following night, after I'd completed my task. Armed with only a towel and an infra-red torch with an invisible 'beam' which would only show up on a special screen aboard the submarine, with which to signal my position on the following night, I stepped ashore from a dinghy on to Hitler's Europe.

I dived into some scrub, just beyond the edge of the beach, and lay there for some time. Everything was quiet, and about half an hour later I moved off in search of the beaches which were very soon to be the scene of the greatest amphibious operation in history.

As I stumbled along in the darkness I gave thanks to Providence for the men in my geographical, photographic and model-making sections who had made me so familiar with these beaches before I ever set eyes on them. I had absolutely no difficulty in finding my way. I really felt quite familiar with the D-Day beaches. Thousands of maps had been printed by the Oxford University Press for use in the invasion—each intended to fulfil a special purpose, and some bore the most inappropriate names, such as Mickey Mouse. They showed approach areas, lowering areas, swept-channels, fire-support areas, target-areas, and masses of other information which form the complicated pattern of a modern battle. Although I'd never stepped upon these beaches in my life, they'd already become more familiar to me than the beaches of England or those where I'd surfed in Ceylon or at the Cape.

The only thing that alarmed me was the startling brightness of the sea; I stopped at frequent intervals to listen, and did my best not to be silhouetted against it. I remembered that dry sand makes a crunching noise, and so I was careful to time the intervals of my steps to the crash of the breakers.

I kept an eye on the luminous hands of my watch to make certain I'd be able to return to my rendezvous before daylight, and I kept reminding myself that I had to reach a hide-out to lie safely hidden during daylight.

I kept clear of the obvious look-out places, and I was helped by my memory of our special model which showed all the

German defensive positions. After dipping my arms into the beaches more than two hundred times, I decided I'd done enough, and made my way cautiously back towards the rendezvous area.

I reached it just before dawn—having first buried my towel—and approached my hide-out from behind in case I'd been spotted earlier and a patrol was lying in wait for me. But there was no one, and I crept into a well-screened pit with a feeling of comforting security. Bushes and scrub hid me from the view of anybody coming up behind, and in front of me lay the sea.

Everything remained quiet until about 8 a.m., when there was a fair amount of activity in the rear areas, but nothing that I could pick out as being of a particularly military nature. I imagined that the movement was simply that of workers in the woods or fishermen going down to the beaches. My greatest need was for a cigarette; foolishly I'd left my food rations aboard the submarine, but I didn't feel hungry.

I passed the time by repeating in my head all I'd discovered about the beaches—the various distances from the sea edge where I'd found traces of peat, where I'd evidence that it existed at the waterline, and so on. I repeated these facts over and over again until I was sure that I'd have no difficulty in pointing out the areas on a map.

It was anything but warm in my little den—unfortunately the weather was damp and cold—and once or twice I thought of stamping round a bit to restore my circulation; but I decided against it. I tried to gauge the passage of time by studying the progress of the sun, instead of constantly looking at my watch; but time still went very slowly.

Finally, however, I dozed off. When I awoke the light was going, and I prepared for my walk down to the beach. I awaited darkness impatiently; but finally it was time to go. There was no activity along the shore and it seemed desolate and empty. I moved carefully down on to the sand, and then entered the water. I walked out until it had risen to my chest, my teeth beginning to chatter with the chilling cold. Then I signalled with my torch.

There was no reply—nothing. I waited, but still there was no sign or sound. I moved out farther, then signalled again. It was impossible to know whether my invisible beam was being picked up. I took another step forward and then suddenly I was too far out, and waterborne!

Now I panicked. In the darkness I'd lost all sense of direction, and I thrashed around trying to keep afloat and at the same time seeking to find bottom. Just when I was about to despair, my feet struck against rocks and I knew I was safe. Although I was chilled to the bone, I desperately tried signalling towards the sea again. It was useless. I looked at my luminous watch only to find that it was now exactly one and a half hours after my rendezvous time.

Despairing, I waded ashore. I collapsed on the beach cold as a fish and exhausted. I don't know how long I lay there, but finally I came to and signalled seawards. Still there was no result. I gave up and scrambled wet and weary up the beach and into the woods. I was now consumed with worry and half-frozen with cold. But apart from these troubles of my own I was impatient to get back with what I regarded as vital information.

My only hope was that possibly the submarine would return for me just before dawn—but how to pass the time now in this exhausted condition, without food, without a cigarette? Again I repeated to myself the report on the beaches, but by now I was word-perfect and this was no diversion. Then I tried mental games of golf round all the courses I'd played on at home and abroad. This proved to be my salvation.

I started off with Rangoon where the first hole gives you a magnificent sight of the famous golden temple, the Shwe Dagon pagoda. I tried to recall whether I used a mashie niblick at the third on the famous Ceylon course. Which was the best way to play the crushed-shell fairway at Aden? How did I win that beautiful set of clubs at Nuwara Eliya in Ceylon, one Christmas day?

Before I knew it the time had come to go down to the beach again. By now I was so cold that entering the water made little difference. This time, within a matter of minutes after my first signal, I heard the wonderful and reassuring sound of oars. Fifteen minutes later I was in the warm wardroom of the submarine, sipping hot drinks and slowly thawing out. Then I learned just how lucky I'd been.

The submarine which dropped me had developed engine

221

trouble, and this one, sent out as a relief, had missed the cove where I was waiting. On the second trip just before dawn the Captain couldn't find the cove and was about to turn for home when suddenly my torch showed up on their screen.

Now here I was, safe and comparatively sound, my head full of information which should certainly help our tanks and armoured forces when the Allied forces landed on these shores.

In the early days after D-Day we were kept busy providing the men of the French Resistance with maps and information on escape routes through the German lines. These routes had to be brought constantly up to date as the Germans retreated. When there was the possibility of Resistance groups joining up with our parachute troops, we had many emergency calls for details of dropping areas.

Then, as the Allied armies advanced, we took on another new job. We sent over several parties of men—'Target parties'—who were parachuted ahead of advancing troops to make a dash for vital factories, scientific research establishments, key commercial firms, and so forth, to secure valuable data before the Germans could destroy them.

My German-speaking American officers were leaders of these parties. They loaded the material they found on to lorries which were then sent back to Oxford; one pleasing lorry-load included a batch of Leica cameras and some most delicious liver sausages. Other parties were sent to France, Belgium and Holland to gather detailed information on the colonies of these countries so that we could start planning operations to free them.

I myself made frequent trips to the Continent to supervise these operations and to liaise with Intelligence officers in the field. By this time we had a large Far East section concentrating on the Japanese war and working closely with a similar one in South-East Asia under Lord Louis Mountbatten.

We'd sent trained staffs out to India, with Commander A. M. Hughes in charge. There was another section working in Washington and a combined American and English team in Australia. Our organisation had spread across the world to every theatre of the war. And to show how much our work was appreciated we'd collected a batch of congratulatory letters from all the Force Commanders.

When the German war ended, I received the C B E, the United States Order of Merit, the Norwegian Order of Freedom, the Order of St Olav, and the French Légion d'Honneur. I also had personal letters of thanks from General Eisenhower and from their Lordships.

These decorations and the letters I received from Buckingham Palace from the Duke of Windsor, whom I had known as Prince of Wales, and from the head of the American Security Forces, showed that my staff had more than proved their worth. They emphasised the importance of carefully gathered and accurate topographical information in modern operations of war.

Now, as I look back over the fifty-four years of my Service career, I remember many things. I recall the inadequate preparations made for operations during the two wars, and for fiascos such as Abadan and Suez since. Often they have only proved how little we learn from past experience.

From this island which for centuries has been a great power throughout the world, our navies, armies and air forces, with a fighting history second to none, have been sent out to stations in all parts of the globe to protect our bases, colonies and trade routes. We thus had generations in which to gather, at our leisure, information about the countries where our forces were stationed—which would now be of vital use. But no one bothered to take these chances and they will not come again.

When the hour came for our forces to land on enemy-held territory, our planners and Force Commanders frequently discovered that the information available about the beaches and the terrain they were to invade was quite inadequate. So the information they needed had to be hurriedly and sometimes inadequately collected in weeks or days, when it could have been carefully gathered over the years.

Thus the I S T D, which was set up in such a haphazard fashion during the early months of the last war, had the job of remedying the results of twenty years of neglect in this field. Time and again, even now, I am reminded of that note I found in one of the files in the Admiralty: "Gone to lunch". It sums up the attitude to Topographical Intelligence work between the wars . . . and since.

But there is another side to this picture; at long last, but perhaps not too late, we are trying to make amends for past apathy. When war came, Britain lacked trained Intelligence staff and the carefully kept files we could so easily have had. But what we did have in abundance, pressed down and brimming over, was our native genius for improvisation.

I remember so many instances, within my own organisation alone, when the quick thinking and enterprise of individual officers found solutions to problems which had seemed insoluble.

In my view it was this genius which won the war.